DELIVERING
INSPIRING
DOCTORAL
ASSESSMENT

SUCCESS
IN RESEARCH

DELIVERING INSPIRING DOCTORAL ASSESSMENT

PAM DENICOLO
DAWN DUKE
JULIE REEVES

Los Angeles | London | New Delhi
Singapore | Washington DC | Melbourne

Los Angeles | London | New Delhi
Singapore | Washington DC | Melbourne

SAGE Publications Ltd
1 Oliver's Yard
55 City Road
London EC1Y 1SP

SAGE Publications Inc.
2455 Teller Road
Thousand Oaks, California 91320

SAGE Publications India Pvt Ltd
B 1/I 1 Mohan Cooperative Industrial Area
Mathura Road
New Delhi 110 044

SAGE Publications Asia-Pacific Pte Ltd
3 Church Street
#10-04 Samsung Hub
Singapore 049483

Editor: Jai Seaman
Editorial Assistant: Lauren Jacobs
Production Editor: Manmeet Kaur Tura
Copyeditor: Jill Birch
Proofreader: Clare Weaver
Marketing Manager: Susheel Gokarakonda
Cover Design: Shaun Mercier
Typeset by: C&M Digitals (P) Ltd, Chennai, India
Printed in the UK

Library of Congress Control Number: 2019944239

British Library Cataloguing in Publication data

A catalogue record for this book is available from the British Library

ISBN 978-1-5264-6501-6
ISBN 978-1-5264-6500-9 (pbk)

At SAGE we take sustainability seriously. Most of our products are printed in the UK using responsibly sourced papers and boards. When we print overseas we ensure sustainable papers are used as measured by the PREPS grading system. We undertake an annual audit to monitor our sustainability.

Dedication

For all those who seek to provide fair and effective feedback to researchers and those assessors and examiners who have shared with us in workshops and at conferences their wisdom, woes and wonderful enthusiasm to improve their practice.

Also, for our families and friends who have borne with patience our neglect of them while we wrote this book.

Contents

List of further resources

Activities

Figure

Information boxes

International examples boxes

Reflection points

Table

Top tips

Voices of experience

About the authors

Pam Denicolo is an Emeritus Professor at the University of Reading, a chartered constructivist psychologist and honorary pharmacist, who provides consultancy on doctoral support and research methodology as well as examining doctorates in institutions worldwide. Previously she established, managed and developed the University of Reading Graduate School, providing a substantial contribution to its Research Methods, Generic Skills and Doctoral Supervisor training. Her passion for supporting graduate students and other early career researchers is demonstrated through her numerous successful doctoral candidates and examinees and her leading roles in national and international organisations such as the International Study Association on Teachers and Teaching, the Society for Research into Higher Education Postgraduate Network, the RCUK Impact and Evaluation Group, several working groups of Vitae including the development of the Researcher Development Framework (RDF), the QAA Doctoral Characteristics Advisory Group, and the UK Council for Graduate Education, all of which have resulted in many publications, presentations and workshops. Through these organisations she met up with Julie and Dawn who became inspirational collaborators on many projects as well as valued friends. Pam provides consultancy and workshops worldwide on doctoral issues. She edits and contributes to the Sage book series: *Success in Research*, aimed at those in the early years of a research career, and co-edits and co-authors with former doctoral researchers a series with Brill/Sense dealing with *Critical Issues in the Future of Learning and Teaching*.

Dawn Duke is the Head of Researcher Development within the University of Surrey's Doctoral College. She leads the team that supports the transferable/employability skills of postgraduate researchers and early career researchers across all disciplines, as well as delivers supervisor training. Dawn received her neuroscience PhD from Imperial College. In 2008, she moved from researching and teaching neuroscience to concentrate fully on researcher development. She has worked to embed and normalise skills training to better prepare researchers for the variety of opportunities available to them. Through her work at Surrey and a partial secondment as Director of Graduate Training for the Southeast Physics Network (SEPnet), she has focussed on bringing researchers together with employers from a range of sectors, integrating this wider range of expertise into training, creating spaces for discussion and experience sharing. Dawn believes that the world would be a better place if the amazing research that is done within our Universities had an even greater impact on policy, society and the economy and is dedicated to enabling the next generation of researchers to take on this challenge. Dawn met Pam through a mutual friend at University of Surrey, and they soon became not only colleagues but also good friends. Then Pam introduced her to Julie and the fun truly began!

Julie Reeves is a Researcher Developer and Lecturer of Academic Development (Research) at the University of Southampton. Prior to this, she was the Skills Training Manager (Faculty of Humanities) at the University of Manchester. She has been involved with the Roberts agenda since 2005, working with postgraduate and postdoctoral researchers and academic staff. Her academic background is in politics and international relations; her doctoral research was in cultural theory and international relations. Her newly acquired knowledge and understanding was put to practical advantage when she taught in Eastern Europe for the Civic Education Project, where she then learned much about differing pedagogies. She is a member of the *Chartered Institute of Personnel and Development* and the *Society for Research into Higher Education (SRHE)*. Julie met Pam through the project to create the Vitae Researcher Development Framework; they became co-convenors of the Postgraduate Interest Network of the SRHE and then they published *Developing Transferable Skills: Enhancing your research and employment potential* together in 2014. Julie met Dawn through Pam, SEPnet and the SRHE, as they provided workshops for newer researchers and their supervisors/PIs. Together they produced a literature review on researcher development for Oxford Bibliographies. All three have been 'partners in crime' ever since!

Acknowledgements

Very special thanks are due to Dr Gillian Houston who not only shared with us the results of her doctoral research into the viva voce but contributed ideas and proof-reading to many of the chapters in this book.

We also owe a special debt of gratitude to Shane Dowle, Dr Catherine Lowe, Dr Naomi Winstone and Dr Edd Pitt who contributed specialist chapters.

We are indebted also to our anonymous contributors of Voices of Experience and to the Tarragona Think Tank (TTT) of the EUA-CDE for advice on their countries' doctoral regulations and processes.

Warm thanks also to the following who allowed us to name them as contributing their Voices of Experience:

Professor Rachel Brooks, University of Surrey

Professor Susan Brooks, Senior Postgraduate Tutor

Dr Mawuli Dzodzomenyo, Environmental Health and Microbiology, University of Ghana, Legon

Susanna Hourani, Professor Emeritus, Pharmacology

Prof Jane Ogden, Experienced supervisor and examiner

Lucie Ollis, 2nd year Health Psychology Doctoral Researcher

Mark NK Saunders, Professor of Business Research Methods

Jingwen Wu, University of Southampton

Professor Zeyun Liu, Beijing Normal University

Last but not least, thank you to Vincent Denicolo, Steve Clowes, Linda and John Reeves, and all our family and friends, and colleagues at SAGE who have kept us going throughout the process.

Prologue

Who might find this book useful?

Our passion is to support all those involved in doctoral education, finding ways to help them not only develop their practice but to enjoy doing so. Those who are involved in doctoral assessment in any form have a key role in ensuring that partner participants in doctoral journeys learn from and are empowered by their experience. It is for those assessors, be they supervisors, progress reviewers or final examiners, that we wrote this book, drawing on our own experience in those and related roles, our research on the topic, our learning from the training workshops we have run for colleagues worldwide and the debates we have had with knowledgeable and concerned colleagues at conferences and institutions in the UK, Europe, Africa, North America and Australia.

One of the key issues that has arisen in those discourses is that, though advice abounds for those who are assessed, there is little support material for those who do the assessing. What does exist is dispersed through internal regulatory documents, articles in mainly education journals, chapters and footnotes in books intended for assessors at other levels in education. There is a pervasive assumption that, having assessed work at taught master's and undergraduate levels and having experienced a doctorate oneself, the implicit 'rules of the game' will have become obvious. This neglects important issues such as:

- The doctorate is an entirely different educational pursuit and experience to any other degree;
- Every doctorate is by its very nature unique;
- Each institution has developed its own procedures and regulations;
- There are different national and disciplinary conventions;
- In the last 20 years the doctoral process has been subject to frequent government and hence funding body intervention as a result of political and economic imperatives;

- Increased and encouraged researcher mobility and the electronic communication revolution have initiated concerns about both global equivalence of support and quality of outcome.

Given this context, it is not surprising that doctoral supervisors/assessors/ examiners and their institutions are anxious to ensure that justice is done, and seen to be done, to the difficult, complex process of developing researchers. However, assessment, continuous and final, is an integral and essential part of that process. That assessment is itself a complex activity involving informed judgement, laced with fairness and combined with sensitive communication. Yet in terms of academic staff development it receives somewhat cursory attention. It is not, therefore, surprising that those invited to assess, or indeed who are persuaded to do so, seek and value information, advice and support to inform their practice and provide reassurance. That is both the purpose and the stimulus for this book.

Voice and vocabulary

Throughout this book we have endeavoured to engage you in a conversation. We have imagined you in diverse circumstances yet each of you with a desire and need to assess not merely competently but well. Therefore, we have drawn on many voices to ensure that this conversation recognises and benefits from a range of perspectives. You may find that you can identify the contributions of the different authors despite our editorial efforts to bring some consistency to the presentation. We hope that, rather than making this a disjointed flow of discourse, it makes it more accessible and enjoyable, inviting you to join in the debate.

Reflecting the diversity in which doctoral studies take place, there are sometimes differences in terminology and of course there is a wealth of technical jargon that might well be interpreted slightly differently according to context and even historical time. To accommodate these challenges to communication we have provided a Glossary of Terms which is not composed of dictionary definitions, rather it explains how we have used the terms in this book, our intended meanings. Further, to aid smooth reading, we have selected some terms to use consistently throughout the book though we recognise that alternative words are used elsewhere. For example, we use the label 'supervisor' to represent a person who guides the doctoral process, providing both support and feedback and inhabiting both a guidance and an assessment role, though the latter is seldom very explicit. We are alert that such persons are called advisors or promoters in other countries. Similarly, we use the term examiners for those who conduct the final assessment though they may be called opponents elsewhere. Again, one aspect of the final examination involving oral dialogue is called the viva voce herein but will be recognised as a defence or 'defense' by some of you. We hope you will bear with us and not find it too difficult to translate as you read.

What is unique about this book?

Though we each have served for many years, and continue to do so, the common purpose of supporting the practice of supervisors and examiners through a range of media and forums, the authors of and contributors to this book combine diverse experiences and knowledge from disciplinary, professional and national contexts. Our backgrounds span the major disciplinary areas, STEM–AHSS (Science, Technology, Engineering and Maths–Arts, Humanities, and Social Sciences) and we hold positions in the professional areas in higher education charged with a doctoral education remit, academic-administrative-staff and researcher development. Sharing those perspectives and combining our experiences of living and working in doctoral contexts worldwide, has enabled us to appreciate both the similarities and differences in doctoral provision that exists across higher education.

Researching with and providing training for colleagues in those different contexts has enabled us to learn from them the issues that challenge and concern them and what reactions have been effective and what have not. It is they who are responsible for our writing this book in response to their requests for an accessible compilation of information, advice and, yes, sympathy and encouragement, to aid the difficult enterprise they undertake as assessors and examiners of the highest university degree. We have sought to do that here but also to weave in reminders of how professionally stimulating and personally fulfilling those tasks can be. They can be personally empowering and confidence-building for those who assess as well as for those who are assessed.

Thus, we have combined practical advice from publications, informal discussions and professional debates, and presented different perspectives on issues by recognising the diversity inherent in contexts and participants. However, this is less a 'how to do' book but more a 'think about and reflect upon' volume, as you will see in what follows.

How can you make best use of this book?

First, be assured that, within chapters and in the appendices, we certainly do provide information and advice that we have learned is useful for assessors/examiners.

The appendices are compilations drawn from multiple practitioners over many years. However, prepare to work with and on that information and those suggestions. To encourage your contemplation, we have provided throughout the book activities and reflection points that we suggest will help you tailor the ideas presented to your own situation and to elaborate overviews and summaries to fit the specific challenges and conundrums that you encounter. To bring the story to life and to illustrate how theory impacts on real-life practice, we have used 'voices of experience' provided by colleagues. We are greatly indebted to them for taking the time and being honest in revealing how it has been for them as assessors/ examiners. Also included throughout the chapters are information boxes and key points/top tips lists that we hope you will find helpful during your first reading and then to refer to when you are engaged in your assessment work.

To help you navigate the book, we have divided it into three sections. In Part I this first set of chapters deals with the fundamentals of the topic in focus – what is meant by 'doctorateness', the attributes we seek evidence for as assessors, the various kinds of assessment involved in the doctoral process, the general regulatory requirements involved in the doctoral research process before the final examination, and the different forms of assessment you might encounter or use during those stages.

The next section, Part II, includes details about engagement with assessment including building rapport with those you assess to create an empowering relationship, ensuring that, despite a range of potential differences amongst researchers, your assessment techniques and pronouncements are inclusive as well as just. We then elaborate on what kind of feedback is useful and appreciated by those who receive it and follow this with a chapter that deals with the difficult issue of providing assessment that is negative. Therein we suggest ways in which both the candidate and the assessor can be supported in handling well potentially fraught situations.

Part III, then, has as its focus the final stages of the doctoral process, including a review of how these differ according to disciplinary and national contexts. We provide detail next about the challenging task of examining a thesis and what criteria you might use for the task. For those of you who will examine in situations that call for a viva voce or any form of verbal defence in addition to written work (with or without additional artefacts), the penultimate chapter presents rationales for their use and advice on how to conduct them well. Finally, we consider what potential forms of outcomes you are likely to encounter, how you can differentiate them and present them to candidates. We emphasise that, despite the implication of the term 'final examination', this is frequently an extended procedure – one that involves feedback, revision and further assessment. We close the book recognising that examiners frequently can enjoy a continuing professional relationship with those they have skilfully and thoughtfully examined.

If you are relatively new to a doctoral assessment role than you will find it useful to work your way through the book from the beginning so that you can reflect on advice and information provided against the contextual background that we provide. You will also be armed with relevant information about general expectations and how to implement the regulations germane to your own situation. Although you might consider deferring engagement with Part III until you are invited to examine a submitted doctorate, we would urge you to read it through. You should pay specific attention to the criteria used in examining a doctorate because those are the criteria that will inform your assessment and feedback during the doctorate. Indeed, even if you never intend to take on a formal assessment role, instead only providing ongoing feedback as a supervisor, it is important to know in advance what criteria will be imposed on your doctoral researchers' outputs and what they need to demonstrate in their theses and defences.

On the other hand, if you are an experienced supervisor and examiner, you might prefer to use the information herein to update and hone your practice, to help you train or mentor less experienced colleagues or, indeed, to contact us to help our future practice and book updates by telling us what we have omitted or misunderstood.

If you are contemplating examining in another culture, either cross-disciplinary or international, you may find it useful to be alerted to the variation in practice that we have alluded to throughout the book but have noted specifically in Chapters 4 and 9. Chapter 11 will be useful if you are not familiar with the various forms of oral examination processes.

Whatever your purpose, we hope you find it helpful that we have begun each chapter by outlining the key points covered in it whilst we provide what we hope are short but accurate section titles that describe the foci for each. Most chapters end with a list of further reading which includes publications that we have found to be useful reference sources for our writing and that we acknowledge as elaborating on the information that we have précised in the chapter.

We hope you will all engage with the activities that involve sharing your experiences and wisdom with colleagues either privately within your own contexts or through the auspices of professional debating during events such as conferences and workshops. It is collegiality such as this that ensures that doctorates are indeed equivalent in quality. It also helps develop doctoral processes into enjoyable as well as educational activities for all participants.

PART I
Engaging with the process

1

What is 'doctorateness'?

In this chapter, you will find, in relation to the doctorate:

- Discussion of prevalent myths
- Exploration of its current nature
- Introduction to significant influences
- Notes about its evolving nature
- Celebration of its diversity

Introduction

When contemplating assessment of something, the first task is to understand what it is that you are assessing, what its dimensions or characteristics are and which of these are vital. For tangible objects that are intended to serve a particular purpose this task need not be onerous, for instance when deciding whether something is big enough for a particular purpose lends itself to measurement. Challenges emerge when some of the characteristics, such as beauty or value or credibility, are a matter of individual perspective, especially when influenced by circumstance and context and when the object is itself largely intangible. Other complexities emerge when something that once was rare and only evaluated by a limited number of experts using tacit, almost secret, criteria becomes more commonplace and subject to examination by a large range of experts who are expected to be able to translate the hints of criteria that come their way, though they seldom have the opportunity of comparing the process with each other. (An example here might be the climb to Everest base-camp.) These descriptions could be applied to the **doctorate** as it was until the 1990s; now we have the additional task of assessing something that is undergoing constant, if sometimes subtle, changes in shape and purpose. Often this is achieved using only wisdom, some of it based on myths, passed down from a small number of peers, alongside our own limited experience.

There are several myths that pervade understandings about the nature and award of a doctorate. One is that the doctorate completes the learning process; having achieved this top award, one has reached the pinnacle of learning. A second myth is that the process of the doctorate is akin to those qualifications that precede it, being simply a larger task, a more substantial project. A third myth, frequently subscribed to by those who should know better, is that the nature of a doctorate, and hence how it should be assessed, has until the challenges of recent times remained the same since it was introduced in medieval times. A fourth myth is that, regardless of discipline, all doctorates are the same and therefore should be assessed in the same way: a doctorate is a doctorate is a doctorate. The final myth, which we shall address first, is that the doctorate is a research **project** described in a large piece of written work of some form.

In the past the research project process and its tangible product, a thesis, became known as a 'doctorate'. Over the last 30 years the focus has shifted so that the thesis has become but one piece of evidence presented in the hope of demonstrating the success of a training process intended to imbue a person with research-focussed skills, abilities, and attributes (together described in Denicolo and Park, 2013 as '**doctorateness**') of someone worthy of the title 'doctor'. However, while a range of people, including doctorate funders and employers, are demanding more of their **doctoral researchers**, often over a shorter registration period, they seem reluctant to define the characteristics of doctorateness beyond those required for their own purposes.

We will address the remainder of the myths in turn while trying to discern just what doctorateness is now. For our purposes doctorateness is that quality or combination of qualities that all successful candidates for the award should possess and be able to demonstrate to those who are assessing them, regardless of discipline and geographical context. Capturing this elusive concept has in recent years challenged new and established academics, as well as those who support and train doctoral researchers, as they seek clarity about their goals and purpose for themselves and their doctoral candidates. Presumably, since you are reading this now, you too are seeking guidance on how to manage doctoral assessment more effectively for the candidates and the wider community of scholars. We will, throughout this book, introduce you to the limited number of other resources to draw on to gain information with the caveat that what there is tends to be couched at a very general, abstract level.

Although a generally accepted aim of doctoral study, as delineated in institutional policy and procedure **rubrics**, is the production of a substantive contribution to knowledge worthy of **peer review** and publication, there have been no universally accepted, detailed and measurable objectives (see more about these in Chapter 2) such as one might find for the award of lower degrees; nor have any yet emerged publicly as the doctorate has evolved in recent years. Perhaps the reason is, we will argue, because doctorateness is a complex mix of many characteristics, which may appear in an infinite range of permutations, providing a challenge to assessors and examiners. This provides one important reason to write this book: to provide a vehicle to explore which elements are essential, intrinsic properties that can be cultivated during the process of doctoral study and to engage you as readers actively in this discussion and debate. While we cannot promise short definitive answers to all of the questions about doctoral assessment that you might have, let us start the process of increasing transparency about doctoral assessment by challenging the other myths about the doctorate.

A transition state in the life cycle

We contend that the achievement of a doctorate signifies, not a completion of study, but the beginning of new ways and **outcomes** of learning. Thus, in assessing the doctorate we are not seeking someone who knows everything about the world, their discipline, or indeed even the focal topic of their dissertation, although by **completion** we do expect some expertise, as we shall discuss in later chapters. Instead, a person holding a doctoral degree is, in essence, an autonomous researcher whose continued learning and its products will be constantly assessed by peer review of one form or another. Thus, assessment of the doctorate must form a bridge between the traditions used to evaluate the process and outcomes of other academic awards and those used by peers, other professionals and employers to review the work of colleagues in all sectors.

To successfully induct a colleague into this wide community of researchers, we suggest that it behoves us to demonstrate, during and on completion of the doctorate, collegiality, modelling how peer assessment can be, and should be, constructive. Thenceforth, they too, as our peers, can make a reflective and productively evolving contribution to the community of scholars in whatever fields, professions and cultural contexts they chose after doctoral completion. Thus, researchers must expect to continue to develop their understanding and practice using skills and knowledge stimulated by the doctoral process.

This reflects the turbulent times in doctoral education that began in the early 1990s and have not yet completely calmed down, even in those countries in the vanguard of the transformation, as described in the following sections that address myths three and four. It involves managing the researchers' expectations about what doctoral assessment and **feedback** involve, helping them to relinquish the predominant need for 'high marks' as they engage in new forms of **evaluation** which differ in kind from those they have encountered previously. We will elaborate on this in the next chapter but let us now remind ourselves about other differences in process between the doctorate and preceding degrees and awards.

Differences in kind

There is little doubt that the learning journey of any doctorate and its intended products are vastly different to those that precede it, including other postgraduate courses, diplomas, certificates and master's degrees, as well as undergraduate degrees. In a previous book, *Developing Transferable Skills*, we recognised that many of the academic skills that are learned as part of those courses, such as study skills, information literacy, critical thinking and problem solving, will serve as a basis for further development at doctoral level. However, such skills will need to be practised in a very different environment whilst simultaneously learning many new skills. We drew on the analogy of swimming, setting achieving Olympic status swimming against swimming across a channel in the vagaries of a natural sea, to compare the undergraduate and taught postgraduate education process to that experienced while studying for a doctorate.

The former involves a large pool of clean, transparent and calm water with clearly demarked lanes, safety procedures and support readily available, with goals of achieving certain distances in a competitive time using specific strokes. The latter involves free-style swimming in deep water of uncertain calmness, unpredictable challenges from shipping and unexpected floating objects, with only intermittent support/guidance available to reach a distant shore which is invisible until almost the end of the crossing. Another illustrative analogy, drawn from current news, reinforces the point that those who are successful at Olympic (undergraduate/taught master's) level may not be immediately successful when the context and challenge changes: Mo Farah, a well-acknowledged champion in 1,500 to 10,000 metre stadium running courses, recognised the different challenges he would encounter in city marathon running, predicting that he would need time to develop new skills. At least in that situation the course is marked out and there is a crowd cheering; if the marathon were cross-country with the destination to be worked out during the process, then it would be more analogous with the doctorate.

The role of assessors during the process is not simply to judge how fast the researchers are covering the distance but how well they are developing new skills, including envisioning their own final destination and how to reach it. It is also to provide feedback to aid them in achieving that goal, while averting tripping up or drowning in the process (generally **formative assessment** –developmental –, with some **summative assessment** – definitive evaluative – at formal review points). The examiners of the submitted doctorate still have the task of determining if the destination is worthwhile and whether the process of getting there complied with the rules, but now they must judge whether the candidate is fit to undertake other such challenges autonomously (summative assessment with perhaps a hint of formative assessment for future work). Both assessment forms, assessment during the process and end point assessment, form the substance of this book but first the issue of whether the doctorate itself has been consistent over time, as indicated in myth three, deserves a mention, if only to begin to respond to assertions such as 'we have done it (assessment) so well so far that it does not need changing'.

The evolving nature of the doctorate

A rapid review of the history of the doctorate reveals that the title doctor had religious roots. A very early form can be found in a religious teaching qualification granted in Muslim nations towards the end of the first millennium. In medieval times the Church and the European universities granted to especially able applicants a licence, bestowing the title doctor, to teach a restricted range of subjects (mainly theology, law and medicine). This licence was considered to have greater prestige than the equivalent of a bachelor's degree.

The term Doctor of Philosophy began to be used in Germany during the 17th century, though the word philosophy had a more generic meaning than it does today, encompassing the seeking of knowledge (from the Greek: love of wisdom) in all fields. As it spread over Europe and further afield various abbreviations developed (D. Phil and PhD being the most common in English-speaking nations) whatever the discipline studied, and training took the form of an apprenticeship over seven years (in common with other apprenticeships at the time). Like other university degrees, doctorates were granted mainly to men with the only exceptions being about half a dozen women gaining doctorates in Europe in the 17th and 18th centuries, largely in Spain and Italy.

The 'modern doctorate' was based on the German model developed further in the USA, the UK and beyond in the latter part of the 19th century. Indeed, not all university lecturers in the early part of the 20th century were required to hold doctoral qualifications, though now these are generally seen as a prerequisite for an academic career. [Aside: The development in the late 20th century of 'professional doctorates' in the UK and elsewhere required the recruitment of experts from the professions to university lectureships. They may or may not have doctorates themselves though increasingly it is perceived as advantageous to do so.] Before we explore further the relatively recent rise in diversification of doctoral degrees and the impact of eschewing the **apprenticeship model**, it is worth considering the warnings provided in the reflections of William James in 1903 – see Reflection Point 1.1 for a brief insight into his argument. See 'The PhD Octopus' in the Further reading for the full version.

Reflection Point 1.1

The 'Tyrannical Machine' of graduate education

Consider the tale told by James and what its significance is for today's situation.

> Some years ago, we had at our Harvard **Graduate School** a very brilliant student of Philosophy, who, after leaving us and supporting himself by literary labor for three years, received an appointment to teach English Literature at a sister-institution of learning. The governors of this institution, however, had no sooner communicated the appointment than they made the awful discovery that they had enrolled upon their staff a person who was unprovided with the PhD degree. The man in question had been satisfied to work at Philosophy for her own sweet (or bitter) sake and had disdained to consider that an academic bauble should be his reward.

> His appointment had thus been made under a misunderstanding. He was not the proper man; and there was nothing to do but inform him of the fact. It was notified to him by his new President that his appointment must be revoked, or that a Harvard doctor's degree must forthwith be procured.

James goes on to explain that the scholar spent the next few weeks writing a metaphysical thesis to try to pass the formidable ordeal of Harvard assessment. Sadly, they could not pass it because, although brilliant and original, it did not 'exhibit the technical apparatus of learning' required in a PhD thesis. The panel advised him to pad out his thesis in the required way and supported his case to the other institution to remain in post while doing so.

James continues thus:

> He was allowed to retain his appointment provisionally, on condition that one year later at the farthest his miserably naked name should be prolonged by the sacred appendage the lack of which had given so much trouble to all concerned.

Accordingly he came up here the following spring with an adequate thesis (known since in print as a most brilliant contribution to metaphysics), passed a first-rate examination, wiped out the stain, and brought his College into proper relations with the world again. Whether his teaching, during that first year, of English Literature was made any the better by the impending examination in a different subject, is a question which I will not try to solve.

… is not our growing tendency to appoint no instructors who are not also doctors an instance of pure sham? Will any one pretend for a moment that the doctor's degree is a guarantee that its possessor will be successful as a teacher? Notoriously his moral, social, and personal characteristics may utterly disqualify him for success in the classroom; and of these characteristics his doctor's examination is unable to take any account whatever.

William James, *The PhD Octopus*, Harvard Monthly, March 1903

Having read James's story, some of you may have been surprised that it was written more than a century ago. We believe that it resonates with similar experiences today, while the more cynical of readers may reflect that brilliance is still overlooked in the seeking of conformity to rules. However, all is not lost: we can do better.

As we alluded, although some things appear to have stayed the same over the last century, many other aspects have changed somewhat, while a few others changed radically. There remained until the early 1990s a tendency for governments to leave doctoral education in the hands of universities, saving their interference for undergraduate degrees issues, and thus institutions developed and refined their own policies and procedures based on either the European model of research conducted under the guidance of a **supervisor** or **proposer**, a master of the craft, or the North American model of a taught component followed by research under the guidance of an **advisor**. In all cases the final product subject to examination was a written piece describing and justifying the research and its contribution to knowledge, known in the European-style system as a **thesis** and the North American-style system as a **dissertation**. [Hereafter for simplicity, we shall refer to the academics guiding the doctoral candidate as supervisors and to the written product as a thesis.] To complicate things, since there was no central coordinating body, both national and institutional differences emerged particularly in relation to the procedures related to assessment, as will be detailed in Chapters 3 and 4.

However, as the 20th century progressed the notion of the lone scholar, usually male and self-funded pursuing knowledge as an interest, became superseded by the requirement for larger groups of people funded by the state to seek knowledge for the benefit of society. Thus, as time passed, funding bodies established by government took an increasing interest in how that money was being spent. An example from the UK is the commissioning by the Higher Education Funding Council for England of a report, now known as the Harris Report 1996, which produced recommendations for assuring the quality and standards of postgraduate study, including the need for institutions to pay attention to providing courses relevant to employment opportunities beyond postgraduate study. Shortly afterwards European Universities became subject to the Bologna Agreement (1999), intended to enable researcher mobility and enhance equivalence, with its sequel the **Salzburg Principles** (2005). These contained a consensus agreement between the 35 participating countries on ten basic principles (see Information Box 1.1.) for doctoral training and support which were to have a far-reaching effect with relevance to assessment procedures, as we shall discuss in the chapters that follow.

Information Box 1.1

The Salzburg basic principles

1. The core component of doctoral training is the advancement of knowledge through original research. At the same time, it is recognised that doctoral training must increasingly meet the needs of an employment market that is wider than academia.
2. Embedding in institutional strategies and policies: universities as institutions need to assume responsibility for ensuring that the doctoral programmes and research training they offer are designed to meet new challenges and include appropriate professional career development opportunities.
3. The importance of diversity: the rich diversity of doctoral programmes in Europe, including joint doctorates, is a strength which has to be underpinned by quality and sound practice.
4. Doctoral candidates as early stage researchers: should be recognised as professionals – with commensurate rights – who make a key contribution to the creation of new knowledge.
5. The crucial role of supervision and assessment: in respect of individual doctoral candidates, arrangements for supervision and assessment should be based on a transparent contractual framework of shared responsibilities between doctoral candidates, supervisors and the institution (and where appropriate including other partners).
6. Achieving critical mass: doctoral programmes should seek to achieve critical mass and should draw on different types of innovative practice being introduced in universities across Europe, bearing in mind that different solutions may be appropriate to different contexts.

7. Duration: doctoral programmes should operate within an appropriate duration in time (three to four years full-time as a rule).
8. The promotion of innovative structures: to meet the challenge of **interdisciplinary** training and the development of **transferable skills**.
9. Increasing mobility: doctoral programmes should seek to offer geographical as well as interdisciplinary and **intersectoral** mobility and international collaboration within an integrated framework of cooperation between universities and other partners.
10. Ensuring appropriate funding: the development of quality doctoral programmes and the successful completion by doctoral candidates require appropriate and sustainable funding.

For an elaboration on these see: http://www.eua.be/eua/jsp/en/upload/Salzburg_Report_final.1129817011146.pdf© European University Association

---

It was from this that the Framework for Qualifications of the European Higher Education Area (EHEA) emerged, which contains the '**Dublin Descriptors**', first proposed in 2002 and adopted in 2005. These are generic statements of typical expectations of achievements and abilities associated with awards that represent the end of each of a (Bologna) cycle or level. Those descriptors related to doctoral education can be found in Information Box 1.2.

Information Box 1.2

The Dublin Descriptors for doctoral degrees (the third cycle)

Qualifications that signify completion of the third cycle are awarded to students who:

- have demonstrated a systematic understanding of a field of study and mastery of the skills and methods of research associated with that field;
- have demonstrated the ability to conceive, design, implement and adapt a substantial process of research with scholarly integrity;
- have made a contribution through original research that extends the frontier of knowledge by developing a substantial body of work, some of which merits national or international refereed publication;
- are capable of critical analysis, evaluation and synthesis of new and complex ideas;
- can communicate with their peers, the larger scholarly community and with society in general about their areas of expertise;
- can be expected to be able to promote, within academic and professional contexts, technological, social or cultural advancement in a knowledge-based society.

(Continued)

Glossary

1.   The word 'professional' is used in the descriptors in its broadest sense, relating to those attributes relevant to undertaking work or a vocation and that involves the application of some aspects of advanced learning. It is not used with regard to those specific requirements relating to regulated professions. The latter may be identified with the profile/specification.
2.   The word 'competence' is used in the descriptors in its broadest sense, allowing for gradation of abilities or skills. It is not used in the narrower sense identified solely on the basis of a 'yes/no' assessment.
3.   The word 'research' is used to cover a wide variety of activities, with the context often related to a field of study; the term is used here to represent a careful study or investigation based on a systematic understanding and critical awareness of knowledge. The word is used in an inclusive way to accommodate the range of activities that support original and innovative work in the whole range of academic, professional and technological fields, including the humanities, and traditional, performing, and other creative arts. It is not used in any limited or restricted sense or relating solely to a traditional 'scientific method'.

There are four points to note about these developments: the elaboration of criteria to describe doctorateness; the increased emphasis on the doctorate being a preparation for a number of employment capacities and sectors, not simply for teaching in higher education; the product of doctoral education being identified as a person with a range of research skills, albeit mainly but not exclusively identified within a written work; and a strong suggestion for a limited timeframe for doctoral completion.

These principles and descriptors have been adopted almost globally, refined/reworded to fit local situations with greater prominence given in ensuing years to aspects that **impact** on national economies. For instance, the Salzburg recommendation 7, for the duration for a doctorate being 'three to four years full-time as a rule', has been adopted firmly by the funding councils in the UK with financial implications for institutions that are, in turn, now greatly concerned with **submission** and completion rates to retain that funding. Although some general defining attributes are now emerging, differences between disciplines can be identified at a broad level in that their representative funders interpret the timeframe slightly differently as well as what counts as evidence of the required attributes. This leads us to consider whether there is equivalence between doctorates from different disciplines, myth four.

Celebrating difference

There has always been an expectation that, although each doctoral study is unique (it must produce a novel contribution to knowledge after all), there is some equivalence between doctorates, no matter the discipline or the geographical location of the awarding institution. Thus, the elusive essence of doctorateness should be demonstrated in, as examples, a dance doctorate that requires a performance, a mathematics doctorate that requires the development of a logical progression, a physics doctorate based on numerical data analysis, a social work doctorate based on the interpretation of interview data and a literature doctorate that involves the deconstruction of text. One reason for having external examiners is to assure that equivalence. However, we note that in the past and commonly now, examiners come from the same general, and often particular, discipline area. It is only in the last 20 years or so, with the advent of multi- or cross-disciplinary doctoral studies that academics have been alerted to disciplinary differences in the way that research is conducted and presented for examination. However, the application of the Dublin Descriptors that can be augmented by disciplinary examination requirements provides some reassurance of, at least basic, equivalence even though there continues to be a range of institutional and national variation in procedures.

In the UK key attributes of doctoral level researchers were summarised in the Researcher Development Framework (RDF) (www.vitae.ac.uk/researchers-professional-development/about-the-vitae-researcher-development-framework), defining the continued development of these attributes at succeeding levels of experience, beyond that expected of new doctoral graduates. Thus, it reinforces our contention that the end of the doctorate is not the end of learning. This framework of 81 attributes with five developmental stages allows for variation in starting points for individual users and across users, with each person encouraged to develop across the range to suit the stages and purposes of their lifelong research journeys. The RDF has been adopted around the world to support the development of researchers, from the start of a doctorate onwards, which is helpful in establishing and maintaining correspondence of doctorateness across borders. Furthermore, the European University Association Council for Doctoral Education is currently discussing a range of ways to work towards greater equivalence by establishing minimum standards of doctoral support, although total standardisation or/and uniformity are being strongly resisted by those who value diversity to address a myriad of different research challenges as well as those who abhor change.

The last caveat is important; clearly there can be differences in approaches, methods, and so on related to research in the various disciplines, while professional doctorates (as those in the UK or in the USA) or practice-based doctorates (as required by different professions) may differ in balance of taught component to research activity. What is critical is that the standard reached, rather than the pathway travelled or indeed its starting point, is equivalent across these variants. However, judging this is more easily written than established in practice. Complexity remains a challenge alongside diversity and this is likely to increase as doctoral research embraces a broader range of subject matter. As was discussed in many UK Quality Assurance Agency (**QAA**) meetings and academic conferences across the globe from the early 1990s, the task is equivalent to Wittgenstein's philosophical treatise on what features determine that something is a game. He noted that there was no rigid definition of a game that excludes everything that is not a game, yet we can still differentiate games and not games (say hopscotch, chess, and card games for instance, from abseiling, commonly described as a sport). Our task is to learn how to differentiate doctorateness from non-doctorateness, both for integrity in the final examination and to provide feedback to guide candidates as they move from one state to the other. Though such assessment is a challenging task, nevertheless it is one that we can accomplish in ways that respect those who try to achieve it. In the next chapter we will investigate further the role and function of assessment in the doctoral process, beginning to formulate more transparent guidance.

Further reading

Denicolo, P. M. and Park, C. (2013) 'Doctorateness – an elusive concept?' In M. Kompf and P. M. Denicolo (Eds.) *Critical Issues in Higher Education*. Rotterdam: Sense Publishers

James, William (1903) *The PhD Octopus*. Available at: www.uky.edu/~eushe2/Pajares/octopus.html

2

What is the role of assessment in doctoral studies?

In this chapter, you will find:

- Identification of meanings of assessment in the doctorate
- The rationales for various forms of assessment explored
- Examples from practice provided
- Demonstration of how assessment and feedback can be positive forces in developing the independence of researchers and for successful completion

Introduction

In this chapter we will weave together knowledge from experienced supervisors and examiners with published research to create example learning objectives for different doctoral stages and discuss how progress towards doctorateness can be supported through assessment and **feedback**. We intend this to empower supervisors and examiners to proactively support the learning and development of doctoral researchers from beginning to end of the doctoral journey.

Uncovering doctoral assessment

The journey to achieving 'doctorateness' is often shrouded in mystery, with reports of it 'just clicking' at some point, as if by magic the person who was not previously 'doctorate standard' suddenly embodies doctorateness. Although this change in a person may appear sudden, in fact if one would more closely observe the journey, the guiding hand of a supervisor would probably be observed, as well as the suggestions, questions and challenges of those within the research community. Undoubtedly, a hard-working doctoral researcher adjusting, responding, rejecting and moulding themselves and their project in response to this wide range of assessment, formal and informal, would also be abundantly evident. However, at very few stages in the doctorate is this assessment recognised for what it is; instead it remains tacit, taking place within the context of supervisory meetings, departmental seminars, and progress reviews, which often seem more bureaucratic than pedagogic.

Perhaps this view derives from a mix of dedication to the myth that doctoral study is a singular and lonely pursuit of independent research, particularly in **HASS** subjects, and the trepidation generated by the word assessment in previous education. Certainly, the notions of assessment being either or both formative and summative (with formative being developmental and summative being final evaluation of outcome towards a standard) are, perhaps, more commonly discussed in the discipline of Education than in other disciplines. However, both kinds of assessment occur at different periods during the doctorate, with formative assessment being the most frequent, and perhaps the most helpful when skilfully used (see Part II). This formative assessment is relatively informal so seldom recognised as assessment, taking place throughout the doctorate, its nature and timing determined mainly by the individuals involved. Summative assessment, on the other hand, tends to be more formal and its nature and timing are often determined by the disciplinary customs and regulations of the Institution (see the next section and Chapter 3). Except for the final assessment, these summative assessment points lack explicit integration within the **pedagogy** of the doctoral journey.

Further complicating matters, there are many variations of the doctoral degree, with differences appearing across discipline and national context. However, research is an international endeavour and those awarded a doctorate degree can take advantage of a global job market. Indeed, to strengthen doctoral currency examiners for doctoral completion are often drawn from an international pool of experts, which helps to create and maintain some international equivalence. Indeed, in some more specialist areas or countries with fewer institutions to choose examiners from, drawing from an international pool might be an expectation or the norm. This being the case, it is important for all doctoral assessors to understand not only the doctoral assessment within their own institution and country, but also to develop a broader understanding of different types of doctoral assessment and their standards and criteria. In this chapter we look at the different stages of progression and their complementary assessment procedures in a general way by focussing on the learning objectives involved, considering how they can be achieved in different ways in different disciplinary and national **cultures**.

Towards a definition of learning objectives for doctoral stages

The frequently tacit nature of doctoral assessment combined with the variable and individual nature of each doctorate can make it challenging for doctoral researchers, as well as those guiding their progress, to identify clear expectations at the various stages of the doctorate. While we would not want to curtail the necessary diversity and originality of research undertaken, we propose that clarity of expectation is key to providing effective assessment of progress throughout the doctorate. When trying to explicitly define these expectations, it is helpful to consider the end target of 'doctorateness' as discussed in the previous chapter. If this is what we are aiming for, then we can work backwards to deliberate on what are reasonable expectations for the various stages leading up to the end.

While defining clear expectations, it is important to remember that doctorateness is not a property of the project, but of the researcher. There may be times when the person is moving forward as a researcher, but the actual research project is not moving forward very much at all. It can be easy, while assessing the progress of the doctorate, to focus on the interesting, innovative research and whether it is progressing. Of course, at times, lack of progress of the research project is indeed indicative of lack of progress of the doctoral researcher; however, this is not always the case and it would be a mistake for anyone, researcher or examiner, to assume so. Therefore, when forming expectations, it is crucial to think about how you evaluate the doctoral researcher's developmental progress, not simply that of the research project which, as we all know, is likely to have its own twists and turns, side-tracks eventually rejected and frustrating recursions. You may have to remind the doctoral researcher of this distinction from time to time.

While we will explore in detail in Chapters 10 and 11 the criteria used at the end point of doctoral study, for our purposes here we will be seeking evidence of the researcher gradually becoming an independent researcher. That is, someone able to use a range of skills to devise, design and conduct impactful/useful research in their field, including dealing with the challenges inherent in research, and disseminate its products in a variety of forms to a range of audiences. Although we expect the actual project to generate some novel information, in this process that project is a learning vehicle, an opportunity to select and hone skills, while the final thesis documents the evidence for those achievements rather than being a simple report about the project. It is thus a unique document with a distinctive purpose.

Now we have explored what is being aimed for, we can proceed to the next sections in which we will examine the various stages of the doctoral research journey, thinking about our expectations, what we consider to be 'good' progress towards that goal and how we can access this at various points, all the while considering the importance of disciplinary differences. Because we understand that different doctorates have different lengths and structures, depending on discipline, national context and institution, as well as the researcher's mode of registration, to better understand expectation at different points in the doctoral journey, we will break stages up into three loosely defined categories; early stage; middle stage and end stage.

Activity 2.1

Your expectations for different stages

What are your expectations for the different stages of the doctorate? Write a list of expectations you have of doctoral researchers in the beginning, middle and end stages of the doctorate. Ask yourself:

- Are they affected by the duration of the research programme, for instance do they differ for full-time or part-time researchers?
- What do you think the key developmental milestones are?
- How are these assessed in your institution?
- What evidence is sought?
- How are these similar and different to those which you experienced as a doctoral researcher?
- Why do you think these differences emerged?

At the beginning

Doctoral researchers enter programmes with a wide variety of backgrounds and experience. Some come into a doctorate straight from a taught programme, either an undergraduate or a master's degree or a professional course, while others have gained years of professional or other work experience before returning to undertake a doctoral degree. Many people travel internationally to find the right doctoral programme for them, bringing with them different cultural expectations and experiences. Yet, despite these differences, in our experience doctoral researchers usually enter a doctorate with one thing in common: they are quite unclear about what is expected of them and how to succeed in the very different learning context of a doctoral degree. After all, they have little to compare it with. Even the very few who have a close relative who has experienced doctoral study will have only a vague, and probably old-fashioned, notion of what it involves now in your context. All of this generates a good deal of excitement and anticipation for doctoral researchers, but also a considerable amount of anxiety and uncertainty, that then adds to the context in which assessment takes place.

Doctoral assessment in the beginning is often hidden, tacit and primarily centred around formative feedback provided by the supervisor. This feedback can come in many forms (see Chapter 4), at different times and can be focussed on a wide variety of aspects from the technical to the theoretical to the practical and may vary greatly across the disciplines (see Voice of Experience Box 2.1). In the beginning, the newer researcher is looking to their supervisor to understand how to succeed in this very different educational experience. Formative assessment is key to doctoral research-ers making a successful transition into this new world of research. It is worth taking the time to actively think about how, when and what type of formative feedback your newer researcher may need to start off well. In our experience new doctoral researchers can find the lack of formal assessment and feedback quite daunting and need to understand explicitly how you will help them understand their progress and provide the feedback they need to improve throughout this beginning phase. Clear expectations are incredibly important to ensure this more informal approach to assessment works well for both supervisor and supervisee.

Voice of Experience 2.1

Feedback in the beginning stage: two supervisors' experiences

I like to get my doctoral students writing early in their doctorate as, in my view, it is only through putting down ideas clearly in writing that we really know we understand. I tell them this is why writing is so difficult; revealing that I find it difficult. I emphasise that none of us write, we rewrite. I also set my expectations of them. I emphasise that I view poor referencing as a sign of sloppy work and stress I only want to read and comment on their best work. I tell them there is nothing more disheartening than, having spent a few hours reading and commenting on a piece of work, for the author to say, 'well I knew I needed to do that'. If the author knew something

(Continued)

needed fixing and they knew how to do it, then why expect me to waste my time commenting about what they already knew!

We chat at length about the nature of feedback they would like to receive even before they have submitted their first piece of writing. They usually talk about wanting feedback that allows them to improve their written argument and highlights any key literature they may have missed. We usually agree the focus of the feedback that will be helpful for the specific piece of writing they are undertaking. For the first piece of work they submit, I warn them that students have said that my feedback seems, at least initially, extremely harsh. I tell them I will be very picky, concentrate mainly on aspects that need improvement, and they will almost certainly take my comments personally; even though they are given in the spirit of helping them develop.

Nowadays, I usually give feedback electronically. This means I can email it to the student to read prior to the meeting so we can have a proper discussion. The feedback is always preceded by a summary outlining those aspects which they have done well and then those where improvement is needed. We can all improve our work. Sometimes if the same issue appears time and time again in the writing I put after the comment 'I will not comment on this issue again'.

I am also happy with the student challenging the points I make – I can get things wrong and make mistakes.

Mark NK Saunders Professor of Business Research Methods

An important aspect of providing feedback to new doctoral researchers is to ensure that it is perceived as useful feedback not harsh criticism. You must establish an open, honest and equal relationship with the researcher, one in which you can discuss their work without intimidating them or making them feel that they must hide things or pretend to understand what they don't. Set out your rules and expectations right at the start and try and find out what their expectations are of you. As well as having formal documented meetings you are likely to meet them informally for brief updates and laboratory guidance very often, particularly at the start.

Trust is key to the relationship and goes both ways. In a laboratory-based discipline you must be able to trust their results as your reputation may ultimately depend on them, so tell them from the start that it is OK to make mistakes if they acknowledge them, record them and learn from them. Equally though make it clear that carelessness and sloppiness either in labwork or in record-keeping are unacceptable. To begin with they may need a lot of practical help and advice, so give them some relatively simple tasks to start with so that they gain in confidence and learn the tricks of the trade. Explain the methods clearly and go through their results in detail, asking lots of questions so that you can gauge their level of understanding. Reassure them if things don't work straight away, and if they make mistakes correct them gently and explain things clearly.

In parallel with developing laboratory techniques the new researcher must learn the essential skills of scientific reading and writing. You need to get them writing something early on so that you can see their level of knowledge and understanding. Give them a stack of papers to get started and show them how to search and evaluate the relevant literature and how to use reference management software *properly*. Get them to write something short to start with, read it before you meet them and go through it in person, explaining any comments you have made and clarifying any points you feel they have not understood correctly.

For both the labwork and the writing make sure that you don't only talk about what they need to improve but highlight what they have done well and give them some praise. They need to feel that a discussion with you is not a test or an interrogation but a valuable opportunity to learn. Don't get impatient if you have to say things more than once before it sinks in, because you do not want to damage their confidence or make them feel that they cannot be open with you about any difficulties. Try to remember what it felt like when you first started; treat them as you would have liked to be treated. Hopefully one day this new researcher will be your friend and colleague.

Susanna Hourani Professor Emeritus, Pharmacology

We propose that thinking about the learning objectives for this first critical stage of the doctorate, the transition into doctoral research, can help bring reassurance through structure and clarity. It can also build trust within the supervisor-supervisee relationship, preventing misunderstandings if they are discussed together in terms of how they could be achieved. Therefore, let us think about what the aims of this first stage are and then consider what are the learning objectives.

We think that a reasonable aim for this stage is that the researcher provides evidence of a firm basis for future progress by ensuring that the design of the project addresses a feasible topic that should produce, through a well-designed process, novel results (**outputs**) that are of value in some definable way. Below we attempt to list some possible learning objectives that doctoral researchers should achieve by the end of the first phase that are broad enough to cross most or all disciplines. We then invite you to compare these to your own expectations (Reflection Point 2.1) and then discuss such objectives with your peers (Activity 2.2).

The doctoral researcher should have:

1. Demonstrated evidence of critical engagement with relevant academic literature;
2. Constructed reasoned arguments for the study and approach;
3. Developed a clear case for the novelty and academic/professional value of proposed research;
4. Demonstrated the feasibility of methodological/philosophical approach, methods proposed and/or experimental technique(s) and chosen analysis procedures;
5. Created a realistic plan of work, which can be completed within the funded period or by an agreed upon completion date, with the understanding that there is a need for contingency planning and flexibility (recognising that novel research never quite goes to plan);
6. Evidenced that research and transferable skills (including writing and analytical skills) are developing at a rate necessary to complete and defend a doctorate within specified completion time period;
7. Provided evidence for availability of necessary resources to complete project.

Reflection Point 2.1

Your review of the learning objectives of the first stage

Do these learning objectives match your expectations of progress in the first stage?

What specific objectives would you add or take away to make this list suit your discipline and institutional context?

Activity 2.2

Share your learning objectives

Discuss your thoughts on the learning objectives for the first stage of the doctorate with your supervisor colleagues. We hope you will join us to contribute to this important international dialogue through networks and online.

First summative assessment

It is increasingly common, internationally, to have a major summative assessment that in many ways marks the end of the beginning phase of the doctorate and the start of the middle phase. This assessment is summative and usually involves assessor(s) outside of the supervisory team. The aim of this assessment typically is to determine if enough progress has been made throughout this first phase of the doctorate, although the way in which these assessments take place and the specific skills tested are highly variable (see International Examples Box 2.1). Most of these assessments test specific learning objectives similar to those outlined in the previous section. This key summative assessment point serves as a gateway in the transition from the beginning phase of the doctorate to the more research intensive and productive middle phase of the doctorate.

International Examples Box 2.1

Three examples of early stage summative hurdles

UK

Confirmation: Confirmation will normally occur within ~12 months of registration as a full-time doctoral researcher. (For part-time researchers, 18 months is more usual.)

The confirmation process is a two-part assessment, consisting of a written report and a viva, analogous to the UK final assessment procedure. Two members of academic staff outside the supervisory team conduct the assessment, with the supervisors playing no role in this assessment. Examiners assess the feasibility of successful completion of the doctorate within the allowed timeframe. To do this they assess the project and the candidate based on the progress made within the first year.

Belgium

First year evaluation: After 9–11 months, the first-year evaluation takes place in the presence of the supervisor and co-supervisor(s) and the supervisory committee. The project and the results obtained so far are presented. The supervisory committee will evaluate if the candidate has enough background knowledge, a critical scientific attitude, has made sufficient progress, is able to present the data in a coherent way with correct statistics and is able to answer questions appropriately. The supervisory committee can make suggestions for improvement of the project and the candidate.

USA

Qualifying Examination: Within the first four semesters a student should pass their qualifying exams. The qualifying examination evaluates the student's ability to integrate their specialty with the broader discipline. Each of the three committee members, normally drawn from internal academic staff other than the advisor, will submit one or two topics (and a reading list), i.e., a total of three to six topics. These will be presented to the student within two weeks of the committee's formation or of its initial meeting. Before receiving the topic/s, it is the student's responsibility to discuss with each committee member potential topics that integrate the student's specialty in order to identify the topic/s and reading list. At the end of three months' (maximum) preparation for all topics, the student will take a closed book, sit-down exam consisting of three questions (generally each committee member submits to the advisor one question related to the reading list).

Please note these are simply examples from universities in these countries rather than representative of the whole country.

This early summative assessment is often an incredibly challenging role for the assessors, who are tasked with assessing a work in progress, a researcher on a unique journey towards 'doctorateness' and a research project that has morphed over the first phase and will undoubtedly continue to evolve throughout the next years. Making it even more complicated, assessors are assessing, not only their colleague's doctoral researcher, but to some extent that person's research and supervision as well. This brings departmental politics into play much more than most other educational assessment situations. However, there is a great need for both critical and constructive feedback at this phase of the doctorate to help define the future journey and, at times, to identify problems that could be detrimental to the doctorate before more time and personal energy are invested in a fruitless endeavour.

Therefore, it is important to ensure that all those who act as assessors are prepared for and supported in this role. To be prepared, all academics within a department should have a shared understanding of expectations of this assessment process. The best way to ensure this necessary clarity is to talk openly within the department and the University, breaking away from the conscious or unconscious tradition of secrecy. We find that once these conversations start to happen, all parties feel a sense of relief at sharing not only processes and expectations, but also uncertainties and fears.

Committing the outcomes of such discussions to writing in the form of written guidance on the assessments then ensures that, as new members of the department come and go, there is a shared understanding that can be revisited and revised as necessary. This written guidance is also positive for the doctoral researchers themselves who can often be anxious going into this first formal assessment and all guidance, on both basic aspects (such as word count) and bigger picture learning objectives, alleviates some stress and allows them to focus on the work they need to do. Some institutions provide the doctoral researchers with templates or pro-forma to be completed in advance, and that forms the basis of the assessment; for instance, one UK institution requires a 6,000-word report in a given template. The learning objectives defined in the above section may be a good starting point for a conversation about these assessment forms, which can be changed and augmented to suite different institutions.

Creating this shared space where all members of academic staff co-create the expectations, can also help to tackle more sticky political issues, such as how to address problems with a research project that is a critical part of your colleague's work. Assessors must feel free to assess and ultimately criticise all aspects of the doctoral researcher's submissions, including those that may be more supervisor driven. This means colleagues must learn to support and value this as a peer-review process. In the next Activity, 2.3, we suggest you explore the procedures in your own context, establishing, if necessary, such a forum for discussion and sharing of good practice.

Activity 2.3

Your institution's first formal assessment of the doctorate

Look at your University's doctoral handbook and/or regulations. Is there a formal assessment of progress marking the transition from first phase to middle phase of the doctorate? If so, are the criteria you, as an assessor, are assessing against made clear? Do you feel these criteria match with what you think is an important measure of a doctoral researcher's progress towards doctorateness? We invite you to discuss with colleagues your institution's practice and your thoughts about how it might be improved for all participants.

It is worth noting that this is likely to be the doctoral researcher's first true experience of peer review (more on peer-review assessment below). They will be looking to both their supervisor and the assessor(s) to learn how to react in this new and sometimes uncomfortable situation. As assessors, providing clear and constructive explanation for your judgements will help greatly. This will demonstrate to the doctoral researcher that the process is not a personal attack, but an exercise to ensure quality. As supervisors, your reaction to criticism will be closely watched. This is a chance to demonstrate reflection and the value of feedback (even though this challenges all of us at times). Peer review is a way of academic life; this first experience is in a controlled environment where all parties can humanely teach our newer researchers the benefits of receiving feedback from colleagues. Another real benefit of the whole process is that it can also be an opportunity to understand the work of your colleagues which can then lead to idea sharing and even future collaboration. For newer assessors it is a fantastic chance to get a better idea of how different doctoral researchers progress and start to build your understanding of different supervisory techniques. The importance of this process for the researcher is clearly manifold, as can be seen in the Voice of Experience next.

Voice of Experience 2.2

Reflection from a PGR on this confirmation and the impact of that assessment

My confirmation review went really well, and I got some really useful feedback. The examiners questioned me a lot about my study design and my study hypotheses and my understanding of the concept I am exploring. In terms of the piece of writing, they had some very constructive feedback on my systematic review and gave me some ideas on how to improve it.

I'm not sure this is everyone's experience, but it definitely made me feel more confident about my ability to complete my PhD (in time and of a good standard!).

It was what I expected as a result of the workshops I attended, and it wasn't anywhere near as scary as people say it is – it felt more like a conversation (if slightly critical) than an exam.

Lucie Ollis, 2nd year Health Psychology Doctoral Researcher

Middle stage: Role of multiple assessors

In general, the middle stage of the doctorate is one of ups and downs, increasing but fluctuating **independence**, and more frequent external assessment of some kind. Progress may occasionally be hard to measure as the researchers' skills and abilities may be progressing at times when the research project itself is stalling or reshaping, for instance as they learn to damage control and/or persist with the project despite challenges. This is often the stage when doctoral researchers become more integrated into their disciplinary research community, moving slightly away from the safety of their supervisor and department with feedback becoming more akin to the peer-review model of a professional. However, there are likely to be periods during which the guiding formative assessment of the supervisor will still be critical to maintain consistent progress amid the normal vicissitudes of a research journey. Summative assessment will, in all probability, continue for most researchers through an annual review process or progress review, which is increasingly becoming formalised through doctoral progress tracking software.

Evolving nature of supervisory assessment

Supervisors remain key assessors of doctoral progress throughout the doctorate, continuing to provide formative feedback. However, as doctoral researchers progress into and through the middle stage of their doctorate, this formative feedback often takes on a different nature, becoming less directive and more facilitative. However, as with so much of these doctoral conventions, this change in approach often happens without explicit acknowledgement. Often this may feel natural to both supervisor and supervisee; however, sometimes the doctoral researcher may feel abandoned by the supervisor, because of the reduction in close working or amount of feedback. The authors have had doctoral researchers come to us in tears, concerned that their supervisors are upset with them or no longer interested in their research because they are spending less time with them and focusing primarily on more junior researchers. Therefore, it is suggested that discussing these changes in formative feedback and explicitly celebrating the growing independence of the maturing researcher is key to ensuring that formative supervisor feedback and assessment continue to be supportive and effective. Furthermore, it is worth discussing the variety of different ways in which a doctoral researcher within this middle stage can obtain additional feedback from others to help move their research and their own professional development forward. Doctoral researchers will appreciate your openness about the process and the reassurance that you are no less interested in them and their research; rather, you are simply noting the change in process to mark their progress.

Peer-review assessment

Besides this informal watching and facilitative assessment by supervisors, external peer-review assessment also becomes a greater part of the doctorate at this middle stage. Throughout this stage and for the rest of their time working in an academic context, researchers receive direct assessment from peers about their conference abstracts, presentations and publications. Learning how to value peer-review critique and utilising it for the benefit of the research is a key skill newer researchers must learn. However, we all know how painful and personal it feels when you read a negative review of the work you have put your heart and soul into. Therefore, everyone involved in supervising and mentoring newer researchers should work to model an appreciation for peer review. Furthermore, if you are in the position to be assessing a paper or conference abstract as a peer-reviewer, it is worth remembering there may be a newer researcher at the other end of this review, someone who needs constructive assessment and feedback to strengthen their research and build their own skills. This by no means is to suggest that the outcome of the review should be any different. Rather, the way in which you provide feedback should be the same as you would do for any doctoral researcher within your department, with detail, clarity and kindness.

As members of your disciplinary community, you are in fact frequently taking on a role of assessor to newer researchers in your general area of expertise in a much more informal and implicit way. Every time you talk with a newer researcher at a conference, ask a question in a seminar or comment on a research poster, you are providing important formative feedback to a newer researcher, whilst also setting an example as a role model. Although it is often not something considered, these brief interactions serve to initiate researchers into the disciplinary community and at times may just inspire and boost the motivation of a doctoral researcher experiencing a mid-stage slump. Often the role of assessor is seen negatively in society; however, particularly in this middle stage of the doctorate where people are just inching themselves out into the external communities of their fields, the opportunity to provide informal feedback that can truly enthuse is a newer researcher is something to take joy in, as exemplified in Voice of Experience 2.3.

Voices of Experience 2.3

Inspiring external feedback

I remember a time in my own doctorate when I was becoming increasingly frustrated with the data analysis. Long story short, nothing was going to plan or seemed to make sense. Then we had our yearly open day where we invited Parkinson's Disease patients and their carers to visit our department and discuss with us the work we were doing to better understand the neurobiology of Parkinson's Disease. I was a little wary about talking to these people, particularly because I felt my research wasn't giving me the answers they would be expecting from us. The day turned out so differently to what I had expected. Throughout the day, I showed a wide variety of people around the lab and talked with them over the microscope about what we were trying to do, but I also got a fantastic opportunity to listen. They told us about living with this disease and how it affected their lives. No one expected answers, they just valued the opportunity to learn what we were doing and to be able to share their experiences with us. Most surprising of all, as they brought this disease to life, which I had been studying in test tubes and slides, I began to think about my data in a different way. They inspired me to think beyond the specific brain area and cell type so commonly focused on in this research area and to think of Parkinson's Disease more as a whole brain disease. This not only got me out of my rut but inspired a new narrative which became central to my thesis.

A Neuroscience researcher

I gave a paper at the British International Studies Conference, the only one, and an important person in my field came along and asked me loads of questions. I really enjoyed his questions but was really surprised when he approached me at the end of the session. First, he invited me to his institution to give another talk and he also asked if I was going to publish the paper. I was absolutely thrilled – I had no idea it was THAT good! For the first time, I had a wider sense of the interest in my work.

A Politics and International Relations researcher

Shortly after starting my PhD, I presented to an academic audience for the first time at the **Doctoral College** Conference. At the time, I was reluctant to engage in any form of public speaking, and the internal conference provided a supportive environment to experience presenting research. A few months later, with new-found confidence, I spoke at the University of Aveiro, Portugal, and went on to present at conferences on a near-monthly basis for the next two years, including every Doctoral College conference event during my time as a researcher. It was through that first conference that I built up the confidence to submit abstracts for external conferences, leading to trips abroad, collaborations, publications, and becoming part of a wider research community.

Presenting at a conference, whether a paper recital or a poster, put me in a position to receive feedback from academics who didn't know me or my research. I have found that the most valuable feedback and insight often comes from those who are outside of my direct area of study. The different perspectives on approaches to research, methodologies, and knowledge of existing studies of interest are of real benefit to new researchers. It is often that the simple questions that go unnoticed by the researcher are asked by the audience at conferences; these can prompt significant changes within the eventual PhD thesis, while also increasing its accessibility.

As a student at a conference the environment offers a great opportunity to engage with experienced researchers and academics who are more than happy to offer advice and guidance. During the final stages of my PhD, I found that I had become the person offering advice to new researchers so that they may benefit in the same ways I did.

A Music researcher

Beginnings of self-assessment

Another form of assessment starts to become increasingly predominant in the middle and then final stages of the doctorate: the ability of the researcher to self-assess their own progress. To successfully utilise the increasingly facilitative feedback from supervisors, coupled with the need to also take on board feedback, criticism and assessment from a wide range of peers, a doctoral researcher must learn to reflect on their own progress and performance and to start to self-assess. This is fundamental to becoming an independent researcher and a professional person, and in fact is the sole purpose of all doctoral assessment. The end point of a doctorate is to produce a person who can independently push the boundaries of what is currently known. To do this, they must be aware of their own progress, be able to evaluate it to identify learning needs, and to seek out external assessment through peer review. It is in the middle stage of the doctorate where this ability typically begins to develop significantly; however, at what point exactly is highly individual and may be driven more from the challenges in research rather than the successes. Accepting that a main purpose of doctoral assessment is to develop the ability to self-assess challenges those involved in this assessment process to walk a tightrope of providing space for learning, at times through failure, with the need to keep the doctoral journey moving forward. For this reason, it is valuable to have the larger discipline community supporting the assessment of researchers throughout this dynamic stage of the doctoral journey. Many institutions ask doctoral researchers to regularly assess their professional skills set and progress using established frameworks such as the RDF, or other professional frameworks, as we shall see in Chapter 4. Such processes are greatly enhanced if, in your role as supervisor and assessor, you support this and show interest in the researchers' view of their progress and development.

Towards learning objectives for the middle stage

The middle stage of the doctorate is probably the most individually variable time in which the novel research projects take everyone on a unique journey, combined with every doctoral researcher's own distinctive professional developmental strengths and weaknesses. Nonetheless, by the end of this turbulent and exhilarating stage, there are certain expectations we can outline to define the skills necessary to tackle successfully the final stage of the doctorate.

Some suggested learning objectives for the middle stage of the doctorate are that the researcher should have:

1. Provided evidence that they are engaging with the planned work with increasing skill, managing the process by keeping to time and to the limits of other resources wherever possible;
2. Demonstrated reflective practice through consideration and application of feedback, both provided by supervisor and through peer review;
3. Enacted contingency plans when research does not go as anticipated;
4. Constructed a coherent narrative of the research journey, articulating expected key contribution(s) to knowledge and developing a draft schema for the thesis;
5. Evidenced a commitment to continued professional development as a researcher through selected skill and experience acquisition;
6. Demonstrated independent ownership of the project with views emerging for professional/career development.

Reflection Point 2.2

Your review of the learning objectives of the middle stage

Do these learning objectives match your expectations of progress in the middle stage?
What specific objectives would you add or take away to make this list suit your discipline and institutional context?

Activity 2.4

Share your mid-stage learning objectives

Share with colleagues and in wider forums your thoughts on the learning objectives for the middle stage of the doctorate so that you can contribute to this important international dialogue. Consider especially, with colleagues and by sharing experience and practice, how the role of assessment facilitates and encourages increasing researcher independence.

Final stage: Towards the finish line

As a doctoral researcher embarks on the final stage of their doctoral research, usually characterised by a great deal of writing and possibly data analysis, with some final bits of data collection, they are well on their way to becoming an independent researcher. However, they will have little idea of the exact requirements for the final thesis and viva. Therefore, they still have a need for formative assessment from their supervisor, before the big end summative assessment.

The doctoral researcher will need feedback on whether they have dealt effectively with results and argued for their interpretations as well as clearly stated the novelty and relevance/potential impact within their writing. An assessment of their ability to discuss and defend their research coherently with various audiences is critical to aid their preparation for the viva. These are all areas where their ability to self-assess will still need to be augmented by formative assessment from their supervisor. They will need to have guidance on preparing for their big day and, most of all, they need help to develop a clear understanding of what to expect during the final assessment stage. (See Part III for detailed guidance on final assessment.)

The learning objectives for this final stage must be based on our universal understanding of the outcomes of a doctoral, such as the Dublin descriptors (see Information Box 1.2). However, whether these descriptors, now over 15 years old, are still relevant and definitive for the doctorate today is a matter for debate. In particular, as the neuroscience researcher indicated in Voice of Experience 2.3 above, the benefits of engaging with and obtaining 'feedback' from the public (as well as communities, organisations, industry and business beyond academia) can be extremely useful to researchers, alongside considering the wider implications and beneficiaries of their research. These are all absent in the descriptors despite becoming increasingly important components of the contemporary doctorate. Furthermore, whether the traditional thesis and viva are enough to assess all the learning objectives of the doctorate is currently being questioned.

Thus, as part of your own ongoing professional development, we suggest that you not only keep abreast with developments in your own context and globally, but also contribute to that debate.

Reflection Point 2.3

Learning from personal experience

Thinking about your doctorate, what was your experience of receiving feedback from your supervisor/s?

(Continued)

Did the assessment reflect the different stages of the project and was feedback adjusted accordingly?

What did you find useful and what would you wish your supervisor could have improved on or done differently?

Further reading

For perspectives on assessment and feedback in professional doctorates:

Costley, C. and Stephenson, J. (2009) Building doctorates around individual candidates' [sic] professional experience, Chapter 13 in David Boud and Alison Lee (Eds.), *Changing Practices of Doctoral Education*. London: Routledge

For perspectives on online doctoral assessment:

Crossouard, B. (2008) Developing alternative models of doctoral supervision with online formative assessment. *Studies in Continuing Education*, 30(1): 51–67. Published online: 29 Jan 2008 (retrieved 29 March 2019)

3

What are the regulatory requirements and responsibilities of doctoral assessors during the doctoral process?

In this chapter, you will be encouraged to:

- Think about how regulation of doctoral assessments helps to assure the standards of doctoral programmes and influences their content
- Consider the assessment roles and responsibilities associated with supervision and progress reviews
- Reflect on how the pedagogy can be rescued from an overemphasis on procedure
- Deliberate on how different assessment roles articulate with and inform each other

Introduction

As discussed in previous chapters, what constitutes assessment at doctoral level is opaque. We hope that our discussion so far has shed some light on the implicit, hidden expectations of doctoral researchers during the key stages of their experience and the junctures at which those expectations are assessed. There is, though, another dimension to doctoral assessments that warrants further clarification: the requirements and responsibilities of you, the assessors. Whereas universities' formal regulations attempt to articulate the roles and responsibilities of those involved in most official summative forms of doctoral assessment (for example, progress reviews and the **viva voce** examination), our experience suggests that these documents can leave assessors, and doctoral researchers, flummoxed. Confusion about procedures probably reflects the difficulties faced by institutions attempting to provide general regulations that are germane and appropriate to a wide range of disciplines while also accommodating the very individual nature of each piece of doctoral research. The very uniqueness of each doctorate defies ready categorisation.

Another reason for the confusion surrounding assessment at doctoral level is that it is seldom referred to as 'assessment'. Instead, a plethora of euphemisms are used throughout the doctoral process to describe assessment, such as 'reviewing', 'appraising', 'evaluating', 'commenting on work', 'giving feedback' and so on. We attempt to shed some light on this by drawing out the different roles you might be asked to take on, that require you to assess doctoral researchers in different ways. Specifically, we draw on our collective experience of crafting regulations, managing the administration of assessments, and 'doing' assessment to bring some clarity to these roles and their associated responsibilities. The different types of assessment attached to the role of the supervisor are explored, before the focus moves to the more formal, summative forms of assessment including progress reviews and the final examination of the thesis. We seek to rediscover the role of pedagogy in doctoral assessment, which tends to be obscured by a focus on process in formal documentation. We conclude that the role of an assessor is diverse and characterised by its fluidity and transformation throughout the doctoral researcher's candidature. First, though, let us turn our attention to why regulation of doctoral assessment exists at all.

Why regulate doctoral assessment?

Doctorates around the world do not exist in a vacuum. As noted in the example of the UK doctorate in Chapter 1, the qualification has become subject to a burgeoning regulatory framework driven by a need to ensure a common standard across disciplines both internationally and nationally (also across a diverse landscape of awards – PhD, DPhil (Oxford doctorate), EdD (Education doctorate), DClinPsy (Clinical Psychology) and EngD (Engineering), to name but a few, the last three being what is known as 'professional doctorates'). Furthermore, while there was at first a need to justify the support of doctoral education via the public purse, interventions in the doctorate from outside the academic realm increased as national governments began to recognise the value and contribution that highly skilled doctoral graduates make to society, culture, policy and economic prosperity.

With respect to assuring a common standard, the Bologna Declaration (1999), the Dublin Descriptors (2004) and the Salzburg Principles (2005) are the key policy initiatives that were intended to catalyse reform of doctoral education across the European Higher Education Area, as discussed in Chapter 1. These closely intertwined processes were underpinned by the noble principle of freedom (protection of academic freedom, freedom of expression, and the freedom of staff and students to move between the universities of member states). An outcome of the process was that higher education institutions across Europe had to commit to aligning their degrees with a common standard to achieve comparability so that the freedoms listed above would be protected. This reformation is an ongoing process with the easier task of introducing regulatory structures taking precedence, at least initially, over winning hearts and minds. An analogy might be setting the course of a huge tanker that then takes some time to actually come around.

It became commonplace across Europe for national regulatory agencies, such as the Quality Assurance Agency (QAA) in the UK, to develop shared regulatory frameworks that used Bologna and Salzburg as their source material alongside the existing good practice in universities. In the UK, the QAA developed the *Doctoral Degree Characteristics statement* (2015) as a reference point to help universities ensure that their **doctoral programmes** and awards were consistent with national and European standards. They also created a code of practice, referred to colloquially as the Quality Code, containing the catchy-titled *Chapter B:11 Research Degrees* (2012), which conveyed the core ingredients needed to run doctoral programmes. This has now been superseded by the latest version in the Advice and Guidance section of the new Code, published on 29 November 2018 (at: www.qaa.ac.uk/en/quality-code/advice-and-guidance/research-degrees).

Like newly developed criteria in other countries, whereas the 2004 version of the research degrees code was a compendium of effective practice agreed by institutions and the UK Research and Funding Councils, the current version is principally used to judge whether a university can be granted the right by government to award doctoral degrees. The completed thesis and, in many countries, oral examinations are the final step through which doctoral candidates are, in theory, assessed against the common standard of 'doctorateness' to ensure that only those candidates who demonstrate doctoral-level thinking are admitted to the award.

In addition to using regulation to assure the standards of doctoral degrees, it has also been used to re-formulate the purpose of doctoral degrees in the UK. Three decades ago the predecessor to the Economic and Social Research Council (ESRC) in the UK reviewed doctoral programmes in the social sciences through an inquiry led by Graham Winfield. The output of Winfield's investigation – the so-called Winfield Report (Winfield, 1987) – identified two tracks running through doctoral programmes: a knowledge track and a training track. Although the report recommended the maintenance of both tracks, over time, it was the training track that came to dominate. The prominence of this track was reinforced by governmental reviews, most notably *SET for Success* (Roberts, 2002) in the UK, which encouraged greater integration of skills training into doctoral programmes. The latter review was enacted to address critiques that the doctorate was too narrow in its scope, preparing award holders to deal only with very specialist issues, and to equip graduates with a range of skills that would enable them to flourish in a variety of career trajectories.

Similar reviews have been conducted worldwide. In Australia, for example, the *Review of Australia's Research Training System* (McGaph et al., 2016) advocated for the addition of broader skills training, closer collaboration between universities and industry at doctoral level, along with opening up placement opportunities to doctoral researchers. In a similar vein, The European Higher Education Area has promoted the triple 'i' agenda to make doctoral education more internationalised (to improve quality), more interdisciplinary (to broaden career prospects and promote knowledge transfer), and more intersectoral (to build-in work-ready skills training to doctoral programmes). In both the UK and Australia, concerns have been raised in academic journal articles and at conferences that the assessment of skills development seldom forms a part of any national version of the final viva voce examination, except perhaps for evidence that the candidate can argue fluently to set the specific project results within the wider frames of the discipline and methodological forms. It does, or at least should, form a part of the regular assessment that occurs through progress reviews though there is some variation in how much attention is paid to this crucial aspect of the doctorate. In an effort to reinforce the importance of skills training as central to the doctoral experience in the UK, the Research Councils mandate that the doctoral researchers in departments in which they sponsor candidates dedicate at least 10 days each year to skills development in addition to any research methods skills training that may be required.

These external regulatory pressures have had an impact on the internal regulations of universities. Most universities, at least within the European Higher Education Area, channel Bologna and Salzburg when they specify the standards of doctoral degrees as well the skills and capabilities that doctoral researchers should have developed when they reach the end of their programme. Taking the UK as an example, most universities' regulations now require that doctoral students attend skills training. In fact, universities amended their regulations from the late 1990s onwards to allow full-time doctoral degrees to last for four years and for part-time doctoral degrees to last for six to eight years. This was deemed to be enough time to allow for skills training alongside the production of a thesis.

A further, and perhaps more controversial, justification for regulation is linked to the marketization of higher education. Although in many countries, the USA and India are examples, there is a 'mixed economy' of public and private institutions, while many countries have high fees for doctoral study, the introduction globally of greater competitive market forces to higher education has shifted the balance of power from the institution to the student or researcher. Through this process, doctoral researchers are considered to have the same rights as consumers, including the right to complain if they are dissatisfied with any aspect of their experience. Those responsible for handling complaints – both within and outside the university – use universities' regulations to judge whether a doctoral researcher's complaint is valid. Although every university has its own detailed appeals and or complaints procedures, they do have important aspects in common. For instance, it is rare for candidates to be able to challenge the final examiners' decision on anything other than procedural grounds; their evaluation of academic worth of the thesis is considered infallible. Nevertheless, appeals and complaints about assessment processes at doctoral level do occur (see Voice of Experience 3.1). Common themes in appeals and complaints relate to the lack of timeliness in reporting academic decisions to doctoral researchers, including the handling of any corrections post-examination, and lack of timely feedback on written work from supervisors.

Whilst regulations aim to protect academic standards and respond to external pressures about what the doctorate should do, our experience tells us that some supervisors and assessors are blissfully unaware of the regulations, and changes in them, until they run into trouble with a doctoral researcher. As one of the authors recalls, when he was a junior member of staff in a quality assurance unit responsible for updating regulations, a senior colleague tapped him on the shoulder and advised him to be very careful when making any changes to regulations because 'people only read them when things go horribly wrong'.

We suspect that a shift is occurring in the use of regulations. Their reshaping to service the wider changes and standardisation of higher education has led to an emphasis on process. Consequently, regulations themselves focus much more on procedural, rather than pedagogical, matters, which diminishes their appeal to the academic community. In what follows, we attempt to rescue the pedagogic aspects of regulation with a view to helping those involved with doctoral assessment.

Supervision as continuous assessment

The role of the supervisor is critical to the success of any doctoral researcher and so it is not surprising that universities across the world are explicit in their regulations about the different strands of a supervisor's role and what the doctoral researcher can expect of their supervisor. Regulatory frameworks tend to be very clear about the operational aspects of supervision focussing on elements such as the composition of supervisory teams (whether they follow the US-inspired supervision by committee model or the team supervision approach that is popular in the UK and Australia); frequency of meetings; the administrative and pastoral requirements of the role; as well as the need to ensure good progress. In our experience, regulations tend to be less adept at equipping supervisors with the tools to do well at what is a demanding and high stakes role.

One activity that tends to get overlooked, or ignored, in regulations is the continuous assessment of doctoral researchers by their supervisors. In fact, as noted in the introduction, the word 'assessment' is very rarely, if ever, used to describe what supervisors do. Whilst terms like 'progress monitoring', 'reviewing' and 'appraising' are much more common and may appear less threatening, the supervisors continuously *assess* their doctoral researchers as a part of the everyday practice of supervision. We suspect that in your supervisory roles, you will regularly be asking yourself questions such as: how is my researcher doing? How is the project going? How are they developing and preparing themselves for life after the doctorate? What comments can I provide on written work to improve it? What advice and guidance do they need at this stage? Are they keeping on track?

The danger of avoiding the word 'assessment' is that doctoral researchers may not realise when they are being assessed and may not respond to feedback in the desired way. Of course, supervisors need to prepare doctoral researchers to handle the very different type of feedback at **doctoral level** – gone are the summative assignments and grades that helped doctoral researchers benchmark their progress in a transparent and structured way in their former lives as undergraduate and master's level students. Instead, assessment by supervisors is more akin to a continuous formative dialogue between the doctoral researcher and supervisor that scaffolds the doctoral researcher's development and helps to elevate them to doctoral standard. It can be very helpful to doctoral researchers if supervisors hold open conversations about feedback including the different and varied forms it may take, including explicit expectations about what a doctoral researcher should do with that feedback. It can also help to use language that is familiar to doctoral researchers and to signal when and how their work is being assessed. We explore feedback in more detail in Chapter 9.

However, not all assessment by the supervisor is formative. At certain points in a doctoral researcher's candidature supervisors may be asked by their university to make a summative assessment of their doctoral researcher's progress and development. Such interventions, as well as the challenges they bring, are explored next.

Progress monitoring: too much process, too little pedagogy?

As noted in previous chapters, one of the key junctures at which doctoral researchers are formally assessed is through progress monitoring such as a confirmation process (previously known as upgrade or transfer when researchers initially registered for an MPhil.) or annual reviews. Such progress monitoring has been heralded as good practice and is commonplace in the UK, Europe and Australia and is emergent in parts of Africa and Asia. Whilst progress monitoring practices vary by institution, they tend to incorporate the following elements:

- a retrospective report on progress;
- a discussion of the doctoral researcher's training needs;
- a plan for completion of the thesis;
- the submission of written work;
- an oral defence;
- an independent review by academics outside of the supervisory team.

Most universities' internal regulations are very clear about the procedures involved in progress monitoring. They specify the frequency of reviews, they provide information about what documentation needs to be submitted and when, and they set out who needs to be involved. It is also common for regulations to state the judgements that assessors can make about doctoral researchers' work. These are critical decisions as they may lead to doctoral researchers being placed on 'special measures', that is, given a specified period to make adequate progress with their doctorate, or even removed from their programme.

Capturing the process underpinning progress monitoring can be very useful for assessors, especially those who are new to it. It can help them feel more grounded, clarify the sequencing and timings of events, understand who else is involved and what their roles are, and it gives them an idea of the required paperwork. Because institutional processes vary, with some moving towards online processes for monitoring progress, it would be a good idea for you to have a look at your own institution's regulations to familiarise yourself with how progress reviews operate in your own institution, as we suggest in Activity 3.1, which provides guidance on important aspects to notice and when deadlines or milestones should or must be achieved.

Activity 3.1

Making sense of progress monitoring

Access a copy of your university's regulations and navigate to the section about progress monitoring. When looking at this section, ask yourself the following questions:

- What are the key stages involved in progress monitoring?
- What are the associated timeframes?
- Are there different types of progress monitoring depending on which stage the doctoral researcher is at?
- What is expected of me as an assessor?
- What material will I have access to in order to judge a doctoral researcher's progress? Is it enough?
- Will I get to speak with the doctoral researcher and supervisors in person?
- How I can get answers to any questions or concerns I might have about a doctoral researcher's progress?
- What are the outcomes of progress reviews? Is it clear what is expected of a doctoral researcher to meet the stated outcomes?
- What paperwork/documentation do I need to complete?
- Where can I get help and support if I need it?
- Is there anything that the regulations do not help me with?

Our experience tells us that regulations tend to be quite adept at describing the procedural aspects of progress monitoring. There is usually ample information about the stages involved and paperwork that needs to be completed, but there is much less information about the pedagogy, the valuable educational process, of the progress review. This raises several challenges for assessors because how to judge a doctoral researcher at different phases of their programme is rarely made clear. This aspect of the assessment remains implicit.

Matters are further complicated by the hidden politics, power dynamics and gaming/internal politics that can influence the different actors' approaches to progress monitoring. It is not unheard of that a 'you pass mine if I pass yours' culture can exist in a department or when it is departmental expectation that reviews are under-valued as only box-ticking exercises. This can make the task of an assessor very difficult either when trying to identify how much progress a doctoral researcher has made or where there might be weaknesses which would benefit from open discussion about both the project and the doctoral researcher's skill-set.

These issues were identified in research from Australia (Mewburn et al., 2014), which found that the key actors involved in progress monitoring – doctoral researchers, supervisors and assessors – are often unclear about the overall purpose of progress monitoring and to whom progress is being reported. Whilst institutions intend progress monitoring to be used to help and support doctoral researchers to submit their theses on time, it is sometimes dismissed as little more than an overly bureaucratic exercise. Supervisors and doctoral researchers might also be reluctant to disclose serious issues such as troubles with the researcher-supervisor relationship for fear of losing face, appearing inadequate or risking reprisal. For assessors, then, handling progress monitoring can be fraught with difficulty, especially when what appears in formal documentation might be a sanitised version of events on the ground.

From our perspective, the limitations of progress monitoring – focus on process, obscuring real issues – relate to its deep entrenchment in the bureaucratic realm. We contend that it is possible, and worthwhile, to emphasise the pedagogical aspects of progress reviews to help both supervisors and doctoral researchers get the most from this intervention. But how can this be achieved? We suggest a few practical things in Information Box 3.1 that assessors and supervisors can do to help shape progress reviews so that they can be used more beneficially for all parties involved.

Information Box 3.1

What assessors can do to improve progress monitoring

- Ask to see written work, such as a draft thesis chapter or article. This will give you tangible evidence of a doctoral researcher's productivity as well as an idea of how their writing and understanding of subject area are improving.
- Provide feedback on the strengths of a doctoral researcher's work and approach, where merited. This can be immensely validating and reinforce their sense of growing independence as a researcher.
- Use the plans from previous reviews to evaluate progress. Where timescales have slipped, use that as a trigger point for a conversation to understand why. Is there an issue with resources/support? Is there a problem with the project design? Is the doctoral researcher being unrealistic about timescales? Do they need to address a skills deficit? Are they experiencing a personal or health-related issue?
- Compare the doctoral researcher's work to a published paper, or a selection of your own work, to develop an understanding of the standard to be aimed for. This helps researchers to deconstruct what 'good' work or progress looks like.
- Solicit doctoral researchers' reflections on their skill-set, requiring self-evaluation where they fall short. Help doctoral researchers to make judicious use of available opportunities available.
- Ask questions commensurate with the stage of research that encourage doctoral researchers to reflect on their projects and progress. Encourage them to justify the decisions they have made with their projects.

(Continued)

- Where you identify issues with the project, give the doctoral researcher clear feedback that they can use to address that problem. What specifically can they do to resolve a problem? You might ask them this and only provide an answer if their answer misses an important point.
- Signpost doctoral researchers to where they can report issues if they feel uncomfortable talking about them in a review.
- Give an honest verdict on the doctoral researcher's progress. There is nothing to be gained by hiding problems or pretending that progress is fine when it is not. All this achieves is deferment of a problem to further down the line when it will become even more difficult to address.
- Do not be afraid to ask for help if you need it. Most universities have Directors of Doctoral Programmes or units such as Graduate Schools or Doctoral Colleges that can provide help and guidance.

Supervisors as assessors can assist in recasting progress monitoring as a pedagogical, rather than bureaucratic, intervention into the supervisory roles. In turn, this can help demystify the doctoral process for researchers. Discussing an upcoming review with doctoral researchers presents a good opportunity to step back from the day-to-day detail of the project to think about the bigger picture. Doctoral researchers can be encouraged to reflect on their project to think about what they would like to get out of the review: what aspects of their activity over the review period they are most proud of and would like to showcase; whether there any aspects of the project that would benefit from the input of another academic or disciplinary perspective.

Even for doctoral researchers who will probably sail through the review, having the opportunity to defend their ideas in front of another academic is good practice for the final examination. Doctoral researchers also find it very encouraging when somebody outside of the supervisory team values their work too.

In Voice of Experience 3.1 below, we share an unfortunate experience where progress reviews had not been used to their fullest potential and, in avoiding issues with a doctoral researcher's project, the assessment had contributed to the researcher receiving a lower award.

Voice of Experience 3.1

Grounds for appeals

It was a sad case in which a doctoral researcher, having failed the doctorate but having been offered a lower degree instead, claimed that, since he had passed at all stages of progress review during the doctoral process, he should have passed the final hurdle, especially as his supervisor was 'famous' and was confident in the quality of the thesis.

The supervisor independently confirmed those points, noting the number of past successful candidates he had supported. Further, the candidate claimed that at no point during the viva was any indication given that the answers he provided to questions were in any way inadequate.

The examiners maintained that the thesis was inadequate, certainly not up to doctoral standard, while, despite every effort being made to encourage and gently lead the candidate through questioning to see for himself where improvements could be made, he failed to elaborate or defend anything beyond what was written in the thesis.

In discussion with academic and administrative staff it became clear that the formal progress reviews were something of a rubber-stamping exercise, especially for the doctoral researchers of experienced, confident academic staff, and were often conducted by junior colleagues 'to give them experience' in doctoral assessment.

After a thorough evaluation of the reports and documents, the independent review panel concluded that, though there were several faults in the system of support during the doctoral process, the candidate had neither produced an adequate thesis nor had used the opportunity of the viva to demonstrate 'doctorateness' so the final examiners had not been at fault. The panel members thus decided that it could not recommend a resit of the viva; they stated that it would not be in the candidate's interest to expend more time and effort on trying to achieve a doctorate with that project.

However, they did strongly recommend that the university thoroughly review its progress review procedures, making them more robust: all internal assessors given training; an experienced assessor included in the review team; a definite expectation that candidates could be 'failed' at any stage; clear guidelines given to candidates about what must be done to bring work up to standard within a fixed, short period. Two points were made. One was that all supervisors, no matter their years of experience, should only supervise as part of a fully-functioning team to ensure that the researchers received continuous, up-to-date support throughout the process. The other was that candidates should be prepared so that they expect that examiners might differ in approach, some being more overtly challenging while others avoid confrontation that might upset the candidate, thus impeding effective responses to later questions.

Independent Review Panel Member

Once the doctoral researcher has reached the stage of submitting their body of research for final examination a number of other regulations come into play. For instance, since the candidate for a doctorate is expected to be able to demonstrate independence as a researcher, institutions worldwide expect that they should make the decision to submit themselves. However, there are few, if any, institutions who would not advise them, if not compel them, to seek the advice of their supervisors in doing so. The regulations about the appointment of examiners and related to the procedures and conduct of the examination are complex, as befitting such an important step, and vary between institutions within and between countries. We provide in Part III a series of chapters that deal with this stage of the process in detail, including discussions that will prepare you for those situations. At this point, we encourage you to take opportunities to examine doctoral candidates, in your own institution as an **internal examiner**, and in other national institutions and those abroad as an **external examiner** so that you can, as a progress assessor during the course of a doctorate, have a better informed view of the quality required of the final outcomes, thesis and researcher.

Concluding thoughts: Assessor, gatekeeper, peer

In conclusion, the role of the doctoral assessor is a challenging yet rewarding one. Throughout a doctoral researcher's candidature, you are invited to evaluate the progress they are making with their projects and development, either in your role as a supervisor or through more formal progress-monitoring procedures. It is an enriching experience to see how a doctoral researcher grows in confidence and moves towards independence as their research progresses. As an assessor, you have a crucial role to play in supporting the researcher through this process by offering feedback at critical junctures, thereby acting as a barometer for progress. This may involve a combination of giving advice when the researcher is falling behind and reassurances when things are progressing well. There may, at times, be a need for difficult conversations that draw on your tact and sensitivity (see Chapter 8), but doctoral researchers have a right to know how they are performing at regular intervals and not only via formal assessment points. Ignoring problems helps nobody in the long run.

In the final examination, your role evolves into that of the gatekeeper. Here, you are evaluating the doctoral researcher through their work to judge if they have met the attributes of 'doctorateness' discussed previously and elaborated in Chapters 10 and 11. Whilst the material submitted for examination and the forms of the examination differ from discipline to discipline and country to country, the end product – the doctoral researcher – should be recognisable across academic fields and geographical locations.

In Chapter 6 we focus on how to build a productive rapport both with your co-assessors and with those you are assessing so that needs and perspectives can be negotiated transparently for mutual satisfaction, within the rubric of regulations that apply in your situation. That negotiation will be a feature of your assessment roles as relationships develop. Building productive relationships with the wide variety of doctoral candidates you may encounter features in Chapter 5, focussing on inclusive practice in assessment of the doctorate. In the next chapter we consider in greater detail the variation in assessment forms and hence roles within and between national contexts.

Lastly, once the doctoral researcher crosses the threshold at the examination and you grant them the right to the pre-nominal, Dr, your relationship evolves once more. At this point, you are no longer the assessor or gatekeeper but their peer. And what a privilege that is!

Further reading

Kiley, M., Holbrook, A., Lovat, T., Fairbairn, H., Starfield, S. and Paltridge, B. (2018) An oral component in PhD examination in Australia: Issues and considerations. *Australian Universities Review, 60*(1): 25–34

McGaph, J., Marsh, H., Western, M., Thomas, P., Hastings, A., Mihailova, M. and Wenham, M. (2016) *Review of Australia's research training system.* Retrieved from: https://acola.org.au/wp/PDF/SAF13/SAF13%20RTS%20report.pdf

Mewburn, I., Tokareva, E., Cuthbert, D., Sinclair, J. and Barnacle, R. (2014) 'These are issues that should not be raised in black and white': the culture of progress reporting and the doctorate. *Higher Education Research & Development, 33*(3): 510–22. Retrieved from: http://dx.doi.org/10.1080/07294360.2013.841 649. doi:10.1080/07294360.2013.841649

Quality Assurance Agency (2012) *UK Quality Code for Higher Education: Chapter B:11: Research Degrees.* QAA. Retrieved from: www.qaa.ac.uk/docs/qaa/quality-code/chapter-b11_-research-degrees.pdf

Quality Assurance Agency (2015) *Characteristics Statement: Doctoral Degree.* Retrieved from: www.qaa.ac.uk/docs/qaa/quality-code/doctoral-degree-characteristics-15.pdf?sfvrsn=50aef981_10

Roberts, G. (2002) *Set for Success: The Supply of People with Science, Technology, Engineering and Mathematical Skills.* HM Treasury. [Online] Available from: http://webarchive.nationalarchives.gov.uk/20091115201121/http://www.hm-treasury.gov.uk/ent_res_roberts.htm [Accessed 23 September 2018]

Winfield, G. (1987) *The Social Science PhD: The ESRC inquiry on submission rates: a report commissioned by the Economic and Social Research Council.* London: Economic and Social Research Council

4

What different forms does assessment take and why during the process of a doctorate?

In this chapter, you are invited to consider:

- The research environment and why assessment matters
- Variation in informal and formal doctoral assessment at key stages in the doctoral life cycle
- Some disciplinary and national differences
- The advantages of different approaches and the insights they provide

Introduction

Doctorates across disciplines, institutions and countries vary greatly in the type and degree to which assessment is embedded in the programme of study, whilst the expectations of the doctoral researchers are correspondingly diverse and mutable. However, all doctorates now contain progress points that candidates must navigate successfully, if sometimes informally. Some include formally assessed, structured components, whereas for others the formal summative assessment component occurs only in a two-part final examination. As supervisors increasingly cross disciplinary and national boundaries either transiently as examiners or more permanently for career progression, this chapter aims to enrich supervisors' and examiners' appreciation for the different approaches used. Before we explore this rich variety of approach, we need to situate assessment in the broader context and consider the growing influential factors that are impacting on the nature of assessment, to which supervisors and assessors need also to be alert.

Why do the research environment and assessment matter?

As we have indicated, studying for a doctorate is a unique experience in Higher Education, which brings both exceptional joys and exclusive difficulties. Whether or not the doctoral process comprises a large proportion of research (as in the UK system) or a more balanced approach with taught components (as in the USA and Canada), overall the doctorate is characterised by a high degree of uncertainty. So much so, that it could be described as a 'high risk pedagogy', although we do not subscribe to that description here; for us, the authors, the whole purpose of assessment is to provide the structural interventions that minimise risk. We accept that there is, however, uncertainty surrounding the outcome; uncertainty of research process and results; and, especially where the doctorate principally contains a research component, then there will be certainly be a good level of uncertainty, for the researcher, concerned with assessing their progress. This last uncertainty is likely to generate questions in the researcher of the nature 'what does progress look like?', 'is this good enough?', and so on. Uncertainty combined with the sustained duration of time spent working on a doctorate is increasingly recognised for leading to high levels of stress and often low levels of confidence among the doctoral researcher community.

Aside from the pedagogic, technical, processual, regulatory and financial reasons for assessment, as discussed in preceding chapters, there has been growing acknowledgement, internationally, of the need to provide better institutional and structural support for doctoral researchers. Recognising that the three, four and more, years spent working on a doctorate not only comprise distinct phases or stages, but also that this is a venture harbouring high levels of perceived and actual risk, there are also attending high levels of personal and emotional investment made by the individual doctoral researcher concerned. Assessment, in all its forms, is one of the decisive factors not only in determining overall success, or completion, but also in playing a crucial role in contributing to a positive researcher experience (the other key factors being supervision and the supervisory relationship, the research environment, and the researcher's attitude and attributes). In our view, assessment can minimise those feelings of risk, and increase levels of researcher confidence and wellbeing. (See also Chapters 5 and 6 in which the contributions of inclusivity and good interpersonal relationships are considered.)

It is fair to say that across Europe and in Australia, the wellbeing and mental health of doctoral researchers (along with all H.E. students and staff) is becoming something akin to a national concern. There have been some studies that have revealed highly disturbing findings about the mental health and wellbeing of doctoral researchers. Most notable is the study in Flanders (2017) that showed

51% of doctoral researchers had experienced symptoms of psychological distress, whilst one in three was at risk of having or developing a psychiatric disorder, and that doctoral researchers were the cohort most at risk educationally from experiencing psychological problems. Surveys carried out within the Universities of Exeter (UK), Berkeley (USA) and Aarhus (Denmark), similarly found unacceptable levels of stress within their doctoral communities. A wider study by Vitae et al. (2018) has confirmed the issues identified in Flanders.These studies indicate and confirm that assessment can and, we would argue, must provide a supportive structure not only to assess the progress of the research but to provide reassurance to the researcher – a major reason why assessment matters.

A structured, transparent approach towards assessment is essential for the development of doctorateness, especially in the terms we define it here as being a property of the researcher. It is also essential for creating an individual who is technically competent and professionally adept. Whilst institutions generally provide access to counselling services and doctoral training programmes increasingly include 'resilience', 'mindfulness' and 'wellbeing' workshops or training in their offer to researchers, we anticipate an increase, also, in the number of institutions and programmes building responsibility for the welfare of doctoral researchers into assessment processes and procedures. Although annual mental and physical health checks may be a long way off in higher education, they are, however, commonplace in the corporate sector; but, if introduced, they would be, we suspect, an institutional responsibility rather than that of an individual assessor. Nevertheless, it is reassuring to see some institutions providing doctoral researchers with additional and separate opportunities for support, as well as introducing tracking software to assist with progress monitoring. Aside from the supervisor, doctoral researchers are being encouraged to join mentoring schemes (if mentoring is not offered by your institution or department, see our companion volume in this series: *Mentoring to Empower Researchers*), being given access to dedicated pastoral care, and even be subject to a formal, yet separate, professional development review. As Professor Susan Brooks illustrates in the Voice of Experience 4.1, an additional structural intervention affords the researcher, and the supervisor, an independent mechanism for review and support, similar, as we shall see below, to systems elsewhere in the world.

Voice of Experience 4.1

Keeping research students on track

We have developed a system for progression monitoring that seems to work well. In brief, the research student produces a written annual report every summer – requirements varying depending on where they are in their programme; for example, doctoral students submit a substantial literature review at the end of their first year, whereas those completing their programme just submit a thesis outline and a brief summary of their plans for completion. In addition, the supervisor provides a report, just 200 words or so, describing progress and highlighting any concerns. The supervisor's report is submitted on a standard University-wide form which is generated centrally, and which flags up any progress issues for that student, for example, if the student should have already upgraded from MPhil to PhD, or if they are nearing the time when we would expect thesis submission.

All students are then interviewed by two academic staff who are independent of the supervisory team – in practice, these are usually the postgraduate research tutors. We talk to the student about how their project is going and explore any concerns they might have. We also formally review their transferable skills development by discussing and 'signing off' their training diary. If all is well, then the students really appreciate independent assessors reassuring them that they are on track. If we, or the supervisors, identify issues with progress or engagement, we can put remedial actions into place – for example, requiring milestones to be met or further review after three months. We can therefore, as a team, support the supervisors in addressing any problems. Conversely, we can act as mediators if the student raises issues around supervision or facilities and attempt to find solutions. Finally, it is one more mechanism by which we can encourage timely submission of the thesis.

Professor Susan Brooks, Senior Postgraduate Tutor

Although assessors may not be officially obliged (yet) to enquire into the professional development or levels of enjoyment a doctoral candidate is experiencing, a responsible and caring one might, and could consider introducing such probing into their processes by reflecting on the questions in Reflection Point 4.1.

Reflection Point 4.1

Whose responsibility is it?

If the personal and professional development of the individual researcher is central to the process leading to doctorateness, consider whose responsibility it is to ensure this is reviewed and investigated. What methods and mechanisms exist in your institution to support this element of researcher development? Are they adequate or could there be better provision, interest and quality assurance in this area? What could you do differently?

What kinds of informal doctoral assessment exist?

In Chapter 3, we indicated the variety of forms the word 'assessment' refers to, including 'reviewing', 'appraising', 'evaluating', 'commenting on work', 'giving feedback' and so on. It was also suggested that, in your supervisory role, you will be probably be continuously raising questions about progress and how everything is going. Although it may not always be an explicit and conscious process, as a supervisor you will be engaging in, what we called, a *continuous formative dialogue* between yourself and your doctoral researcher; you can be certain that your supervisee will be holding a similar internal dialogue with themselves, as well you might too. Perhaps seldom articulated, these internal dialogues do proffer an opportunity for informal and evaluative exploration. They can stimulate being transparent about subjects often taken for granted (such as how long it takes you, as a supervisor, to prepare a presentation, or what feedback you receive from your peers). Such discussions build trust, demonstrate your authenticity, in view of your openness and vulnerability, and would facilitate both you and the researcher to express thoughts at different stages of the process.

Sharing experiences regularly and at key stage points in the process, such as at the time of the researcher's first public or departmental presentation, first conference attendance, first proposal submission, first annual report, and so on, affords you the opportunity to demystify the process for the researcher (and mitigate some of the uncertainty mentioned above). Reminding yourself about how you felt at a similar stage or time, might also give you an insight to their perspective on progress and development, although we all should be alert to the unconscious bias that others are like us. Informal interactions should not be underestimated for the role they play pedagogically, developmentally, intellectually and emotionally. In a process with limited structure, such interactions form the framework around which more formal interactions can be included and they are entirely in the assessor's gift to create and provide. However, a note of caution is required. As indicated in Chapter 5, for some researchers an informal interaction – such as a chat in a corridor – can be confusing in its status and may need to be clarified. Whatever your assumptions are, they are only yours; so, it is always better to enquire and explain if necessary.

Building on the 'first times' mentioned above, we will briefly consider other kinds of informal assessment that can occur at different stages in the doctoral researcher life-cycle.

At the beginning

The very early stages will be concerned with introducing the researcher to the processes and procedures of research, the department, discipline and institution. Much of this early assessment period will be formative – checking what should be happening is actually happening and that the new researcher understands the range of things they may need to do, as well as providing advice and guidance on what to do next. In some institutions, for instance at the University of Vienna, the supervisor and doctoral researcher agree on the frequency of feedback meetings and this is then contained in a 'doctoral thesis agreement'. Whilst many institutions and supervisors around the world have expectations that by the end of the initial stage overall, proposals will be approved, **ethical** approval forms will have been submitted, some written work will have been drafted and commented on, most will only have a formal review point towards the end of the year. The exceptions will be those countries where the doctorate begins with coursework or Comprehensives; for instance, for some institutions in Canada, the USA and Ghana, passing core and elective courses in the beginning stage is mandatory, and the structural support of formal assessment is in place.

In places where the early work is only informally assessed, the development of the project plan and **literature review** provide opportunities in all disciplines for feedback and mark the beginning of a joint effort and relationship. For some suggestions about how this can be made more rewarding for all those taking part, see Information Box 4.1 below.

Information Box 4.1

Planning for enjoyment!

In our book, *Success in Research: Fulfilling the Potential of Your Doctoral Experience*, we have an activity for researchers: 'Your First 100 Days – Personal Checklist' (2017: 39), which provides considerable detail about the many, often small but essential, things they can do to help their research start smoothly. You could use this list, or construct your own, as a tool for what might need to be included in the project plan, which will then facilitate a discussion about what will happen when. Encourage your doctoral researcher to draw up a Gantt chart or timeline with milestones, and to uncover the research process. Taking inspiration from our Scandinavian colleagues, where research teams seem to have regular coffee and cake meetings (fikas in Sweden), be sure to include enjoyable events such as conferences, science festivals, doctoral celebrations – including lots of coffee/tea and cake!

We know, from our own experience and from other colleagues worldwide, that the literature review causes uncertainty for many doctoral researchers, and yet is often not discussed with a supervisor or until it is written up. Frequently, we hear of researchers being given a long reading list or told to 'read around the topic' or 'immerse themselves in the literature' and then asked (or told) 'to do a literature review', yet many do not know how to undertake this task at doctoral level. Having feedback on how it is progressing, if they are reading enough, if what is being read is appropriate, and helping them to understand what they are reading for, and especially how to read critically, is beneficial for the doctoral researcher's developmental progress. This activity forms the basis of many research skills, including analysis, evaluation, synthesis and problem-solving, and provides a good opportunity for the supervisor to begin to help the researcher adopt effective doctoral writing skills which can be further honed throughout the middle and end stages.

Middle stage

It is the middle stage where regular and visible monitoring, with deliverables, seems less variable across disciplines and institutions and is welcomed by staff and researchers since it provides reassurance of progress or an opportunity to address problems. For many this is an annual system, but some institutions have mandated more regular committee or panel meetings – for instance, in one Turkish university the Thesis Advisory Committee, comprising the supervisor, an internal from the department and an external, from within the University but a different department, are required to meet every six months to review progress, prepare a written progress and verbal report, and give feedback to the researcher. In Belgium, a similar evaluative process occurs, with the same supervisory committee, during the first and second years; after three years a doctoral plan is submitted in advance and the committee extended, and the candidate makes a presentation to the committee; following a discussion with the candidate, the committee deliberate in private. The candidate must pass all these milestones, although they can have two attempts; failure at any point results in termination of the doctorate. In the UK, the current common practice is for an annual review conducted by academics external to the supervisory team, but some institutions are working towards a six-monthly review of some kind as the requirements for timely completion bite harder.

Final stage

At this stage, formal assessment is focussed on the examination and the processes that lead up to that. Many institutions, for example across Europe, including Austria, Belgium and Germany, require doctoral candidates to take part in public defences of theses. What is interesting about some of these, for instance Austria and Spain, is that this is an examination in two parts: there is a review or examination of the thesis *prior* to the candidate being allowed to proceed to the second, final and public examination (see International Examples Box 4.1 below). Others, like the UK, South Africa, and the University of South Australia (the first institution to introduce the oral defence in Australia), hold a single examination process; whilst the thesis will have been reviewed prior to the examination, the candidate does not know the outcome and the oral defence is a private affair with select attendees. Other countries' examinations require an initial presentation from the candidate; for instance, a Turkish colleague says it is quite usual for the candidate to make an oral presentation to five examiners accompanied by PowerPoint presentation and handouts. This contrasts with the UK viva, which is usually without audio-visuals and largely discursive, although in some disciplines there might be performative elements, and a few UK institutions have introduced an initial presentation, but this is far from the norm.

All these forms of final assessment have stressful aspects that could bear some research in terms of whether a closed viva or a public one is more or less empowering/traumatic for different researcher types, so all need careful preparation in which the supervisor ensures that the candidate knows what the process involves and provides detailed guidance on thesis construction and content and formative feedback on rehearsals for whatever kind of performance, if any, is required. The attendance of doctoral researchers at such public defences is viewed as extremely useful, formative preparation for them as are practice viva voces.

International Examples Box 4.1

Three examples of final stage formal assessments

Please note the examples are drawn from specific institutions and may not be representative of all institutions in the country.

Austria

The doctoral candidate and supervisor can suggest up to three expert reviewers, ideally external to the University. The Studienprases will then appoint two reviewers, who are initially presented with the thesis. Once the reviewers have positively assessed the thesis and all other curriculum requirements have been met, registration for a public defence of the thesis can be made. The public defence is open to the public (family can attend for example). An examination committee is formed of at least three people; usually the supervisor and one of the reviewers form part of the committee, who will examine the public presentation and award a grade. If this is positive, the candidate is awarded a doctorate, and can celebrate with a conferring ceremony.

(Continued)

South Africa

At least three examiners review the thesis and once their reports have been received, an examination committee is formed and chaired by a non-examining member of Faculty, a professor. The oral examination takes place in private – the supervisor may attend but cannot contribute to the process. The viva usually begins with the candidate giving a brief overview of the study, followed by questions from the examiners. Sometimes it is not possible for the examiners to be present in person, so they connect via telephone conference. The result is only finalised after the viva, which usually lasts between 40 and 60 minutes.

Spain

The completed thesis (and accompanying short report) are sent to two external referees for review, usually acquaintances of the research group. The referees are not members of the final Viva board, but can suggest changes or additional work; therefore, in view of this assessment, the supervisor and candidate can be confident that the thesis is successful and that the only variable will be the final mark (Latin honours). The viva voce normally consists of an oral presentation to the board (about 1 hour), followed by questions from the board (1–2 hours). The audience can include family and friends, members of the department, other doctoral researchers.

Forms of assessment

In all forms of assessment, no matter if it is formative or summative, or at what stage it takes place, it should be considered and tailored to the individual and the context (as we shall explore further in Chapter 7). Marks or grades of performance, such as those given in 'Comprehensives' in North American institutions and for the public defence of the thesis in Austria and Ghana, are definitive (accepting there may be challenges); whilst assessors' reports and the way information is conveyed to the researcher are thoughtful pursuits or should be. Now we enter the realms of feedback; how you might approach this as an assessor and the language and method you could use will be discussed in detail in Chapter 7. Here it is enough to note that feedback is designed to assist/improve performance, boost confidence, reduce anxiety, and leave the recipient with a clear idea of what to do next.

Feedback can be verbal or written; it can be explanatory (signposting what something is, how it should be and why); descriptive (as providing a summary of the situation); or aim to improve understanding (with questioning, contrasts and discussion). Good practice in feedback matters, because this is the main vehicle in the learning process. Since the doctorate is a delicate learning process, in so far that is an incremental developmental process, often implicit but always with intense personal/emotional investment, constructive and useful feedback is essential.

Precision and clarity are vital – writing feedback down before delivering it verbally will enable you to check if the way you intend to deliver it will be received well and what you are trying to convey is clear.

Giving feedback in a small review meeting or one-to-one supervision is the best way to deliver both positive and negative feedback (see Chapter 8). Some institutions have clear expectations about the regularity of feedback (from once a month, through stipulated quarterly meetings to annual reviews all structured around informal interactions with supervisors), and most expect this to be flexible and change through the life cycle and stages. For instance, several UK institutions recommend meeting every two weeks in the beginning and only moving to monthly meetings when appropriate. Others suggest at least once-a-month official supervisory meetings focussed on the individual's personal and project development, not counting social, laboratory or departmental meetings. When doctoral researchers are part of a team, such as in a laboratory or group setting, then additional care needs to be taken not to embarrass, humiliate or isolate researchers by ignoring them or declaring their deficits in public. One-off informal comments or asides or negative non-verbal behaviour can be highly impactful in these settings, so that one needs to be mindful of the group reaction as well as that of the individual concerned.

Self-assessment and self-awareness

As we emphasise in Chapter 7, feedback at the doctoral level should be evaluative rather than judgmental to encourage self-awareness and self-assessment. Some institutions provide additional tools or frameworks for self-assessment. **Vitae** provides an excellent one in relation to attributes and skills in the online **Researcher Development Framework** (UK) package. Teaching standards frameworks, if they are undertaking teaching duties, or other professional bodies' frameworks, help to recognise the standard and professional quality of progress. Similarly, academic needs analyses and skills audits all support the growing self-awareness and self-assessment process. You could use the EAT framework described in the Information Box 4.2 below, to encourage self-assessment and to co-design an assessment agreement with your doctoral researcher. All these, however, require a debrief; everyone needs to discuss their thoughts with a more experienced person, you as assessor, supervisor or mentor.

Self-coaching only gets one so far; we all benefit from being challenged by a different perspective, that unexpected question, the view of us that we do not see ourselves. To be able to self-assess is an important professional habit for up-and-coming researchers to acquire. In your assessment role, you can enquire into this formative form of assessment whilst also indicating that self-drive and self-awareness need not be, nor should be in our view, isolated and lonely undertakings. Knowing when and from whom to ask advice is part of the doctorateness we are trying to engender. So not only should self-assessment be encouraged, but the habit of reviewing and reflecting with critical friends and others is a habit to cultivate – one that is useful for the remainder of one's professional life. Given the widespread acknowledgement of the volume of activity in the middle stages, encouraging this practice may occur during informal interaction. It may need to be made explicit to researchers that there is nothing new here; self-assessment is just a more personal version of receiving feedback on unfolding doctorateness. Yet, this is a vital component of the final outcome, the professional development of a researcher, and an important form of assessment.

Information Box 4.2

Create your own formal assessment process

Professor Carol Evans has created the Evans Assessment Tool (EAT), a self-regulatory framework, which is a free resource under a creative commons licence (see www.southampton. ac.uk/rap/eat-resources/eat-frameworkindex.page). There are score cards for lecturers and 'students' that you and your doctoral researcher could use to assess how confident and informed you both are of key areas. Co-designing assessment practices, like supervisor or doctoral agreements, is a powerful, dynamic and empowering approach to assessment practice.

Insight and variation

There can be a tendency to focus on the research rather than the researchers' experience and more on the process rather than pedagogy, yet by the end of it all, doctorateness is about the individual person. To achieve this requires a range of support, including institutional support. Insights and learning from other institutions can benefit researchers, research and assessors enormously. Thus, we close this chapter and this section of the book by sharing examples of good practice that have impressed us in our travels and discussions with colleagues in other institutions in the UK and further afield.

International Examples Box 4.2

Supportive practice ideas

- The co-design of a supervisor-supervisee contract, that outlines duties and commitments, expectations and anticipations, serves to provide an opportunity for clarification at the beginning of the partnership and is even more useful if it includes a 'flexibility clause' that allows for review and updating at regular intervals.
- Co-supervision and collaborative supervision that includes regular meetings of the whole team, including the researcher, to share concerns and joys about the process makes the process more collegiate and allows for differences to be aired and tentative ideas to be shared in a collaborative climate.
- The introduction of tracking software is growing and welcomed by some supervisors; feedback from doctoral researchers suggests that they like the fact it manages the formal assessment process equitably and makes the process transparent. The software empowers them to nudge or remind their supervisors to meet requirements on occasion.
- Regular, formal and independent reviews held every six months or quarterly in addition to annual reports, whether held with other faculty members, external staff, or academic tutors, seem crucial for identifying problems early and providing support to the researcher.
- High-quality annual reviews are essential, as a comment from a colleague in Belgium shows: *The strength of our system as I see it, is that the critical yearly assessment will make for better 'doctorateness' because it is formative. Supervisors do not want to lose face and so prepare their candidates well; and internal jury members can guide and advise when there is still time to change and improve.*
- The use of an independent chair in any form of viva, defence or presentation provides assurance of due process and support for all present if things go amiss.
- The presence of at least one supervisor in the viva voce, at the request of the researcher and on the agreement of the external examiner/s, can boost confidence and reduce candidate anxiety. However, we recommend that the supervisor is seated out of the sight of the candidate to ensure that non-verbal signals, no matter how well meant, do not distract from the process.
- A report to the candidate on the acceptability of a thesis prior to any presentation, viva or defence can result in a more confident performance. If there are corrections to be made, these should be prepared and accepted beforehand so that the candidate can enjoy this final rite of passage into the college of research practitioners.
- The public defence of the thesis undoubtedly demystifies the final examination for doctoral researchers in a way that the 'secret garden' approach, described by Vernon Trafford and Shosh Leshem (2008), of the closed examination cannot. The openness and transparency of such approaches can only be beneficial in terms of facilitating a supportive and reassuring research environment. In countries in which a closed viva is preferred, efforts should be made to clarify the process for all concerned, including allowing/requiring candidates to report on their satisfaction with the organisation and conduct of the process.

Further reading

Lee, A. and Danby, S. (Eds.) (2012) *Reshaping Doctoral Education: international approaches and pedagogies.* Abingdon (UK) and New York (USA); Routledge

Nerad, M. and Heggelund, M. (Eds.) (2015) *Toward a Global PhD? Forces and Forms in Doctoral Education Worldwide.* Washington: University of Washington Press with the Center for Innovation and Research in Graduate Education

Vitae in partnership with the Institute for Employment Studies (IES) and the University of Ghent (2018) *Exploring wellbeing and mental health and associated support services for postgraduate researchers.* Available at https://re.ukri.org/documents/2018/mental-health-report/_ (retrieved 31 March 2019)

PART II

Success is in the detail – empowering during the research process

5

How can assessment be made inclusive?

With contributions from Catherine Lowe

In this chapter, you are invited to reflect on:

- What is meant by inclusivity and why assessment needs to be made more inclusive
- How to make assessment inclusive:
  - in assessing a research proposal
  - in providing formative feedback
  - in progress reviews
  - in confirmation examining
  - in assessing the thesis and viva voce
  - beyond accommodating disability

Introduction

Historically, we have accepted researchers with disabilities, of different faiths, nationalities or from non-typical backgrounds as long as they *integrate* with the institution's systems and structures. In contrast, *inclusion* today requires us to modify structures and systems to enable most people to succeed. It is underpinned by UN Article 24 that states persons with disabilities are not to be excluded from reasonable adjustments and access to tertiary education (2006, UN Convention Rights). In the United Kingdom the Equality Act (2010) states the protected characteristics that are not to be discriminated against. These are:

age; disability; gender reassignment; marriage and civil partnership; pregnancy and maternity; race; religion or belief; sex; sexual orientation.

It also highlights a legal requirement to make anticipatory reasonable adjustments for those with disabilities, removing or avoiding anything that places a disabled person at a disadvantage compared with their non-disabled peers. Best practice, therefore, would be to take an anticipatory position and review current assessment systems rather than reacting when a researcher draws attention to their specific difficulty. There will always be a requirement for some bespoke reasonable adjustments, but the idea of inclusion is to incorporate the majority of adjustments into our everyday assessment practice. Such adjustments are also of benefit to the wider researcher community beyond those we have a legal obligation to support in specific ways. This chapter invites you to reflect on current practice and to consider ways to amend it so that researchers can demonstrate their ability without being disadvantaged by matters of faith, culture, where English is a second language, and for those with protected characteristics under the Equality Act. For clarity, the chapter will select examples from the realm of diagnosed disability, but we hope you can elaborate and extend our advice and suggestions to embed inclusive practice for all into structures and systems of assessment and examining to enable all doctoral researchers to demonstrate their abilities and to achieve their potential. (See also Chapter 8, *Delivering Inspiring Doctoral Supervision* in Further reading.) We will widen the discussion in the final section after considering some specific examples of processes in which we could make our practice inclusive.

Inclusive practice in assessing a research proposal

If your own master's student is producing a doctoral research proposal, then it is likely to be created in discussion with you, follow your institution's requirements, and be of an area of interest to the department. However, if the proposal, whilst equally appealing in terms of concept, is submitted by an international student, or someone who has a Specific Learning Difference such as dyspraxia and has disclosed this in the application, then the proposal may not conform to your expectations about what it should look like and how the ideas should be conveyed. You can reflect on these issues through engaging with Activity 5.1, which may help you avoid dismissing a potentially stimulating proposal and doctoral researcher.

Activity 5.1

Considering proposals inclusively

How can we ensure such proposals are read without thinking about the disclosure or that the applicant's first language is not in the language used in the institution?

How can we prevent possible discrimination?

Reflection

Does the research proposal have to take a prose or essay-type format? Could it be tabulated so that candidates respond to an explicit question in each section? This subtle change might enable the applicants to demonstrate their research idea, current knowledge, etc. without spending huge additional effort in trying to present perfect prose. Of course, the eventual thesis and journal articles need to be written clearly, but as long as the required language test (such as the International English Language Testing System – IELTS) score is met, or that the applicant with a Specific Learning Difficulty acknowledges their requirement to use assistive technology or specialist tuition where available, then we should not be dissuaded from considering the application in competition with other research proposals.

In addition to reflecting on the format candidates are expected to use for submitting their research proposal, one could also reassess the guidance provided for submitting it. You might consider whether it gives explicit guidance so that a candidate with Autistic Spectrum Conditions (ASC) who may need clear, literal language can demonstrate their critical engagement with the field, and defined research area. Is it typed in an accessible font for those with reading difficulties? (One of the most accessible and most widely available fonts is Arial; others include Calibri, Century Gothic, Helvetica, Tahoma and Verdana. All these fonts are 'sans serif' fonts. They have none of the little decorative lines, serifs, that are found on letters in some fonts like Times New Roman or Georgia.) Is the text in a consistent style so that those using technology to 'read' the guidance to them can 'listen' to a flowing guide rather than having to re-set equipment for different texts? A quick UK google search of the words *research proposal* reveals a range of guides, extracts of which are produced in Activity 5.2.

Activity 5.2

Comparing guidance on a section of research proposals

The following extracts are from some guides on the literature review section of a research proposal. Reflect on each one's strengths and weaknesses. How do they compare with your own department's guidance?

(Continued)

Extract 1

Literature review (minimum 500 words): This short essay is supposed to provide some context/background to your dissertation. It will also provide your supervisor some insights into what you have been reading, where you are coming from, and how you plan to contextualise your research project.

www.surrey.ac.uk/politics/files/Proposal_guidelines.pdf

Extract 2

You should provide background information in the form of a literature review which sets the context for your research to help the reader understand the questions and objectives. You will also be expected to show that you have a good knowledge of the body of literature, the wider context in which your research belongs and that you have awareness of method-ologies, theories and conflicting evidence in your chosen field.

Research proposals have a limit on words or pages, so you won't be able to analyse the whole existing body of literature. Choose key research papers or public documents and explain clearly how your research will either fill a gap, complete or follow on from previous research even if it is a relatively new field or if you are applying a known **method-ology** to a different field. Journal articles, books, PhD theses, public policies, government and learned society reports are better than non-peer-reviewed information you may find on the internet. The University's Library hosts online guidance on getting started with researching, managing your sources, and practical information on finding what you need in search engines.

www.ed.ac.uk/files/imports/fileManager/HowToWriteProposal090415.pdf.

Extract 3

You should explain the broad background against which you will conduct your research. You should include a brief overview of the general area of study within which your proposed research falls, summarising the current state of knowledge and recent debates on the topic. This will allow you to demonstrate a familiarity with the relevant field as well as the ability to communicate clearly and concisely.

www.birmingham.ac.uk/schools/law/courses/research/research-proposal.aspx

Reflection on the activity

These examples highlight the different levels of guidance provided. To enable your guid-ance to be understood by as many people as possible, avoid colloquial jargon, and try to use literal language: some people with Autistic Spectrum Conditions will find inferences very difficult to understand. You might consider a table format whereby the candidates answer explicit questions which may ensure everyone has a clear understanding of what they are responding to. You would still receive a longer piece of writing yet ensure the candidates are providing the information you seek.

Inclusive practice in providing formative feedback

Formative feedback for researchers differs from that given to those on taught degrees where there are usually formal fixed points for comment. Feedback for researchers might take the form of an unplanned discussion at the coffee machine, occur in supervisory meetings, progress reviews, by email or be written comment on a document. Because of this it may be useful to set ground rules so that the researcher understands the time they might have to wait for feedback on a draft chapter, or the timeframe within which they might expect a response to a quick email question. Ideally, confirmation in writing of discussions, meetings, etc. contributes to clarity, particularly that the researcher has understood your recommendations and suggestions. Many researchers find it empowering to send summary emails, but someone with a poor working memory or slow processing speed may find it helpful for you to send the confirmatory email rather than them. Regular reviews of planned work also enable the researcher to stay focussed. Sometimes enthusiasm for experimental research by both the supervisor and researcher lead to months of laboratory-based work that is more relevant to a paper than the main area of research for the thesis. Reviews keep everyone's minds on the main task.

Activity 5.3

An example of dealing with a challenging situation

Your researcher has an autism spectrum condition and seems to be misinterpreting your guidance, and wants explicit 'what to do, step-by-step instructions'. S/he is also finding it impossible to present his/her research to departmental peers which forms part of the informal assessment process all researchers are required to undertake. This is due to overwhelming social anxiety.

Reflection

It is so important for researchers to become independent that it would be helpful to explain 'the journey' in the early days of the first year, and to remind the researcher of this as they progress. Written literal summaries of meetings are helpful, along with introducing choices of direction even if they are unwelcome.

Instead of a public presentation for the informal peer assessment, the researcher may be able to present their work to one or two people rather than the crowd. They may be more comfortable filming their presentation for others to watch. Questions could be emailed for the researcher's response.

Inclusive practice in progress reviews

Consider the experience of the researcher who provided the Voice of Experience 5.1.

Voice of Experience 5.1

My experience of support after diagnosis

My experience of being an adult learner with a new diagnosis of dyspraxia (physical co-ordination and planning issues) has been mixed. Issues with my writing and organisation skills were picked up by my supervisor at about nine months into my PhD. It took six months to get my assessment as the University's Disability and Neurodiversity Service (DANS) initially assessed me for dyslexia. However, with persistence I was diagnosed and was awarded Disabled Students Allowance.

One-to-one support from the DANS is invaluable to me. However, in my experience, dyspraxia is a hidden disability which is hard to define and to relate as each person's needs are different. Therefore, in my progress reviews, although I am improving all the time with DANS support, I still feel that I am penalised for my disability to sequence and to organise my work in a linear way. For example, a lot rests on Gantt charts, and although I do meet deadlines in a timely fashion, it's not in the ordered (linear) way that my supervisors would like me to. Also, I am only just beginning to realise my strengths and weaknesses and to assert my needs with my supervisors.

I am also aware that a PhD attribute is to be organised with my work, which in my way I am, but in my supervisor's eyes, I'm not always so. Concern about this sometimes leads to unhelpful micro-management, whereas I would work well if left to get on with it alone (another attribute of a PhD candidate I believe).

Because Dyspraxia is so hard to define and to pin down, I think it is hard for supervisors and myself to recognise my needs. Had I been diagnosed earlier in my educational career (I'm 58), it might have been easier to identify the provision I need. It is a frustrating journey, but also rewarding, as I'm learning to cut myself some slack and to justify the need to do this. Also, when a very linear sequential thinking supervisor praises me for my creative brain saying that she is not able to think that way because she is too sequential in her thinking, I take that as a compliment. I guess in the review process there needs to be room for the creative strengths that people with dyspraxia bring to the PhD world. For example, our creativity, being able to see things from different angles, and often, even though the tests may not recognise it, we are very bright. It would be a shame to waste mine and others' talents. Indeed, if this were to be the case, academia and the world would be a poorer place.

2nd year PhD researcher

Reflection

It is to the credit of the supervisors that they noticed the way the structure of this researcher's written work did not match the articulate way topics could be verbally discussed, and recommend the researcher contact the Disability service. As assessors we can be mindful of the possibility of undiagnosed Specific Learning Differences (SpLD) that can lead to unexpectedly poor written work, or time management, etc. and suggest early referral for screening for SpLD.

Progress reviews, whilst intended to track progression, are perceived as yet another 'test' for researchers like the one in the previous Voice of Experience:

> I find them quite stressful even though evaluating the targets set six months ago and agreeing new targets is useful.

Reducing unintentional stress benefits all researchers, but for those with severe anxiety, it is paramount. Inclusive reasonable adjustments range from the physical location, time of day, to how the discussion during the meeting is recorded, and how work is presented and discussed.

Consider some more scenarios in Information Box 5.1.

Information Box 5.1

Examples of challenges and possible adjustments

Scenario 1

Situation: A researcher who uses crutches and is partially sighted has been invited to meet you in your new second floor office at 4.00pm in winter.

Possible adjustments: Check the lift access is nearby to your new office or relocate the meeting to the ground floor; consider the lack of daylight in winter late afternoon. Could the meeting be held earlier in the day?

Scenario 2

Situation: Your researcher has disclosed they have AD(H)D (Attention Deficit and Hyperactivity Disorder) and dyslexia.

Possible adjustments: Ensure researcher is as least distracted as possible by enabling them to sit not looking out of a window, or next to a door. Keep checking they are still engaged in the current conversation and draw them back if necessary. Consider allowing the meeting to be recorded so that it can be re-listened to if required. Consider acting as the minute taker so that the researcher can focus on the conversation rather than attending to note taking. Send confirmatory summaries of the actions expected at the end of the meeting in addition to the usual supervisory paperwork held in the department.

(Continued)

Scenario 3

Situation: Your researcher has failed again to attend a progress review meeting on their progress but have disclosed in the past that they have extreme anxiety.

Possible adjustments: Discuss the anxiety: many people can explain the triggers and how they might be alleviated. If the situation becomes overwhelming for the researcher, seek advice from the institution's wellbeing service on how you might support the researcher. Arrange a less intimidating environment: would the researcher feel more comfortable in a different location? Would it be possible to provide written commentary on progress before the meeting so that the researcher knows what to expect?

___

Inclusive practice in confirmation examining

Whilst progress reviews can result in the researcher being asked to leave due to unsatisfactory academic progress, the confirmation process is the formal assessment of the feasibility of on-time completion of the doctorate based on progress within this first year. It is normally a peer-review process by which academics outside of the supervisory team read a report written by the doctoral researcher about their progress thus far and their plans for future research. Then the candidate is often examined by viva voce. If both the confirmation report and viva are essential components of this assessment, then the doctoral candidate must perform satisfactorily in both elements to continue with their doctorate. Our next Activity, 5.4, and Voice of Experience 5.2 will, we hope, help you to make these occasions more inclusive.

Activity 5.4

___

Considering equal opportunity for success in confirmation examining

Review the potential Confirmation learning objectives listed below and consider how to ensure all researchers are given equal opportunity of success:

The learning objectives (LO) of the Confirmation

1   Demonstrate evidence of critical engagement with academic literature;
2   Construct reasoned arguments for study and approach;
3   Develop a clear case for the novelty and academic/professional value of proposed research;
4   Demonstrate the feasibility of methodological approach, methods proposed and/ or experimental technique(s);

5   Create a realistic plan of work, which can be completed within funded period or agreed upon completion date (not to be longer than 48 months for full time or 96 months part time);

6   Evidence that research and transferable skills (including writing and analytical skills) are developing at a rate necessary to complete and defend a doctorate within specified completion time period;

7   Provide evidence for availability of necessary resources to complete project.

Reflection

The quality of grammar, spelling and quality of sentence structure do not officially form part of the learning objectives for the written report. What is stated as required is the demonstration of critical reading and reasoned argument. The achievement of the ability to write in a scholarly way is assumed or implicit in each objective. Therefore, there is little required in terms of 'reasonable adjustments' to this part of the Confirmation process. However, as the 'voice of experience' below comments, the sheer additional effort and time required by, for instance, a dyslexic researcher to produce the report is not reflected in the process. Those with declared disabilities should be using assistive technology and/or the support of their specialist SpLD tutors where available. Frequently a researcher is writing in their second language. Although it can take a little longer to understand the content, the English they use rarely prevents the argument from being conveyed.

Voice of Experience 5.2

The confirmation process from the viewpoint of a researcher with dyslexia

I feel that my dyslexia impacted greatly on my performance and found the confirmation process a challenge. The general outcome was not that I lacked the knowledge required, but the ability to express that through my written work. I found that getting all my thoughts down on paper in a cohesive and structured manor [sic] very difficult. The extensive reading and referencing required for the literature review chapter was the hardest part as reading the vast amount of papers whilst maintaining focus was demanding. In the confirmation viva, I found it very intimidating, as I knew the writing would be brought up as a common problem, even though that's where the majority of my efforts were spent. Due to the amount of time I dedicated to the confirmation process, I feel this directly impacted the progress of my research, putting it on hold for longer than intended. If I had been diagnosed before my confirmation process, I think that I would have gotten the necessary help that would [have] allowed me to better utilise my time efficiently. To improve the process for PhD candidates with dyslexia, I think that allowing the focus to be shifted away from the writing and more towards the understanding, knowledge and overall content should be considered.

A 2nd year PhD researcher

The Confirmation process provides two assessment methods so, in theory, someone might balance a comparatively poor piece of written work with a strong oral examination. However, we need to be mindful that it does not help someone with both a Specific Learning Difference and extreme anxiety. It would be fair to raise a concern over the quality of the written work, but not to dwell on it in the viva. Perhaps the comments on the written work might focus on the content rather than grammar, sentence structure and spelling. You might make a small comment at the end to note that you can see how the disclosed SpLD has impacted the work, and check that assistive technology is being used to help the researcher with the organisation and structure of their written work.

Inclusive practice in examining the thesis and viva

Voice of Experience 5.3 is written by a PhD researcher awaiting her viva voce and reflects on her research journey in total rather than just the viva.

Voice of Experience 5.3

My dyslexia and my doctoral research

- My dyslexia in fact helped my research because it meant that I thought more out of the box for the problems I was facing. It did hinder my progress with regards to writing and reading. Reading – it was very difficult to read up on all the literature to begin with, as I was slower than the other PhDs and was expected to do it at the same pace. Writing – I took longer to write my thesis than others, but I started earlier to allow for this.
- Supervisors – My supervisors didn't accommodate for it in any way. I think they had forgotten I had dyslexia after the first week! So, if it hadn't been for my specialist study skills tutor and the support from DSA [Disability Student Allowance in UK], I would have really struggled!
- Suggestions for examiners – I would say that they need to leave time for the candidate to answer and perhaps visually write down the question if the candidate is struggling to understand, because dyslexia can make the thinking process slower than a normal person.

PhD researcher

Two senior professors were approached in different institutions to ask for their voices of experience about how they make anticipatory inclusive accommodations when examining researchers. Both replied that they felt the nature of the viva voce means that each examination is unique and therefore adjustments are tailored for everyone as required. Indeed, in one author's experience, when approaching a possible external examiner, attention was drawn to the candidate's disability and offers were made to provide guidance on reasonable adjustments for the examination. A candidate may choose to disclose their condition to the examiners, in which case advice from the Institution's disability service should be sought on what accommodations are recommended. In the case of examining a Deaf candidate the disability service should be able to arrange for the examiners to meet the British Sign Language (BSL) Interpreter before the day of the viva.

The viva is naturally stressful but for those with mental health difficulties, Specific Learning Differences, or autistic spectrum conditions, their level of stress will already be heightened, and the viva may increase it to nearer their tolerance threshold. A way to help them manage this would be to give them time to refer to their thesis and notes before responding to a question. They could be encouraged to jot things down during the viva. You might provide them with a list of questions, or to ask them one question at a time, or to rephrase the question if the candidate appears not to have understood. It might be that the candidate needs to be accompanied by someone known to them for reassurance. For a candidate with AD(H)D you might find yourself having to repeat questions and draw the candidate back when they may have gone off on a tangent. All these practices are quite standard within vivas, you should just ensure that you are being sensitive to the needs of your candidate and using this flexible nature of the viva to support the individual needs of the candidate.

The exam room itself is something to consider. In addition to being mindful of the accessibility of the room for those with mobility difficulties, some people are hypersensitive to light (particularly overhead LED lights), sound (especially sudden noise), and smell, whilst others may need to be near a lavatory and have breaks in the viva to attend to personal need. Extreme anxiety may cause the candidate to 'freeze' in a formal exam environment and a reasonably confidential but alternative setting might have to be found. The easiest way to address environmental issues is to discuss the planned location with the examinee well before the exam day.

Inclusive practice – beyond accommodating disability

Most universities now have doctoral populations that are increasingly globalised and diverse. This will continue to challenge our understanding of inclusivity and our **sensitivity** to a variety of individual needs. For example, it is important to consider significant religious occasions and rituals, for example Friday afternoons, or periods of fasting. It is sensible to arrange the time of vivas so that they do not conflict with prayer or fasting times. Some cultures demand that women must be accompanied when in the presence of unrelated men, which might have implications for the way a Confirmation and a viva voce are conducted. People may have specific caring responsibilities, making times when children need to be dropped off or picked up particularly challenging, especially for researchers who do not have family support in the immediate area.

In fact, inclusive practice can be more readily achieved for everyone by discussing with candidates before significant events what constraints they may have on their time and how the process can be made less stressful and more inclusive. This conversation is one that should be had with all candidates. We make assumptions about people because of their outward appearance; however, this is not always indicative of their needs. Doctoral assessment should be about academic rigour, not about creating artificial barriers that favour certain people and disadvantage others. These types of conversations may feel uncomfortable and can be difficult to engage, particularly because many of us come from cultures where inclusivity is not openly discussed. Therefore, building supportive relationships with those you are assessing is critical. The next chapter will discuss the building of these critically important relationships within the variety of doctoral assessment contexts.

Further reading

The following websites are UK-centric. There may be complementary ones to fit your location but these will provide a basis for understanding if you have difficulty locating others.

Dyslexia: The British Dyslexia Association (www.bdadyslexia.org.uk/)

Dyspraxia: The Dyspraxia Foundation (https://dyspraxiafoundation.org.uk/)

AD(H)D: The National Health Service in the 'living with' section provides guidance for adults with AD(H)D (www.nhs.uk/conditions/attention-deficit-hyperactivity-disorder-adhd/)

Autistic Spectrum Conditions: The National Autistic Society (www.autism.org.uk/)

Mental Health Difficulties: Mind (www.mind.org.uk/)

Blind: Royal National Institute of Blind People (www.rnib.org.uk/professionals)

Deaf: British Deaf Association (https://bda.org.uk/help-resources/)

Faith: This guide explains the legal framework but also lists the key facts and observances for the more common faith groups (www.acas.org.uk/media/pdf/d/n/Religion-or-Belief-and-the_workplace-guide.pdf)

6

How can you establish rapport and respect in doctoral assessment?

Guest authors: Naomi Winstone and Edd Pitt

In this chapter, you will find out about:

- Key relationships necessary for supportive and effective assessment
- The doctoral researcher's role in the assessment process and the importance of building her/his capacity to seek and use feedback
- The relationships between assessors and supervisors, as well as co-assessors
- Examples from practice
- How assessment and feedback can be positive forces in developing the independence of researchers and for successful completion

Introduction

The special nature of the doctorate means that doctoral researchers, and the processes they are involved in, are very different to those who are taught at other levels in the academy. Although in many countries doctoral researchers have been referred to as 'students', in others they are colleagues. Even in the former situations the intent is to develop them to an equivalent status. Yet in all cases they are in the position of 'colleagues as learners'. Issues of power and control become especially acute in this context, so this chapter addresses ways in which a productive rapport (a deeper affinity and relationship of trust) can be established between assessors and those they assess. Further, assessors frequently work as a team, so we address the development of constructive rapport between assessors to ensure recognisably fair and compassionate process and outcomes.

Why relationships matter in assessment

Some assessment situations are characterised by minimal interpersonal interaction. In some **massified** forms of undergraduate education, students' work is marked anonymously, and neither marker nor student may be aware of the other person's identity throughout the whole process. However, in doctoral education, there is no anonymity, meaning that the development of rapport between the doctoral researcher and those who will be assessing their work is important in ensuring that the process results in empowerment rather than disempowerment.

The nature of different relationships in doctoral assessment is also complex. Your role may involve assessing the work of doctoral researchers in your capacity as a supervisor, as an internal examiner, or as an external examiner. Of course, there are other important relationships, such as the informal peer-review networks that doctoral researchers may develop amongst themselves. Whilst the specific nature of the relationship between the doctoral research and each of these partners in the assessment process might differ, what they all have in common is the likely influence of power dynamics, and the potential benefit of developing rapport in order to empower the development of the doctoral researcher through the assessment process. Activity 6.1 invites you to think about rapport in the context of doctoral assessment.

Activity 6.1

Conceptualising rapport

What does the term 'rapport' mean to you in the context of assessment? How might our approach to building rapport in doctoral assessment differ from other contexts, for example, undergraduate assessment?

In a formal sense, rapport can be defined as an authentic relationship characterised by sensitivity to the emotions of others, shared purpose and effective communication. A key challenge in building rapport is how to balance the creation of this authentic relationship whilst concurrently occupying a position of power as one who can pass judgement on the candidate's work, whether formative or summative. These unequal power relations may lead to negative impact on the self-esteem of doctoral researchers, posing a threat to the authenticity of learning partnerships, as doctoral researchers may resist exposing gaps in their knowledge or skills. In Voice of Experience 6.1 Professor Ogden discusses her experience of doctoral assessment relationships.

Voice of Experience 6.1

The role of relationships in the assessment process

PhD assessment is about maintaining academic standards, protecting the discipline and promoting good work. Or so they say.

But when I am in the viva room as either the chair or the examiner, or nervously waiting in my room as the supervisor, the assessment process is far more about maintaining the respect of the examiners whilst protecting the student and promoting the best dynamic possible in the room given the people whom we have been chosen to be there. And all of this is about relationships.

First – take the external examiner. They have been invited in as an expert in the field who is also (hopefully) fair-minded and without any agenda. But they need to be managed. They may not only be an examiner but also someone who may feel underskilled, out of their depth and worried whether they will be good enough. They may feel the need to impress the older, more experienced internal or to show a more junior internal how it is done. Or even suspect the internal of nepotism and need to compensate by being extra tough. They may also respect the supervisor and want to prove that they were worth inviting or they may hold some long-standing grudge for a grant rejected or some unjustified comments on a paper. They are human so may also take against the student if they remind them of one of their own who they found irritating, if their own work hasn't been cited or if the student is deemed aggressive and defensive, even if this is just the result of nerves. People are people and none of us can leave this behind when we examine.

Second – take the internal. Although the rules state that both examiners are equal it rarely plays out like this and the internal role is often as back-up and to see that fair play is done. But the internal also has their own issues to manage. They probably know the supervisor well which can have all sorts of consequences depending on whether this relationship is good or bad. Likewise, the student will be known to them and they too will have their own history of interactions. Relationship management raises questions such as should the internal impress the external by being clever, the student by being kind, or the supervisor by being a bit of a pushover? It is a challenge if you want to be liked by everyone.

And then there's the student who is nervous and needs to be reassured. But they might have heard that the internal can be vague, that the external is tough and may have the words of their supervisor ringing in their heads that they want to impress and please even if they are not actually in the room.

All this in one small and often windowless room. Yet we all know that people perform better if they are calm, confident and settled. So, before the viva I often become everyone's mum – praising and hugging students, thanking and complimenting examiners and making sure that everyone has a drink, knows where the toilets are, and that the room is laid out to make everyone feel at home. Then once the viva has started I seem to turn into a couple's counsellor – smiling, nodding, encouraging, making jokes to break the tension, asking easy questions to get the student talking, expanding upon my fellow examiner's questions to make them clearer, watching the tension in the room rise and fall and bringing it back to a gentle equilibrium to keep everyone at their best. Oh – and I even have to manage myself! Am I trying to impress? To prove myself? Am I irritated? Am I bored? Who do I like or not like in the room?

> PhD assessment is about standards. Theses must be good enough to sit on the shelf along with the others. And when we read them in the cold light of our office we switch on our critical faculties and enjoy finding the flaws and thinking of clever questions. But in the examination room everything changes and here we have three human beings with all the dynamics that this brings. So being a good examiner means having a critical faculty and asking clever questions. But more importantly it means managing the room and making sure that the relationships in that room enhance rather than undermine the student experience and the conclusion that is drawn.
>
> *Prof Jane Ogden: Experienced supervisor and examiner*

Power dynamics in assessment

Any process of assessment, whereby one person's work, thinking, or creative output is subject to the judgement and appraisal of others, is a likely location for power dynamics. However, the power dynamics in doctoral assessment differ to those at earlier stages of university education because, once doctoral students have gained their qualification, they in many cases become of equal status to their assessors. However, assessors still occupy a position of power over doctoral researchers, as gatekeepers to successful completion of the doctorate.

The dynamics in this relationship led Australian universities in 2018 to agree on a set of principles for respectful supervisory relationships, explicitly noting the power imbalance and how it may lead to sexual harassment or affect wellbeing (see Further reading at the end of this chapter for details).

Power asymmetries in assessment, where assessors and students occupy the status of 'expert' and 'novice', respectively, can work positively if the relationship is framed as that between experienced and less experienced co-workers; a collaborative relationship where both parties are working towards the same outcome. This requires the building of trust in the assessment process, where assessment is interpreted not as passing judgement on the student or trying to 'catch them out', but as a genuine transformational endeavour.

Trust is integral to developing the student's confidence in accepting and discussing their weaknesses, misconceptions and areas that require development with their assessors. If there is a trusting relationship, then even difficult feedback conversations are more likely to be interpreted as supportive and developmental.

Building rapport in assessment as a supervisor

The assessment role of a supervisor may in some ways appear to blur with the general supervisory process. Rapport in assessment involving supervisors and their doctoral researchers can be achieved through a model, where the supervisor is supporting the doctoral researcher as an 'academic-in-training'. Through frequent cycles of assessment and feedback, supervisors are in a powerful position to shape the doctoral research experience.

Clarifying expectations and roles in the assessment process

A transactional, transmission-focused model of assessment in which an assessor provides and delivers comments on the work of a student is in many ways unhelpful. This model places emphasis on what the assessor does, without clarifying what the student should *do* with the comments they receive. As a supervisor, you will likely provide many iterations of formative feedback to your doctoral researchers on drafts of chapters, manuscripts and the final thesis. Building an effective assessment relationship requires supervisors and their doctoral researchers to agree expectations of each other's roles, and to seek further clarification where necessary.

When a doctoral researcher passes you a piece of writing for comment, establishing an effective assessment relationship involves clarifying expectations such as how long the doctoral researcher can expect to wait to receive your comments. Being realistic is essential to ensuring a transparent assessment relationship; if the doctoral researcher has an idea of likely turnaround time this will help them to plan their time effectively and decide what other tasks they can be undertaking whilst you are reading their work.

It is also important to discuss with doctoral researchers your expectations of their role in the feedback process. Do you expect them to passively wait for the comments you provide, or do you expect them to be more proactive in seeking and eliciting specific feedback? For instance, you could jointly agree that they will declare what kind of feedback they need in relation to a piece of work, such as an indication that the draft is on the right lines or a detailed review of the content. Agreeing this in advance is beneficial for two reasons. First, it gives the doctoral researcher a clear expectation of what you will provide in terms of the nature, detail and volume of comments. Second, it ensures that the comments you provide are of use to the doctoral researcher and enable them to clarify their own skills and understanding.

It is also essential to clarify your own expectations in terms of what the doctoral researcher will do with the comments you provide. This may also require you to consider whether you want to return comments in person to talk through your feedback or return a marked-up document via email. Do you expect them to revise the draft in response to your feedback? Do you expect them to access skill-development opportunities, for example? Setting out roles and expectations in advance will support doctoral researchers to understand how they can use feedback exchanges to improve their work over the course of the doctorate.

Empowering doctoral researchers through feedback exchanges

As a supervisor, except for in a very few national contexts such as the USA or Germany (see Chapter 9), you will not be involved in the summative assessment of the doctoral researcher's final thesis. However, you will be an essential player in the ongoing cycles of formative assessment that take place on a continuous basis throughout the doctorate. Perhaps towards the end of the doctorate, feedback exchanges will be in many ways indistinguishable from those in which you engage with your professional collaborators and co-authors. Dialogic interactions go further than being a conversation or discussion of key concepts, towards more of a shared responsibility to consider, reason and deliberate ideas as a collective.

In many ways, doctoral supervision is like a coaching process. Supervisors initiate students into scholarly debate and critical discussion through feedback exchanges, so feedback processes in doctoral assessment are about more than just providing comments on students' work. A key consideration for empowering students through feedback exchanges is to create an environment where the student feels quite comfortable discussing their work, unpacking errors, and being open to taking a different tack if necessary. Such an approach mirrors more of a professional conversation than merely monologic transmission of comments. Indeed, it implies a relationship of trust which, as Kay Guccione's work illustrates, is critical to the success of the supervisory relationship.

Based upon the concept of a therapeutic alliance in psychotherapy, the educational alliance considers the quality of the relationship between supervisor and student. The strength of the alliance has been considered to be the greatest predictor of future success. The educational alliance encompasses:

> (i) the learner's belief that there is a mutual understanding of the purpose or goal of the relationship; (ii) the learner's belief that there is an agreement about how to work toward that goal and the activities involved; and (iii) the learner's liking, trusting and valuing of the preceptor and belief that these feelings are mutual. (Telio et al., 2016: 934)

Within the assessment process, the strength of the educational alliance, including beliefs and trust, is crucial in predicting whether researchers will engage and respond favourably to the feedback they receive.

Building rapport in assessment as an internal examiner

Most academics are at some point invited to act an internal assessor for a doctoral researcher for an upgrade or confirmation viva, or for the final viva itself. In this context, internal assessors may be familiar with the work of the doctoral researcher if, for example, they are part of the same research lab or group. The internal assessor may also know the supervisor well as a fellow colleague. This role can again require consideration of rapport and ensuring that the process is empowering for the doctoral researcher. This is especially true for an assessment at an early stage of the doctoral journey, such as the upgrade/confirmation viva, as the doctoral researcher will meet you again and it is important to make sure that the ongoing relationship is positive.

Establishing a positive environment for the doctoral researcher

An important part of assessment throughout the doctoral journey is to build a sense of mastery in students, through less vital assessment experiences as a way of building confidence for crucial assessments. For example, the confirmation or upgrade process acts as a good practice-run for the final viva, and feedback on written work can act as a skill-building opportunity for the scholarly peer-review process.

Whilst assessment processes such as the confirmation/upgrade viva might be less daunting than the final viva, they are nevertheless an important rite of passage and so doctoral researchers are likely to benefit from an authentic and challenging yet supportive experience. The most important thing you can express as an internal assessor is a sense of interest in the doctoral researcher's work, and communicate that you are taking the process seriously, even if in some cases it is a 'given' that they will pass the confirmation/upgrade process. Asking authentic viva-type questions gives students the opportunity to experience this style of questioning, and to formulate within their own minds the importance of their thesis and research plans. In Voice of Experience 6.2 a recent doctoral researcher recounts her/his experience with the UK confirmation process, taking place between 12–15 months of full-time registration.

The confirmation viva

My confirmation viva was full of mixed experiences and emotions. Whilst I was made aware in the early stages of my PhD that I would need to pass the confirmation, there was limited guidance about the process and the level of work I needed to produce. I spoke to fellow PhD researchers who had passed their confirmation to get an indication of what was involved and what I needed to prepare, but expectations about the work required and the confirmation varied wildly. Fortunately, nearer to the event, my **principal** supervisor offered invaluable guidance and support, drawing upon his experiences as a supervisor and examiner about what he felt made for a positive confirmation experience and what the panel might expect from me. Even with this guidance, I still felt unsure as to whether I had done enough and was adequately prepared for the confirmation.

On the day of my confirmation, as I sat nervously outside the office waiting to be called in, my supervisor informed me that the chair of my supervisory panel had accidently scheduled the wrong date and the confirmation had to be rescheduled. I was devastated. Not only had I worked hard work in preparation, but I had experienced stress and sleepless nights in the lead-up to the confirmation. ... Am I doing enough? What if the work isn't good enough? Am I going to be made to leave the PhD programme because I am not up to scratch?

When the rescheduled confirmation took place, the supervisory panel were immensely apologetic and sympathetic to the stress the situation must have caused. Whilst I appreciated their apologies, after a surprisingly positive and successful experience of the confirmation (which I passed), my imposter syndrome managed to creep back in, where I convinced myself that I had only passed the confirmation because the panel felt bad for rescheduling. It took several months for my supervisor to convince me that I passed the confirmation on merit. With hindsight, I recognise that my supervisor was right, and despite some of the tribulations relating to my confirmation, I can look back on the event as being highly beneficial, not just preparing me for the final viva but for helping me tackle imposter syndrome.

Upon entering the room for the confirmation, the panel briefed me on how the process would work. They would begin by their initial thoughts and then explore points further; this was almost exactly what I experienced in my final viva where I was given an outline of what to expect; therefore, seeing a similar pattern between the two events was highly reassuring for me during the final viva. In my experience then, the confirmation viva offered an authentic opportunity to experience what I might expect in the final viva, which reassured me instantly on the day. At the time, whilst I felt that their questions were challenging, when the panel shared that they had intentionally put me through my paces to prepare me for the final viva, I was grateful that they had pushed me. Not only was I placed in a better position to feel prepared for the final viva, their comments acted as invaluable feedback which enhanced the final thesis.

*A **postdoctoral** researcher*

Building rapport in assessment teams

Acting as an internal examiner also involves managing relationships with co-assessors. Regardless of whether you know your co-assessor, or if it is the first time you have met them, establishing working relationships and agreeing roles are valuable processes that enable the assessment team to work in a synergistic, not antagonistic, partnership. The pre-viva meeting, whether for a confirmation/upgrade viva or for the final viva, is a good opportunity to build rapport with your co-assessors, rather than expecting it to develop during the process of the viva. It is helpful to agree in advance between yourselves the line of questioning that you will each adopt, and your initial thoughts about the nature of the work you will be assessing.

It is natural that there will be points on which you disagree. As an internal examiner, you may hold subject-specific expertise, whilst the external examiner may have specific expertise in the methods adopted in the research, or vice versa. Equally, you may both hold similar expertise but view the work of the doctoral researcher in different ways. Maintaining rapport in an assessment team requires a recognition that different opinions are valid, and that the views of different assessors should be complementary, not necessarily identical.

Many doctoral researchers report that they pick up on the dynamics between their assessment team, and this can influence their experience of assessment. A doctoral researcher in a study by Hartley and Fox (2004: 730) reflected that 'There was a "leader" and a "follower". The leader was more inclined to ask the most searching questions (bad cop) and the follower to ask approving questions (good cop)'. Effective rapport in assessment teams involves adjusting your approach so that you are responding not only to the candidate's responses, but also to your co-assessor's approach. You may have a series of questions that you intend to ask and an idea of their sequence but working with co-assessors involves functioning as a unit, not as independent people.

If you find that a co-assessor's style is quite critical, then you may feel it is appropriate to balance out their approach which a more encouraging tone, to provide a challenging yet supportive environment for the doctoral researcher. There are also rare situations where, as an internal examiner, you are paired with an external examiner with a competing agenda. An example of this type of situation is represented in the scenario in Activity 6.2. These dynamics can be difficult to manage, and this serves to illustrate the importance of building rapport with your co-assessor before the formal assessment takes place. Effective rapport between assessors is in turn likely to facilitate the creation of an effective rapport between assessors and the doctoral researcher. Activity 6.2 illustrates an assessment scenario exploring the dynamics between co-assessors.

Activity 6.2

Managing difficult dynamics

1. Read the scenario below.

Deborah entered the viva with a sense of confidence. She had already published two of her studies, and she was looking forward to having the opportunity to engage in scholarly discussion with her examiners during the viva, and to celebrating later with her family and friends.

As soon as she entered the room, she could sense tension in the air. She knew John, her internal examiner, well having worked as a teaching assistant on his introductory statistics module. But he wouldn't meet her eye as she walked in.

The external examiner, a very eminent professor in her field, gave her a wide smile as she walked in. 'Do sit down, Deborah', she said, gesturing to the empty chair across the table. John continued to look intently at the papers in front of him, avoiding eye contact with Deborah.

As the viva got underway, Deborah quickly realised that something was wrong. She was asked none of the questions she had meticulously prepared for; instead, the external examiner aggressively questioned Deborah's findings. Deborah tried to respond, but never felt that she was giving the 'right' answer. John said very little, continuously rustling the papers in front of him.

By the end of the three-hour viva, Deborah was exhausted and totally despondent. By the time she returned for the examiners' verdict alongside her supervisor, she had no idea what the outcome would be. Once again, John avoided eye contact with Deborah, although she did notice him exchange a glance with her supervisor.

The external examiner wasted no time in cutting to the chase: 'Unfortunately, Deborah, we feel that major revisions are required in order for your thesis to meet the requirements for the doctorate'. Deborah instantly felt sick. 'We acknowledge that you have had your work published, but as your examiners we are questioning your original contribution to knowledge, and we are going to request that you collect more data, resubmit your thesis, and undergo a further viva.'

At this point, the external examiner looked across at Deborah's supervisor; a look that only later would Deborah understand.

After Deborah had contacted her family and friends to let them know that they would not be meeting to celebrate the outcome, she went to see her supervisor. 'I'm so sorry, Deborah', she said. Deborah was puzzled, as in no way could she blame her supervisor for the outcome. 'John is distraught – when he met with the external, she explained that on no accounts would she sanction the award of the doctorate. I think I know why.' Deborah held her breath. 'I suggested her as your external as she is the world's leading expert in our field. I wanted you to feel validated by the process, in having the opportunity to discuss your work with her. Two years ago, I examined a thesis written by one of her students. I gave quite extensive suggestions for revisions because the student had misinterpreted one of the core theories in our field. It seems that your external was angry with me for questioning her judgement as a supervisor, and this may have led her to use your viva to settle the score.'

(Continued)

2. Think about the following questions for reflection and debate:
   - Why do you think John, as the internal examiner, might have felt powerless to act in this situation?
   - What actions would you advise Deborah to take in this situation?
   - To what extent can internal examiners temper the judgement of external examiners?

In workshops with colleagues, the main themes that emerged from discussions about the scenario in Activity 6.2 were:

- The importance of selecting appropriate examiners, both internal and external;
- Appropriateness includes, in addition to expertise, recognition of human frailty;
- The need to inform, train and support through regulations all examiners so that they are empowered to make principled stands;
- The powerlessness of the candidates in such situations, which led to consideration of a growing need to appoint **independent chairs** and/or to record examinations in some way to protect candidates' rights.

Maintaining relationships with colleagues

Internal assessors are often close colleagues of the doctoral researcher's supervisor. In a survey study of 88 PhD graduates, Share (2016) reported that in 83% of cases, internal assessors were colleagues of the supervisor from the same department or school. This can add a challenging dynamic to the assessment process, where it might feel as if you are not only passing judgement on the doctoral researcher's work, but by association, the guidance given by your colleague in their role as supervisor. Your role is as an impartial assessor and remaining open and transparent is the best way to manage relationships with your colleagues when assessing the work of their doctoral researchers.

Building rapport in assessment as an external examiner

The final viva examination is the pinnacle of the doctoral research journey, which raises the stakes of the assessment for the candidate. High-stakes assessment situations bring to the fore power dynamics between candidates and their assessors and can be intensely emotional environments. Building rapport as an external examiner can be more challenging than as an internal examiner, as you will not likely have had chance to build rapport with the candidate and your co-assessor prior to the viva day. In this section we consider how through your role as an external examiner you can create an environment where doctoral assessment is a positive experience for candidates. Activity 6.3 challenges you to think about how different expectations of the viva may impact rapport and doctoral researcher experience of the assessment process.

Activity 6.3

Sensitivity to expectations

The following quotations are comments by doctoral researchers participating in a study by Wellington (2010), in which they expressed positive and negative expectations of the viva. How can external examiners be sensitive to each of these different expectations through the ways in which they interact with candidates? What implications do these perspectives have for building rapport with the candidate as an external examiner?

- 'I want to learn from it – I want it to be a quality experience.'
- 'It's a chance to shine.'
- 'It could help me to build my career, and my publications, through contact with the external examiner.'
- 'I might fail.'
- 'My mind might go blank and I'll want to leave the room.'
- 'Examiners may have their own agendas.'

Empowering the candidate to perform

Creating rapport and an effective assessment environment for candidates is not just important in ensuring that the assessment itself is a positive experience. The assessment experiences of doctoral researchers, especially in the final high-stakes viva, can have a profound influence on their identity and confidence for their future academic careers. An intensely negative experience can lead doctoral researchers to doubt their suitability for an academic or other professional career, whereas a challenging yet positive experience can empower candidates to pass through the threshold from student to professional researcher.

Empowering the candidate to perform is not about making the experience easy for them; instead, it is about ensuring that the viva is an authentic experience that validates their identity as an academic researcher. Consider these two polarised experiences in Reflection Point 6.1.

Reflection Point 6.1

Variation in viva experiences

Contemplate the two experiences below reported by participants in a study of viva experiences reported by Hartley and Fox (2004):

> The real viva was a nightmare. More of an interrogation, and, in the end, I felt worn down to the point of not being able to defend my study. The experience put me off ever going through it again and, indeed, doing any further research. (p. 735)

> In a way the real one was a let-down, but not because of anything to do with the **mock viva**. The real one was a lot easier than I anticipated, and in the end, I was kind of disappointed that I was not given more of a grilling. (p. 735)

As an examiner you will meet candidates with different expectations, so you need to prepare to deal with them effectively. Offering the candidate the respect you would offer to a new colleague is part of the skill; treating them in a way that you would prefer to be treated yourself as a professional is another important facet of effective examining.

The experience for both participants in Hartley and Fox's examples was negative; the first, because they were given a 'grilling', and the second, because they were given an 'easy ride'. As an external examiner, you can provide an empowering environment by balancing challenge with encouragement, for example by:

- maintaining eye contact;
- acknowledging what the candidate is saying through non-verbal responses such as nodding, smiling, etc.;
- avoiding the temptation to interrupt the candidate;
- showing genuine interest in the candidate's work;
- asking challenging questions, but in a non-confrontational way;
- building the candidate's confidence through staged questioning, building on their answers;
- creating an environment where the candidate is enabled to enjoy the viva experience.

Because of the levels of investment in a doctorate and the high risk involved, the viva is often an intensely emotional experience for candidates. This is one reason why, as an external examiner, your facial expressions and other non-verbal signals can easily be magnified and misinterpreted by candidates. Facial expressions such as smiling, accompanying nodding and active listening, leaning forwards, tone of voice, encouraging turns of phrase (i.e. tell me more) and mirroring can all help the candidate to demonstrate their potential. Conversely, your ability to build rapport with the candidate can be impeded should the candidate be experiencing strong emotions that limit their eye contact with you, as illustrated in the scenario in Activity 6.4.

Activity 6.4

Dealing with emotion

Consider the following scenario.

Andrew was a very experienced PhD examiner. For Liam's viva, where he was acting as an external examiner, he was paired with Leanne as the internal, an equally experienced examiner. For both examiners, Liam's viva was unlike any they had experienced before.

Liam seemed on edge from the start; he shuffled into the exam room and his hands were visibly shaking. Andrew decided to kick off the viva with a question that he had experienced as effective in putting students at ease: 'So, Liam', he smiled, 'perhaps you can begin by telling us the overall story of your thesis? What do you see as being the main outcomes and learning points for the field?'

Liam gave a good answer; he successfully outlined the implications for practice that emerged from his research. But he didn't make eye contact with either examiner. Instead, he looked beyond them, fixating on a tree outside the window. Andrew wasn't quite sure how to react to this behaviour. It felt uncomfortable; Andrew had over the years developed many strategies for building rapport in the viva, remembering clearly how the eye contact and reassuring nods from his own external examiner many years ago had put himself at ease. Without being able to communicate non-verbally with Liam, he felt himself floundering over his questions and finding it difficult to show his interest in Liam's findings. Leanne, who knew Liam well, also failed to secure eye contact with him. She could tell something was wrong but didn't know what to do about it.

It was when Andrew moved to the questions he had prepared about Liam's statistical analyses that the atmosphere in the room changed dramatically. 'Could you explain to us why you chose to separate out these groups for your analyses, please?' Liam continued to stare at the tree outside the window, his eyes clearly welling up with tears.

'Would you like to take a short break, Liam?' said Andrew. 'You're doing really well, and it's fine to have a bit of a breather if you like.'

Liam stood up and walked out of the room. Andrew and Leanne looked at each other, not quite sure what had happened. 'Did I say something to upset him?', asked Andrew, concerned. 'I can't see how', said Leanne, 'you've been really supportive'. Five minutes later, Liam returned to the room. He continued to respond to questions whilst staring out of the window, and both Andrew and Leanne were wary of upsetting Liam again. They asked the key questions they had prepared but ended the viva sooner than planned. When they later told Liam that he had passed, he looked shocked, but thanked them for their support.

Questions for reflection and debate:

- How else can you build rapport in a viva situation, beyond eye contact and other non-verbal cues?

(Continued)

- Given Liam's behaviour, what would you have done to develop a supportive environment?
- When Liam returned to the room, what would you have done to start afresh in building rapport and putting Liam at ease?
- What are the disadvantages to Liam of Andrew and Leanne's decision to keep the viva as brief as possible following the interruption?

Building rapport with candidates through the doctoral assessment process requires assessors to develop emotional literacy; the ability to recognise and respond to the emotions of the candidate. Activity 6.5 allows you to explore emotional literacy further. This is particularly important if, as an external examiner, you are in the position of having to deliver bad news to the candidate. (For more on that topic see Chapter 8.) The relational dimensions of assessment, and the 'educational alliance' that we discussed earlier, are crucial to supporting candidates to manage emotion in the process.

Activity 6.5

Emotional literacy

In a paper published in 2016 (187–8), Share reported a variety of emotional responses to the viva expressed by doctoral researchers. For each quotation, consider why the candidate may have experienced that emotion, and how each emotion could be promoted/minimised.

Positive emotions

- 'Elated. It was surreal. I was a little in disbelief that something so massive and all-consuming was finally over. I cried a lot.'
- 'Happiness, excitement, relief, tiredness, sense of shock that it was all finally over.'

Negative emotions

- 'Absolutely the worst experience I have ever had. I felt undermined and professionally stripped.'
- 'Absolutely traumatised. It was a horrible experience, and it has had long lasting effects on my self-confidence, both personally and professionally.'

Neutral emotions

- 'I was relieved that I only had minor revisions to undertake, but it was not the excited reaction that I would have expected.'
- 'A bit deflated –"Well that's that". I was pleased that I had gotten through but I didn't really feel anything emotionally.'

From the last two activities you will recognise that being an examiner can demand more than 'simply knowing your stuff'. If you found responding to the situations and questions difficult, as any of us would, you may find it helpful to discuss these scenarios with groups of colleagues so that you can all learn from each other and share support when confronted with such all too human situations. We certainly do not suggest that you should let the possibility of having to handle them put you off being an examiner. We provide more ideas about how to handle negative outcomes in Chapter 8. One important thing to remember, though, is that as an examiner, you are in charge of how you deal with the process. Do not let it run away with you but consider giving everyone an opportunity to reflect on what is happening by calling a break and then addressing explicitly but sensitively what the problem seems to be. Leaving problems to fester never solves them.

Supporting the final mile

The role of assessor in supporting the doctoral researcher does not end at the point of delivering the final verdict. Assessors continue to support doctoral researchers by advising on the nature of corrections required, giving guidance for publishing the research, and even acting as a referee for the candidate's future job applications. (See Chapter 12 for detail about this process.)

In the immediate aftermath of the viva, the primary concern of the doctoral researcher is likely to be ensuring that they know what they need to do in order to be able to satisfy the specific requirements for corrections. It is important to recognise when sharing the outcome with the candidate, the release of emotion, such as relief and euphoria, may mean that students are not in an ideal cognitive state to take in detailed comments and information about corrections. Thus, it may be better to summarise the necessary corrections, leaving the real detail for your (obligatory) written report.

What you want to communicate is that the corrections are achievable, and for candidates to feel empowered to enact each comment and make the necessary changes. In some cases, the necessary changes are more substantial, and may involve the collection of more data. In these cases, again empowerment is key, so that doctoral researchers know exactly what they need to do to meet the requirements.

Recommending the award of the doctorate, either directly or subject to the completion of corrections, is an enjoyable task for an external assessor. When communicating this news, you are essentially welcoming the doctoral researcher into the disciplinary community. In so doing, you may also wish to offer to be a future referee for the candidate or provide guidance to support the candidate in publishing their research. Hopefully, your relationship with the candidate will continue as you see them at conferences, events, and perhaps even as part of a collaborative research team in the future or in a professional capacity outside academia.

Conclusion

Building rapport and effective relationships with fellow assessors and with doctoral researchers is crucial if formal and informal assessment processes throughout the doctoral journey are to be a source of learning and empowerment for doctoral researchers.

For doctoral researchers, their experiences of assessment during the PhD are likely to serve as an initiation into the scholarly peer-review process. Furthermore, if candidates progress to pursue an academic career, their experiences of assessment are also likely to influence the approaches they take to doctoral supervision and assessment in the future, while in other professional capacities it will influence the way they interact with others, provide feedback and manage professional relationships. Thus, by demonstrating rapport, empathy, and interest through interactions with doctoral researchers and co-assessors, you will be modelling effective relationships in doctoral assessment that may well influence the next generation of doctoral assessors and professionals in your disciplinary ambit.

Further reading

Guccione, K. Trust Me! Building and breaking professional trust in doctoral student-supervisor relationships, The Leadership Foundation. Available at: https://www.lfhe.ac.uk/en/components/publication.cfm/SDP2016Sheffield (retrieved 08 April, 2019)

Hartley, J. and Fox, C. (2004) Assessing the mock viva: the experiences of British doctoral students. *Studies in Higher Education, 29*(6): 727–8

Share, M. (2016) The PhD viva: a space for academic development. *International Journal for Academic Development, 21*(3): 178–93

Telio, S., Regehr, G. and Ajjawi, R. (2016) Feedback and the educational alliance: examining credibility judgements and their consequences. *Medical Education,* *50*(9): 933–42

Wellington, J. (2010) Supporting students' preparation for the viva: their pre-conceptions and implications for practice. *Teaching in Higher Education, 15*(1): 71–84

7

What feedback is useful and how can it be negotiated?

In this chapter, you will find:

- The meanings of 'critical', as used in academic jargon, explored
- Emphasis on the need to negotiate expectations and forms of feedback
- Consideration of how feedback is received by individuals
- Clarification of the use of staged, formative and summative feedback
- Discussion of frequency, response rates and development of feedback
- Debate on the need for consistency between assessors' feedback

Introduction

In Chapter 1 we relayed a story in Reflection Point 1.1 from William James about how a brilliant scholar failed in his first attempt to write a thesis because he struggled to produce it on his own, not knowing the rubric that a traditional thesis encompasses. He succeeded with his re-submission once he had had feedback from the examining panel. For him, feedback was critical in two senses though it is sad that he, and many like him in succeeding years, had to wait for the final exam to discover what would have made an acceptable thesis. In common with those of us examiners today who must refer theses for further work that could have been avoided had good feedback been provided earlier, James expressed his chagrin at having to disappoint a promising colleague. We hope that in some small way, the readers of this book will contribute to reducing the occurrence of this sorry state.

Critical feedback is, from our academic perspective, something to be wished for. The comments, suggestions and corrections from our fellow authors and editors have certainly helped us to produce this and our previous books and journal articles. Nevertheless, for new doctoral researchers, it can be interpreted as something to be evaded if possible. This is often because, due to prior experience of critical feedback, they understand the word 'critical' as being either negative evaluation, even disparaging commentary, or for those with health professional backgrounds something that is life-threatening, or at least very grave, depending on the context. In academic parlance, we use the term critical to mean analytical, diagnostic, and crucial to the development of ideas. Thus, we sometimes remember to say, 'let me give some *constructive* feedback' but, because we are so accustomed to peer review, we often forget such niceties. As we discussed in Chapter 2, it is important that we make our implicit assumptions explicit – that our criticism, be it critical observations and/or critique, is intended to facilitate improvement – and remind researchers of the empowering pedagogy behind progress reviews.

Stage- and person-appropriate feedback

No matter their age and professional background, most doctoral researchers are relative novices in relation to research and certainly about the doctoral process itself. We have tried to alert them about what to expect in our recent book in this series, *Fulfilling the Potential of your Doctoral Experience*, but your group of researchers may not have read that yet! We advocated there that they negotiate with supervisors how best they can work together, including a recommendation to be joyful when they receive copious feedback to help them craft and hone their work. However, joyful responding is a challenging skill to master, and it is likely your doctoral researchers will need your support to learn how to react positively to criticism and to be open to challenges rather than taking them personally. To help support this learning process, we recommend to supervisors and early stage assessors that they introduce their feedback in ways that will encourage rather than destroy further efforts, motivating rather than intimidating them (see Voice of Experience Box 7.1 in the next section). Recall the EAT framework from Chapter 4: you could sit side by side with your doctoral researcher to explore the different aspects of assessment, including feedback. Before you read that, though, think about the need to tailor feedback to individuals' needs and predispositions by working on Activity 7.1.

Activity 7.1

What stimulates you to improve?

Think back over your lifetime of learning experiences. Do not restrict yourself to academic learning, for those experiences may not have been the most positive. Try to identify occasions when you really wanted to do better at some task. What factors prevailed at the time that motivated that striving for improvement? What was said, what feedback made you keen to enhance your product or upgrade your effort? How could you incorporate similar motivators into your assessment process?

Recognising that some things will work more effectively for some people than for others, ask friends and colleagues what kind of process and feedback helped them to achieve improvement, then you can build up a repertoire of ideas to use flexibly when the occasion demands it.

Feedback from supervisors

Although the main point of feedback from supervisors is formative, to help the researcher improve their practice, there is no denying the summative element; to help someone meet a prescribed standard it is necessary to evaluate their current place in relation to it. However, it is important to remember that, in most cases, at least in the early stages while trust is being developed, doctoral researchers will be more acutely sensitive to the summative aspect than the formative one. Because there is a lot to learn about the process of research and the conventions of recording it in writing, such researchers feel vulnerable (see Chapter 6). This is exacerbated by the dearth of available information about the objectives and criteria by which they will be judged other than the high hurdle that they should produce a publishable, significant contribution to knowledge. It is in this context that your feedback will be interpreted. For some perspectives from doctoral researchers, see Voice of Experience Box 7.1.

Voice of Experience 7.1

Contrasting feedback experiences

Compare these three experiences.

1. Whenever anyone mentions the word 'feedback' my heart does a little lurch. I would carefully craft my work, submit it, then wait several weeks before my supervisor returned it. Into my head pops the feedback I got – on the top right-hand

corner of the first page: Fine. That's it – the little scrappy writing of one word. That was all my effort was worth. No information about how to make it wonderful, as I wanted it to be. It was the same for my annual reviews, so I had to wait three and a half years in tension wondering if I was anywhere near doctoral standard.

Successful doctor A

2. I didn't realise until I spoke to other students that my experience wasn't the norm. I would submit work to my supervisor who would respond telling me when I could expect to have it returned – usually within a couple of weeks at most. At first it would be covered with smiley icons to show the bits she liked and question marks with annotations, such as 'could you be more specific?' or 'what evidence could you put forward to support this?' to challenge me to improve other parts. As time went by we got to a more short-hand form, and more friendly tone sharing reflections on progress, but I always felt I knew what was on the right track and what needed some review.

Successful doctor B

3. I shall always regret giving up on my PhD but after two years of receiving nothing but negative comments all over everything I submitted, I felt I would never get it right, so I was wasting my time and money heading for failure. My supervisor tried to dissuade me from withdrawing, pointing out that I had passed my first-year review, but I think that she just didn't want to look bad by losing a student.

A researcher who withdrew – C

Both A and B successfully submitted their theses, but one lived through the whole research process in constant tension while the other gained confidence as a researcher. The confidence of C was so badly challenged that he gave up entirely although he had lots of feedback which was probably, despite his interpretations, intended to help him to succeed. Let us be clear here – each doctoral researcher is different in her/his degree of tolerance of negative feedback, patience to wait for feedback, willingness to negotiate what kind of feedback is helpful, and comfort with the rate of development in feedback at any specific research stage. Therefore, both A and B might have given up if experiencing the same as C, or A might have stuck out the feedback regime of C, and so on. Nevertheless, it is not unlikely that C might have stayed had he had more positive feedback and if A had had more elaborated feedback, that doctoral experience may have been more fulfilling.

Hence, when considering how we might give feedback, including the timing and form, we first need to consider the researcher's needs at their actual stage in their studies and in relation to their general resilience. In the early stages they are all likely to be anxious, no matter whether they show it or not, because they are dealing with a great number of unknown factors. Whether you are reading this as a supervisor or a new doctoral researcher the value of clarifying expectations about the feedback process is evident. The aspects it would be helpful to negotiate at each development stage in the process are:

- What sort of work benefits from feedback?
- What kind of feedback is most useful and why?
- How frequently should work be submitted?
- How quickly might feedback be available?
- How might the researcher respond to it?

We will address each of these in what follows, but first two important points: 1) be very clear from the beginning that the feedback process will evolve over time as the researcher gains skills and confidence and the requirements of the research change; 2) realise that each doctoral researcher and doctoral project is unique, therefore, negotiation will always be critical to ensure feedback is truly useful. We advocate strongly that from the start all researchers should write about what they are doing and why and begin to prepare draft chapters to gain feedback on the research process and the writing style required of a thesis. However, they should be alerted that what passes at each stage will require revision later during the final stage of thesis writing. We have heard many cries of dismay from researchers along the lines of: 'My supervisor has gone crazy – all my chapters have been acceptable or good up to now but suddenly, so near the end, it seems I have to re-write them!' They had gained a mistaken impression that the 'final write-up' process involved merely sewing together everything they had produced so far.

Fortunately, equally often we have heard from researchers that, on looking back on previous writing, they realise how far they have come and how they now can improve on what they wrote in earlier times: how things make different sense in retrospect and how much more cogently they can write about it. The key to guiding your doctoral researchers to respond more like the latter example is to involve them in the practice of continually re-negotiating the process and ownership of the feedback procedure. Note that the latter example shows a researcher who is self-evaluating and driving the final drafting process, whereas the former example is of a researcher who feels the need to re-draft is being 'imposed on them'.

In re-negotiating feedback for this final stage, we explain to our researchers that a completed thesis should take the form of a retrospective review of the research process that flows as a story so that the reader can follow the important points of development. This means that some issues that might have seemed crucial or overwhelming at the time, including disasters and re-starts with new ideas, may fade into a few short paragraphs in the final tome. In contrast, what is written during the process needs to include all decisions taken and outcomes, with considerable emphasis on the rationale with supporting evidence. This will become important in the final stage reflections even if it does not all appear verbatim in the thesis. We suggest they have an imaginary guide, an alter ego, on their shoulder whispering into their ears: 'Why, and what is your evidence?' Although some former doctoral researchers refer to this voice as their supervisor embedded in their head, it is actually their own voice now able to self-evaluate and push the quality of their work to doctoral standard. Supervisors providing feedback in the form of these questions, in addition to compliments on well-structured and defended arguments throughout the earlier stages, can help the development of this voice.

Forms of submitted work and styles of feedback

Let us now return to our first proposed feedback discussion point: what form of work might be useful to submit for supervisor evaluation and comment. The Voice of Experience A above spoke of carefully crafting work for submission to the supervisor and that is one form of work that supervisors can give useful feedback on, but it is not the only kind. Indeed, in the early stages it might be more useful to consider, for example, drafts of ideas for discussion, a plan of work and outline project design and deliverables (as discussed in Chapter 4) for consideration or an outline of an intended argument or preliminary chapter for general feedback before more effort is expended on polishing. Whichever form is chosen, both researcher and supervisor/s need to be explicit about its intent and what is expected in response. Therefore, open communication about feedback within the context of a positive relationship, as described in Chapter 6, is vital.

For a draft of ideas, the feedback response might simply be a date when the ideas can be discussed, accompanied by a general indication of what might be useful to consider before that discussion. An argument outline might benefit from a note of what is effective in it, what could bear elaboration and what has been omitted, perhaps with some suggestions about general order of points and guidance about resources such as specific literature that might be informative or provide stronger evidence. Similar, but more detailed, feedback on content and on structure would be useful for a draft chapter, perhaps with a note that vocabulary and grammar have *not* been commented on since the chapter is not yet in polished form. The key is listening to your doctoral researchers about what they feel they need feedback on and communicating openly with them about what you think is important for their development at any given time.

For language issues such as syntax and punctuation, each supervisor has different views about how much feedback they would ever be prepared or able to give, and how often they will repeat the same comments, but every researcher deserves to know if their presentation form is good or requires some improvement to meet the formal doctoral thesis standards and where/how they might get help to achieve that. Such comments would be most appropriate after the researcher has had time to polish their drafts a little further in the light of first (or second) feedback, though they might value first being directed to good completed theses in your department as guidelines for style. For instance, there are disciplinary traditions about what tense and voice to use in a thesis, as well as the general need to write in a more formal way. It is valid to put the responsibility for developing writing skills onto your doctoral researchers; however, they need to know this is an expectation, and they are also likely to need to know where they can go for additional support outside of the supervisory team, if necessary. They will also need ongoing feedback from you to oversee their development, even if you are not actively teaching them basic academic writing skills.

If you have not already done so, alerting them that writing requires many drafts is important. No one is born to write in an academic style; it is a specialist form with a language that requires effort to master. Indeed, you might remind them each time a draft is as good as it need be for that stage that it will need updating and polishing later. To remind yourself of this process and, indeed, to locate examples that you might share with your researchers, we invite you to engage with Activity 7.2.

Newer researchers often have very high opinions of the skills of those already titled doctor or professor. They think that, because we are well-practised in the skills of the profession we represent, we sit at our computers and rapidly type out our journal articles or books or research proposals. We might wish that were true but know in practice that several, often many, drafts lie between the good idea that precedes writing and the final draft that is sent to the editor, publisher or funding body. Nor may novice researchers realise the frequency with which these are returned for improvement in the light of critical feedback! To induct them into this learning experience common to all writers, it can be helpful to share with them the comments you have received from peers before such submissions and the further feedback you might have had from reviewers. You could also share with them drafts from previous doctoral researchers (with their permission, of course), as described in Activity 7.2 below, prefacing that activity with an explanation that translating ideas from one's own thoughts to something written that makes sense to others is indeed an art and craft to be practised over a lifetime.

Examples of drafting

The most accessible examples for newer researchers may well be examples of draft chapters from their peers who precede them so, if you have not already, gain permission from those you have provided feedback to on draft chapters to share these, with their accompanying comments or track changes, with new recruits to demonstrate the development of writing over time. These need not be complete chapters; instead short sections that demonstrate specific points can be valuable teaching tools. You might start to collect such examples to use as the need arises.

Perhaps the most impactful examples, though, will be samples from your own writing that has been critiqued by peers. Choose a few samples that demonstrate how feedback from others helped to clarify and elaborate your writing.

We can attest to the great relief expressed by the less experienced author-contributors to our books in this series when a chapter contributor – a very experienced writer and publisher – allowed us to share the editorial comments on his first draft. You can read more about the value of such co-operation in one of our series books: *Success in Research: Inspiring Collaboration and Engagement*.

An important outcome of Activity 7.2, is that researchers see how feedback helps to drive writing development. If you are confident enough to share your own work with feedback from colleagues or peer-reviewers, this extends this lesson to help them realise that we are always developing our ability to communicate our research, and feedback is always an important aspect of this. Sitting side-by-side with your researcher and deconstructing their feedback and yours, or making comparisons with a previous researcher's work, would be a highly inclusive and formative approach to learning. Becoming an independent researcher capable of self-assessment, does not mean we no longer need feedback, it means we are aware of when it is important to seek out the feedback we need. It is this ownership of the feedback process that we are trying to instil in our doctoral researchers.

As the research/er advances, different kinds of feedback take priority as the thesis/argument itself develops, moving:

- from comments on what could or will be done and why;
- to what is being done and what it is achieving (or not, and why);
- then on to what it all means, including reflections on what could be improved if repeated and why;
- what the impact of the results might be;
- and what further research should emerge from it, with a scattering of a few more 'whys'.

These reflections will benefit greatly from the researcher's earlier notes of the details of reasoning and steps forward and back in the process, which should reassure them that previous writing efforts served a purpose. Encouraging them to periodically review previous versions or old chapters, will help them to recognise how far they have travelled and help to hone their ability to self-assess. Finally, feedback will concern the final content and structure of the thesis and some discussion about overall strengths and weaknesses to prepare for any viva that might follow submission in some countries, and for future publications.

As they move throughout the doctorate, your feedback will not only guide their progress but help develop their reflective ability and serve as a model for research evaluation. This modelling process is critical, as the true purpose of assessment in the doctorate is to support the researcher to become a self-assessor, able to evaluate their own progress and the substance of their research as well as that of others. Having your feedback to emulate is one way to achieve this but, in addition, it is important to introduce questions gradually into feedback that encourage the researcher to judge fitness for purpose and value, or lack of it, for themselves before you share your views. The more your doctoral researcher is involved in discussions about feedback and actively involved in the feedback process the better this model will work for them.

See Information Box 7.1 for a summary of the value of different general feedback types.

Information Box 7.1

Value of general feedback types

Example of feedback	Improvement value
68%	Marks alone give no indication of what to improve and how.
Not critical enough	This is an example of judgement without description. Without fully understanding what 'not critical' means or what would make it 'critical enough', the doctoral researcher will not be able to use this feedback effectively.
Good use of references for supporting evidence	Praise for aspects that have been done well encourages repetition and understanding of what is expected so they can self-evaluate in future.
Consider your sentence structure to highlight the comparison, such as: 'On the one hand [this]; on the other hand [that].'	The provision of examples of good practice help the development of good practice enabling future self-evaluation.
What recent research might strengthen your argument here?	Questioning can help researchers find their own answers and encourages their development as a self-evaluator.

Temporal aspects of feedback

The frequency of work submission is also to some extent subject to supervisor/researcher preference and stage of the research process. However, to build confidence both in each other and in the doctoral process, it is useful in the early stages of research to have frequent evidence of, and reassurance about progress, albeit based on small pieces of work. The researcher does need to know, though, that the purpose is to make a good start and that more elaborate but less frequent submitted work will become the norm later. Some may be surprised to learn that in later stages they may be working on several things simultaneously, perhaps collecting or analyzing data while drafting a chapter on Lab/fieldwork and honing their methodological arguments, although in our experience part-time researchers are quite adept at multi-tasking.

Their perusing of previous successful theses might have engendered the delusion, one that pervades public understanding outside of academia and research enterprises, that research happens in a logical order with each stage wrapped up tidily before the next is embarked on. Sadly, the registration time allowed is now short for doctoral research while the vagaries of the process of data availability and collection means that any potential downtime in data collection must be filled with other productive work. Happily, such a process accommodates the times when, psychologically or physically, a researcher is full of energy or depleted in it. All of us experience the vicissitudes of suddenly being inspired, too drained to do more than check references or enjoy the comfortable tedium of checking through transcripts for grammar and spelling.

Throughout these different phases and different types of work being submitted, a two-way dialogue about what is required and how this fits into the researcher's development is helpful. Even more empowering is to encourage the doctoral researcher to create their own aims and targets for their work in collaboration with you from the outset, contributing your experience to ensure both progress and achievability, then gradually supporting them to do so as they become more confident.

The current pressures to ensure timely completion of doctorates do lead to repercussions for the supervisor, including pressure to provide feedback within shorter timeframes. To be able to manage this added pressure to successfully provide your doctoral researchers with the feedback they need, whilst balancing your other commitments, we suggest negotiating with your researchers about which issues need the most urgent feedback for progress to be achieved in one realm and what can wait to be dealt with later. A wise supervisor will ensure that, at these busy times, negative feedback is well balanced with positive feedback and examples demonstrating the expected standard, if possible. We do expect our researchers to be resilient but sometimes a suggestion that a chapter requires a complete re-draft with many changes, can be demoralising, especially if the researcher does not understand how to make the situation right. A mentor, other than you, or peer mentoring can be very helpful in these circumstances, as a source of additional support. You should draw on as much resource as you can to assist your researcher, rather than assuming all tasks yourself, as well as encouraging them to build their own network of champion supporters.

Furthermore, when there are other setbacks with the research, some feedback may be able to wait until the calamitous experiment is re-started, or the lost data rescued, or a revised interview schedule approved to cope with unforeseen circumstances. However, the researcher would benefit from knowing that any delay in feedback is a deliberate ploy to complete important jobs first, rather than disinterest, or forgetfulness (though we know this can happen too!).

Reasonable response rates and researcher reactions

Although supervisors must adapt their response rates to their own workload at any time, as well as to the needs of the researcher's project, it would be reasonable to expect them to negotiate in advance the provision of feedback within less than one month for larger pieces of work and considerably less for smaller sections or queries. Indeed, many supervisors undertake to turn around drafts within two weeks and to respond to queries on email within a week unless they inform the researcher in advance that they will be at a conference, on holiday, or other special circumstances.

We would suggest that, when negotiating such things, you make it clear that the researcher should be working on other things while they wait. It can be very annoying to spend time making helpful comments on a script to then only be told that the researcher has, in the meantime, produced a new version. It would be of mutual benefit if, along with your feedback, you gave a clear indication about when corrections or updated versions of corrected work will be required: whether the researcher should address your comments immediately or wait until they are blending that work into the final thesis, for instance. An immediate response would apply, for instance, if the required amendment is for plans for the ongoing research process but if the requirement is simply for a polishing of presentation that could wait until the full thesis is compiled near the end. A requirement for the tightening of argument could await a less busy time in lab/field work and so could be negotiated.

A further example of reciprocity is asking your researchers to give you feedback on the value/helpfulness of your feedback! Beyond the query about whether they found it useful you could probe further to find out in what ways it was helpful and how you could improve your feedback. As well as discovering how to improve your own practice with these researchers this would model professional reflective practice for them, thus contributing to their professional development.

Your own professional development as a supervisor can be extended by taking opportunities to act as a reviewer of other researchers' progress in more formal settings either for interim reviews or as a final examiner. We describe the feedback required in these roles in the sections that follow.

Feedback from review /interim assessors

Assessors specifically chosen to evaluate doctoral work at identified stages (often an annual review and sometimes a more formal assessment in the early/mid stage of the doctorate) are expected to provide both summative feedback, whether the researcher has made sufficient progress by that point, and formative feedback, either how to achieve that sufficiency if not yet apparent, or how to progress further. These two forms of assessment feedback are more balanced in this role than in the supervisor role while usually the role, and the nature and volume of the feedback, are more constrained than that provided by the supervisor since they are bounded by specific institutional guidelines/regulations. The person taking such a role is generally expected to be independent of the research under review so to provide an objective, 'outsider' perspective. Often these guidelines or regulations deliberately model final assessment procedures to provide practice for the researcher (and, if incidentally, for assessors). Thus, as we discussed in Chapter 4, the procedures may incorporate an oral presentation and/or an opportunity for questioning by the assessors, in addition to a specified written synopsis of progress, perhaps including a sample chapter. At this point you might find it helpful to engage in Activity 7.3.

There is an important sub-text to these opportunities to provide feedback. That is, that this feedback should provide guidance on what the researcher could do to improve their writing and research activities and stimulation to do so. In short, good feedback is feedback they can do something with to move their doctorate forward. It should induct researchers into the peer-review process so that they can emulate it in their minds when reviewing the literature (what is good about this work and how could it be improved?), when listening to conference presentations and, significantly, when reading their own drafts of their work.

Activity 7.3

Your institutional regulations about interim doctoral assessments

Even if you are not yet ready to take on the interim assessment role for a doctoral researcher, it will be useful to you as a supervisor in preparing researchers for such assessment to know when and how interim assessment is conducted in your establishment and what to prepare for it. Seek that information and consider what the process involves. Then consider what evidence you would want to see in any researcher-provided documentation, and in a presentation if included, to demonstrate that they are on track, for that stage of registration, to achieve a doctorate. You could also consider what questions you might ask and what answers would satisfy you in the light of the quality of that presented evidence.

The quality of the evidence provided for the review and of the responses to questions within it form the focus of your, the interim assessor's, feedback. The regulations will guide you in what summative alternatives are available, but they are likely to include three general levels: progress is satisfactory; progress is somewhat short of satisfactory, but it would be achievable with some specified effort; unsatisfactory progress with a recommendation for withdrawal of registration. Because of the very serious implications for the candidates, their supervisors and, indeed, the reputation of the institution, as elaborated in Chapter 8, the last one is the least frequent and is likely to require very careful delineation of the reasons why the work does not meet the standard required of that stage of study. All these stakeholders want to be sure that the decision is based on clear evidence and fairly assessed. It is usual that some form of 'special measures' is instituted if unsatisfactory progress is the verdict, such that specific activities that produce the required improvement must be undertaken over a restricted time period such as three months. Thus, the quality of feedback is critical in many senses of the word.

Of course, the same requirements of feedback relate to the other possible decisions, although the outcome is less drastic. For those making **satisfactory progress**, information about what aspects of the work specifically has led to that decision will be appreciated and useful to found future work on. However, for those in the middle group, good-quality feedback is extremely important rather than merely helpful. As we noted in Information Box 7.1, researchers will, of course, need to know what has been omitted that should be included, what must be done that has not been, and what requires removal or amendment, possibly with some exemplar or illustration to help them by making the abstract more concrete. In addition, they will very much need to know what must and what can remain as it is so that they recognise that they have done something of value. Again, we will address this further in Chapter 8.

When compiling this feedback, that should be in written as well as presented in oral form, do take notice of the time allowed in the regulations for any changes to be accomplished: prioritise those things which really must be done to achieve satisfactory status and include any others as suggestions that might be incorporated by a later date. Finally, be very clear to the candidate and the supervisors involved about the deadline date for the required responses and who will make the judgement on the adequacy of those responses – the whole panel or a specific member, depending on the conventions of your department/ institution.

Feedback from final examiners

As we will discover in Chapter 9, the final assessment of the doctorate within your institution, or within an institution that has invited you to be an external examiner, can take one of many variations in form. These forms are determined by the traditions within a country, the regulations of the award-granting institution and conventions of the discipline. However, the outcomes cover the range between outright Pass with no corrections, or an allowance for typographical errors to be addressed, to outright Fail. As with internal reviews, those passing will appreciate acknowledgement of the key points of excellence in their work. Similarly, there will be a requirement for those who fail to be provided with clear, unambiguous detail about the deficits of the work. Correspondingly, those candidates required to do additional work, ranging from relatively minor corrections to a major work for resubmission, will need unambiguous, detailed feedback on the requirements, and by when they must be submitted, so that they can reach the doctoral standard. There may be a further category – those candidates offered a lower degree as an alternative to a doctorate, with or without required corrections; they will need to know in what ways their work does not, and cannot be amended, to achieve doctoral standard but is perhaps, and for instance, worthy of recognition for a master's degree. We will elaborate on these potential outcomes in Chapter 12 while in Chapter 10 the review of criteria that delineate doctorateness will provide guidance and what needs to be specified for corrections or re-submissions. In the chapter that follows we consider not *what* feedback to provide in these less than positive circumstances, but *how* you might convey it. Before you read that chapter, you might find it helpful to engage in Reflection Point 7.1.

Reflection Point 7.1

Feedback feeding forward

In feeding forward it is important to focus on the future and not dwell on the past. Carol Dweck's work (see Further reading) recognises that praise and praising processes, strategies and effort are highly motivating for people and encourage a growth mindset. Reflecting on a piece of feedback you have given recently or will give soon, how could you use it to focus on the future or a future action, and what could you say, or change, that would make it more helpful and inspiring for the recipient to hear?'

Doctoral rites of passage

A rite of passage is an experience that marks the transition from one phase of life to another, for instance in many religions and cultures there is some form of ceremony, from a physical ordeal or challenge to a social celebration that marks the transition from youth to adulthood. The doctoral examination is frequently described as the rite of passage into the intellectual community of scholars. Whether the candidate comes through the process feeling empowered to begin a new career stage or left feeling somehow short-changed depends on how the examination is conducted and what feedback is received.

We have heard colleagues, significantly successful academics in senior positions, confessing to having had an imposter syndrome (see Voice of Experience 6.2). Of course, many personal attributes and circumstances can contribute to this feeling of unworthiness but, equally certainly, the process of and feedback during and following the final examination of the thesis can stimulate or exacerbate this feeling. It may surprise you that one colleague puts it down to having had a very short and easy viva examination that resulted in a pass with no corrections required while another had a longer viva with questions that did not seem to refer to the most important aspects, for her, of the thesis, though again this was a pass with no corrections required. Both of these were examined in the UK, but another European colleague had a public viva following a request to add a few short additions to his thesis after submission, but neither those additions nor the questions in the viva addressed a part of his research procedure that he, in retrospect and rightly or wrongly, felt was weak.

These examples indicate that for satisfactory theses honest feedback is required that recognises the excellent aspects and those that are good and how they compensate for the less-than-perfect facets (recognising that all research projects have some of those). For those theses that require more work, comprehensive feedback is vital that will enable doctoral requirements to be met if corrections are completed satisfactorily, but that feedback can be couched in ways that leave the candidate inspired to do so. This will be addressed with advice on how to give really bad news in the next chapter. But first an addendum to recognise that feedback is based on assessors' individual perspectives founded on accumulated experience.

Consistency of feedback

Frequently it is only when scholars reach the doctoral level that the relativity of knowledge and the challenges of different, sometimes conflicting if not simply contrasting and shifting, **ontologies, epistemologies** and **paradigms** become evident. This can come as a surprise to researchers previously convinced that experts in disciplines agree and contribute to an accumulation of facts. However, recognising the complexity of research problems, an increasing number of projects involve interdisciplinary research with supervisors from different backgrounds advising researchers and thus the potential for divergent views has increased.

Since it is becoming increasingly common for supervision to be conducted by teams of academics or academics with industrial/professional collaborative supervisors, it is important to consider how to deal with potentially inconsistent or even conflicting feedback. Certainly, it can be confusing to novice researchers to receive apparently conflicting advice or comments on their work from different illustrious sources, be they supervisors or independent assessors or combinations of those groups. In the past we have advised supervisors to discuss any disagreements privately to present their researchers with a clear, uncluttered response to avoid the researcher being forced into choosing one over the other or finding a mid-pathway. However, research conducted in Denmark (Dr Sofie Kobayashi) on the supervision process strongly indicates that it is useful for researchers to become aware of these differences of opinion, especially as they engender much fruitful debate in the academy. Perhaps this is because when difference of thought and perspectives are discussed openly and transparently, it empowers doctoral researchers to feel free to develop their own unique stance.

If differences are debated, but also accepted as valuable, researchers can utilise feedback from various sources and self-assess their work to create their own position. Thus, we suggest that supervisors introduce such divergence at a time and in a way that demonstrates a collegial approach rather than a confrontational one, encouraging the researcher to weigh the evidence and form their own defensible opinions. Similarly, independent reviewers and supervisors should attempt to remain professional and consider the position of the candidate by keeping any rancour from debates about different opinions in public. A worthy goal of doctoral education is to develop skills of intellectual argument alongside a healthy appreciation of different forms of knowledge and a life-long enjoyment of learning from others.

Further reading

Dweck, C. (2017) *Mindset – Updated Edition: Changing the Way You Think to Fulfil Your Potential.* New York: Ballantine Books

Godskesen, M. I., Wichmann-Hansen, G. and Kobayashi, S. (2017) Doctoral supervisor education in Denmark: aiming to foster reflective practitioners. *Doctoral Education Bulletin*, Spring(9): 6–7

Kumar, V. and Stracke, E. (2017) Reframing doctoral examination as teaching. *Innovations in Education and Teaching International 2017.* Available at: http://dx.doi.org/10.1080/14703297.2017.1285715

Reeves, J., Henslee, E, and Starbuck, S. (2020) *Success in Research: Inspiring Collaboration and Engagement.* London: Sage

8

How can you deal well with less positive assessment outcomes?

In this chapter, we encourage you to:

- Consider potential causes of poor outcomes and their variety at different stages
- Recognise that disappointments happen and need careful, sensitive management
- Think about fairness and transparency in the light of changing situations
- Evaluate ways of handling negative outcomes to empower rather than demean the candidate
- Reflect on living with the consequences of hard decisions
- Draw on the experience of other professionals who must deliver bad news
- Identify support available for supervisors and examiners for dealing with the need to communicate negative outcomes

Introduction

This chapter honestly and openly deals with the hardest assessment tasks anyone involved in doctoral assessment can face – having to convey to a doctoral researcher that, at some point during or at the end of the process, they have not reached the necessary standard. It is possible that you may go through your career without having to hold one of these conversations because they are quite rare but, if you intend to act as an independent assessor or external examiner regularly or supervise many researchers, then it is something worth preparing for. We also hope that some of the advice within this book about assessing and then identifying problems early, along with the wide range of tools and techniques we introduce in our sister book, *Supervising to Inspire Doctoral Researchers*, will also help you to minimise the occurrence of these negative outcomes.

Candidates are often surprised to learn that most assessors find it hard to give bad news; yet seldom do assessors or examiners really want to severely criticise or fail someone's work. In fact, they usually recognise and regret that their responses, though intended to be fair decisions, cause disappointment and heartache. It is less worrisome, and more motivating for all involved (including the candidate, examiners and supervisors), if they can provide feedback (see previous chapter) that enables the development of a more sophisticated piece of work that then falls within the range that is considered acceptable for a given set of criteria at a specific education level. In what follows we discuss such possibilities, as well as even more difficult situations when corrections are technically not possible or when the candidate is not capable of making them, in their own or the assessor's eyes. We explore these challenging aspects of assessment as well as ways of dealing with the impact (emotional and intellectual) that they may have on assessors as well as on candidates.

As we have seen in previous chapters, most assessment at doctoral level has a formative element with an outcome that allows for correction/revision of submitted material for re-evaluation. Even at the final stage there are more potential outcomes (see Chapter 12) that allow revision than those that are either complete failure or an offer of a lower degree (which might seem like complete failure to the candidate). Indeed, in percentage terms candidates receiving those latter two outcomes are few (for evidence of this see the Voice of Experience 8.2 later in the chapter), with the vast majority gaining some opportunity to reach the final target of a doctorate. [Chapter 12 in this book and Chapter 7 in Houston, 2019 (see Further reading) provide more detail about the range of results and how they are implemented. The latter particularly evidences disciplinary differences in interpretation.] These more positive outcomes are aided by rigorous and appropriate assessment at earlier stages so that problems are resolved during the process rather than at the final stages. Let us, then, deal with continuing or in-course assessment first.

Managing borderline and unsatisfactory progress as a supervisor

In Chapter 7 we considered the supervisor role as an in-course assessor and emphasised the need for honest, critical feedback that eventually develops the candidate's ability to self-assess. Most of the time this feedback will be encouraging and be intended to help the doctoral researcher move forward; however, there may be times when providing honest feedback may mean telling someone that their progress towards the doctorate is inadequate. Assessing and communicating unsatisfactory and even borderline progress is particularly challenging for supervisors because, naturally, we all want doctoral researchers to succeed. However, as mentioned in Chapter 3, not being honest about problems is not helpful to anyone. It is unlikely that the candidate will improve their research practice until they are alerted to faults. In demanding situations, like being engaged in a doctorate, people stick with doing things the way they know how until someone or something stimulates them to improve. For everyday circumstances that 'someone' should be one of the supervisors and the 'something' should be constructive feedback.

It is now common that institutions have some type of procedure in which the supervisor can officially inform their doctoral researchers about a perceived lack of progress, with additional guidance on how to recover momentum over a fixed but short period. For instance, some UK and other European institutions include such procedures in their Postgraduate Codes of Practice, usually giving the researcher three months to reach specific, remedial objectives. This procedure is used to avoid the situation deteriorating between official review points which may be many more months ahead. If informal objectives are set in motion before the official review, time can be saved or major problems forestalled, by either resolving them in advance or persuading the candidate to take the option of a more graceful exit.

Because of the individual nature of the doctorate, in terms of both the research and the professional development of the doctoral researcher, it can be hard to know when to say progress is unsatisfactory. This is especially true when looking at progress on a weekly basis. Making specific targets/objectives for longer periods of time, over a month or several months, can help identify trends of lack of progress as opposed to the odd tough week here or there. It can also help identify when a certain research approach is not working so that a contingency plan can be invoked. We suggest that targets be well aligned with overall learning objectives for the specific stages, mentioned in Chapter 2. If this is done, it will be easier to identify real problems with progress throughout the changing doctoral journey and to communicate this to your doctoral researcher promptly.

Assessing problems in the first year of doctoral study can be especially challenging for a supervisor, because it is reasonable to expect a doctoral researcher to take time to acclimatise to the very different world of doctoral research. This is particularly true for a researcher who may also be adjusting to a new culture or returning to study after a substantial break or learning to balance a number of roles or personal/professional issues (see Chapter 5). However, this transition is critical to future success; habits formed in the first few months in terms of working patterns and expected progress can stubbornly last, therefore, ensuring good progress from early on is important. See Voice of Experience 8.1 for some potential troublesome areas to watch out for in this first year.

Voice of Experience 8.1

Potential first year problems

I have worked across the entire University for more than a decade now, supporting a cohort of over 1,000 doctoral researchers as they progress through their doctorates. This view does mean I see the problems as well as the triumphs on a faster and more massive scale than I did when I worked within a single department. I also can see patterns, helping me identify where problems commonly occur. In the first year of the doctorate, most people have a wobble or two. This may feel worrisome both for the doctoral researcher and perhaps for the supervisor as well, but usually some supportive advice and guidance from the supervisory team is all that is needed to get the researchers back on track. However, there are some signs that a problem may be more serious, and a supervisor would be well placed to watch out for these.

One area concerns critical engagement with the literature and the ability to start to understand limitations of published work as well as the research the new doctoral researcher is starting to develop for their own project. A very stubborn stance on what the expected outcome of the project will be, or an inability to see both strengths and weaknesses in different research approaches, are possible signs of a problem. If this occurs, setting some clear targets for engaging with literature along with some short, written, comparative outputs can help develop these skills, as well as perhaps encouraging participation in a reading group, journal club and/ or seminar series. If, after a couple of months, there is still no improvement, it may be time for the supervisor to invoke 'unsatisfactory progress' procedures. Of all the skills researchers are expected to develop in the first year of their doctorate, across disciplines these critical, analytic skills are crucial.

In the science disciplines, the other areas to which to be alert are the ability to adapt to the research lab culture and the resilience to troubleshoot inevitable technical problems. In AHSS subjects, understanding the links between ontology/epistemology/theoretical frameworks and the methodology and methods of the individual's research project, is also a challenge area. These too are skills that are critical to the respective disciplines and must show progressive development within the first year.

Of course, some doctoral researchers lack the necessary discipline to work independently, without the structure found in other levels of education. This is usually the easiest of the problems to fix, but it does sometimes take a strong wake up call. Doing a doctorate should not mean working 60–70 hours a week every week of the year, but they will need to be treating it like a full-time job in order to succeed.

Researcher Developer in Research Intensive University

In general, unsatisfactory progress procedures should never be the first action taken by a supervisor if they observe one of the above problems or any other problem with progress. It is important to create a positive, open relationship which helps the doctoral researcher to reflect on their own progress as described in Chapter 6 and to give good formative feedback as discussed in Chapter 7. However, by the time the assessment of unsatisfactory progress is made, it should not come as a surprise to the doctoral researcher. These problems should have been discussed in the team with the researcher more formatively and it should be clear to both the doctoral researcher and supervisors that progress is not being made.

Once a doctoral researcher makes it past their first year, it is optimal that they have the core skills and a solid research project to take them to successful completion and an award of doctor at the end. However, there can be later stage problems with progress. Sometimes these are caused by well being issues, or life issues outside of the doctorate. If this is the case, it is important to support the doctoral researcher in taking the time they need, most likely by temporarily withdrawing from the doctorate, to sort these out. (There will be guidelines and regulations in your university related to this.) Personal problems can present themselves like problems with progress, and it will be important for the supervisor to work to disassociate life problems from doctorate problems.

As discussed in Chapter 2, there can be mid-stage slumps while, as the researcher nears the end of the doctoral journey, there can be challenges around analysis and thesis writing that highlight some unforeseen skills weaknesses. Two of the biggest struggles across all disciplines after the first year are: 1) coping and succeeding with the expectation of increasing independence; and 2) maintaining motivation throughout the whole doctoral journey. At times these two can be hard to differentiate but working out what is the true problem is important because an inability to become independent is much more problematic in terms of final assessment outcomes. However, if it is a motivational issue, harsh feedback about progress may make it worse. The loss of motivation could be the result of feeling overwhelmed, perhaps they have too much information and are not sure how to deal with that; it can also stem from a loss of confidence and/or sense of direction, which will need to be approached with sensitivity. As with the first year, it is important to begin with support and guidance in a formative manner, using summative assessment only if other forms have failed. (See our previously mentioned sister book on supervision in this series, for more ideas, tips and techniques to support doctoral researchers across the various stages of their doctoral journey.) See Reflection Point 8.1 to think about whether it is time to make the assessment of unsatisfactory progress.

Reflection Point 8.1

Judging whether progress is unsatisfactory

If you and your co-supervisors become concerned about the progress of one of your doctoral researchers, here are some questions to ask yourselves.

(Continued)

1. Are objectives being missed repeatedly? If it is rare, or a relatively new occurrence, see Chapters 5 and 7 for guidance.
2. Is the problem continuing despite you trying different approaches and ways of communicating feedback? If you have not tried different approaches, see Chapters 6 and 7 for guidance.
3. Have you been concerned about progress for several months, despite communicating with your doctoral researcher that there is a problem? If you have not communicated the problem, they may not be aware, so see Chapters 5 and 7 for guidance.
4. Are you concerned their thesis will not be of doctoral standard? If you have identified specific problems and articulated them clearly with little or no response, you should warn the researcher about the unsatisfactory progress procedures.

If you have answered yes to one or more of the questions above, you really must seriously consider making the formal assessment that satisfactory progress is not being made. Despite differences in systems, internationally, three things are extremely important in such circumstances:

1. Seek support. This support may be through others in the supervisory team, departmental colleagues, through faculty/university administrators who understand the necessary procedures and policies and/or support services involved in providing researcher development and pastoral care. Seek out anyone who can support you. You are not alone in this and there will be a range of expertise within your institution to help you. (See Appendix A for more suggestions.)
2. Openly discuss this assessment with the doctoral researcher. They have a right to know the seriousness of the problem. Information Box 8.1 provides pointers on how to have such difficult conversations.
3. Make a formal record of this conversation and your advice to the doctoral researcher. The advice you give will depend on the severity of the problem and the options allowed through your institution.

Information Box 8.1

How to deliver bad news to a doctoral researcher

Both giving and receiving bad news is hard, so prepare well.

It is a good idea to write down what you want to say and then review it to make sure it is clear and appropriate (considering whether you would want to receive it in that way). Then deal with the situation keeping the following points in mind.

- Honesty and sincerity are key concepts for such situations.
- Choose an appropriate context to deliver upsetting news.
- Ensure that enough time is available for discussion and consolation.

- Set expectations from the beginning by tone and words (assertive, not confrontational).
- Find out what the doctoral researcher already recognises as inadequate in their work.
- Get to the point: do not delay, avoid or use evasive language but be clear and straightforward.
- If people become emotional, just stop and give them time and a place to compose themselves. Do not rush because you feel uncomfortable.
- Be sympathetic: let the doctoral researcher know that you understand their distress.
- Respond to their reactions calmly and firmly.
- Provide details that support the decision. These should be provided in writing after any verbal delivery.
- Be prepared to answer questions about the problem/s.
- Note any positive outcomes that might mitigate or lessen the impact of the decision.
- Determine and inform about specific next steps, how they will be achieved and by whom.
- Help them to 'save face' when possible by discussing what the rest of the world needs to know and in what form. Be mindful that they may be under pressure from, for example, family, employers or governments so, although the decision must be made with integrity, how it is conveyed is significant.
- Provide time and space for them to come to terms with the outcome.

This conversation with your doctoral researcher will not be easy and should be shared across the supervisory team. In Chapter 5 we discuss a variety of techniques that can help you as a supervisor create a relationship which is honest and built on reflective and transparent expectations. This foundation is extremely important to being able to convey messages about unsatisfactory progress to your doctoral researcher, if the need ever arises.

Remember that doctoral research is not for everyone; many extremely bright people are not well suited to doctoral study. It is very important to have high standards and a rigorous admissions process (see our companion book, *Supervising to Inspire Doctoral Researchers*) to minimise the chance of a doctoral researcher not being a good match to the doctoral process. However, this is not a guarantee. If a person is not going to succeed in reaching doctoral standard, establishing this as early as possible is a positive thing. However, making that assessment can be hard for a supervisor and difficult to hear for the doctoral researcher. Nevertheless, no matter how difficult, it is a caring thing to be honest with people and to tell them when they are not succeeding as researchers whilst not undermining them as people. It is cruel, and immoral, to allow someone to continue struggling who, unless major changes happen, will never meet the standard necessary to be awarded the title doctor. The way you manage this is important for how they will feel about themselves thereafter.

Dealing with negative outcomes as an assigned examiner during the doctorate

There are times when the supervisor may not recognise a critical problem with a doctoral researcher's progress because they are too close to the student and the project to objectively identify the weakness. This, of course, is one of the main reasons we have a peer-review system in academia. External eyes are sometimes clearer and provide needed objectivity. Unfortunately, it is also occasionally true that some supervisors relegate the provision of less positive feedback to an unsuspecting colleague nominated as a formal independent assessor, preferring not to be the conveyor of bad news themselves. (Of course, we would not expect this to be the case for anyone after reading our books!) Sadly, in these cases the outcome frequently then comes as a greater shock to the doctoral researcher who may believe that they are doing quite well so far since there has been little information to the contrary, or they have not been alert to hints.

As discussed in previous chapters, although the precise nature varies by institution/ discipline/country, it is likely that colleagues outside of the supervisory team will be involved in assessment checkpoints along the doctoral journey, intended to ensure that the researcher is on track for a successful completion. This mitigates against problems with supervision, low availability of resources and a less-than-supportive research environment, as well as identifies specific weaknesses in the doctoral researcher and their progress that have not been addressed by the supervisors, whatever their motivations. For all these reasons, if you are an assigned examiner who is tasked with assessing the progress of colleagues' doctoral researchers, you are undertaking a very important task.

As mentioned in Chapter 2, this is often the first experience doctoral researchers will have had with the peer-review process. Therefore, it is critical that you act with integrity and skill in assessing progress and providing feedback to the doctoral researcher. The previous chapters considered how to establish a good relationship with the doctoral researcher you are assessing and how to provide helpful feedback in situations where the outcome is generally positive, even though you may well have to relay some constructive criticism.

Remember, a negative assessment is not the norm, because, most of the time, an assigned assessor acts to confirm that progress is indeed on track, while adding specific insights into the project and the professional development of the researcher. However, if you uncover serious concerns about the research project or the development of the doctoral researcher, then it is important to all parties involved that you do honestly discuss problems or potential problems with the doctoral researchers. It may be that your discovery of these problems will enable them to address the issues early and, therefore, avert a negative outcome at the end of the doctorate.

Because the candidates might be nervous about such assessment, it can be helpful to build up in a research community an atmosphere that recognises the value of external feedback on the progress of the research and thus the reputation of all involved, from candidate to the institution. Equally, it is important that the academics involved, the supervisors and the assigned examiners, have established a relationship of mutual trust and openness to both giving and receiving feedback. This would be an opportune moment to engage with Reflection Point 8.2 to consider your own context.

Reflection Point 8.2

Building a culture that values external feedback

Think for a few minutes about the opportunities that the wider research community provides for us as academic researchers to learn more and improve our practice.

You might have included feedback from conference participants, peer review of written material, responses to funding proposals, and of course feedback about your work, or your behaviour and its impact on others from critical friends when engaged in intellectual discussions and debates. All these forms of feedback, albeit that they are sometimes irritating, and can be annoying or painful, enable us to improve our practice (see Chapter 7). Peer review is, indeed, part and parcel of our professional way of life (see Chapter 3 'How to make the peer review process work for you?' in our sister book in this series: *Publishing for Impact*).

Now consider your own immediate context – the department in which you and your doctoral researchers work. How often is such peer review discussed? Are colleagues transparent with each other and their researchers about the amount and value of peer review, or do they tend to keep it hidden, as if it were disgraceful? How honest are you in your public feedback to colleagues presenting seminars, or do you avoid such feedback entirely or provide it only in private? Does the level of honesty on both sides reflect the levels of trust and respect you and your colleagues have for each other? If you receive suggestions for improvement do you overtly welcome them … or … perhaps grumble to yourself? How would a colleague react to fellow academics, those who are assigned assessors of their doctoral researchers, concluding that enough progress had not been made or that there was a fundamental problem with the person's development or with the research project? If you were acting as an assigned assessor for a doctoral researcher supervised by other colleagues in your department, would you feel like you were able to say that the doctoral researcher was not of the expected standard? What if the supervisor(s) was a senior colleague? What if the supervisor was your department head/line manager?

It should be a priority for all academic members of staff to build a community that fosters an environment where all researchers from doctorate level to full professor are freely able to discuss research and exchange ideas. Peer review among colleagues should be collegiate, not competitive. However, we do acknowledge that we do not live in Utopia and there can be internal politics. We would suggest that, before taking on any role that requires you to assess a colleague's doctoral researcher, you think very hard about the questions raised in the last paragraph of Reflection Point 8.2. If you do not feel you could freely fail a colleague's (perhaps a very senior one) doctoral researcher, you should not accept the role as assessor. This is true no matter how unlikely it is that you would make a failing assessment. You must not put yourself in any situation where your academic integrity conflicts with your career progression.

As an assigned assessor, when you realise the work you are reviewing is causing you concern, it is important to review all the regulations surrounding possible outcomes and to consider seriously what you believe is possible for the doctoral researcher to do in order to salvage the situation. The positive aspect of peer-assessment during the process of the doctorate is that, even if a serious problem is discovered, there is often the time and ability to fix the problem(s). Activity 8.1 has a list of questions to ask yourself as an assigned assessor when concerned about the doctoral researcher's progress.

Activity 8.1

Questions to clarify and address concerns about progress

Concerns about the doctoral researcher's knowledge or skills:

1. What skills exactly do you feel they are lacking, i.e. critical thinking, academic writing, research-specific skills?
2. How far away from the expected level are they for their stage of the doctorate? How did you reach this conclusion and what evidence supports it?
3. What opportunities might there be for them to get help in developing these skills or knowledge?
4. Could there be an underlying reason for this problem, i.e. an undiagnosed disability (see Chapter 6), or lack of specific expertise to teach this knowledge/skill within the supervisory team or department? What assumptions might have been made about the candidate's ability/knowledge?
5. Realistically, do you think it is possible for them to gain the necessary standard within a reasonable amount of time? If so, how can this be supported?

Concerns about the feasibility or practicality of the research project:

1. Does the work have reasonable potential for producing an original contribution to knowledge?
2. If not, would modifying of the project make this original contribution possible?

3. Do you think it will take too long to complete the project?
4. If so, could you suggest a contingency plan that would help ensure the possibility of an original contribution in the time remaining?
5. Are there elements within the project that you think pose a great risk of not producing a result that could be used in the thesis (understanding that a negative result is an acceptable answer)?
6. If so, could you suggest a way to eliminate or reduce those elements but still ensure an original contribution?
7. Being honest with yourself, are you biased against the research approach in any way? If so, perhaps you are not the best person to make this assessment.

Concerns about resources in the research environment:

1. Are you concerned that the supervisory team does not have the appropriate expertise? Would another co-supervisor help the situation?
2. Are there additional resources that you think would help support success? How accessible are these?

The above questions can help you start to think not just about specifically what the problems are, but also how you may be able to support doctoral researchers and their supervisors to find solutions, ideally before any serious delay to the doctorate itself occurs. In general, problems with the research project and/or lack of resources, although potentially politically awkward to discuss, are not too hard to fix if all parties are willing. Problems with the doctoral researcher's skill level may also be addressed given high-quality feedback (see Chapters 5 and 7) and a supportive environment. Recognition that the success of any project is not solely dependent on the knowledge and skills of the candidate conducting the research but is also dependent on the support of people and other resources, can alleviate some of the pressure on candidates in these situations. Then they can make good use of any feedback offered to enhance their own development and to lobby for more appropriate support and resources if necessary.

However, the result may not simply involve feedback for improvement; it may recognise that the project itself is not viable or that the candidate is not best placed to continue to conduct it. If this is the case, although difficult, it is a kindness and a professional obligation to be honest with the candidate. As mentioned above, there is nothing worse than continuing to work year after year if success is improbable or perhaps impossible.

Nevertheless, doing the ultimately kind thing is often a personally demanding professional response so you should draw on other resources to sustain your own wellbeing and to help you deal with challenging situations. We provide some guidance on where you might access such resources in Appendix A.

Dealing with negative outcomes as a final assessment examiner

Should you be unlucky enough to have to examine a thesis that is a long way from being 'good enough' for a pass and also quite far from needing only relatively minor corrections (currently almost the customary outcome), then the choice of outcome is major corrections, or a lower degree (a master's of some sort) or a fail verdict. Fortunately, especially in institutions in which regular review and feedback is taken seriously, the last two outcomes are rare, while experienced supervisors are convinced that major corrections are becoming more frequently imposed.

In a context in which low completion rates result in financial sanctions on institutions, the haste to submission accounts for some major corrections when both the candidate and the supervisors lacked time to complete all the detail, proof-read, acknowledge alternative perspectives in interpretations and recognise important omissions. Managing and monitoring the process closely usually reduces the need to rush to finish, except where unforeseen circumstances disrupt a well-planned pace of work. With or without the need for further amendments/corrections, the case of an offer of a lower degree is frequently the result of the supervisors' and candidate's (either or both) lack of knowledge about the criteria for a successful doctorate or their vain hope that something, some form of novelty, will come along at the last minute to raise the level of relatively mundane research.

The few cases of complete failure are the result of the candidate being unable for various reasons to demonstrate ownership of the research and/or its report in the form of a thesis. These range from the candidate constantly only following direction from a supervisor without understanding, to more serious demonstrations of lack of integrity such as inventing data, using others' research or having someone else write it up. In between these extremes are numerous inadequacies with the approach, method and/ or analysis which negate the claimed results and interpretations, which can be the result of inadequate structural support, the candidate's limited ability to understand the requirements, or weaknesses in the research project or question, or a combination of these problems. For such cases, it is likely, and sad, that the supervisors had ignored, or been insufficiently alert to, warning signs to take earlier action. At this point you should consider the illustrative points made in Voice of Experience 8.2.

Voice of Experience 8.2

Reflections on inadequate submissions by an experienced examiner

It is not only our professional duty to reciprocate the efforts of colleagues who examine our doctoral researchers by taking on the role of examiner ourselves, but it can also be a professional joy to see our discipline move forward while welcoming new researchers to the field. However, there is frequently a sense of frustration when we must disappoint candidates by criticising their work for errors or omissions when these could or should have been pointed out earlier by their supervisors.

Yes, by the time they submit their theses the candidates should have become independent researchers. However, if they were not given critical advice earlier or given to understand by omission or commission throughout the process that certain dodgy procedures or unrefined, unevidenced arguments were acceptable, then I feel like failing the supervisors instead of the candidate. Sadly, the system doesn't allow that, and we cannot just let theses/candidates pass who haven't reached the standards even if it is not their fault. That would diminish the achievements of those who did attain doctorateness despite having to leap many hurdles, and sometimes despite poor or negligent supervision.

As time has gone by, though, I do try to make clear in my reports that I would have expected a timelier intervention, long before submission, to improve the problem areas. I hope that this then stimulates the supervisors concerned to do a better job in future.

Australian Examiner

This examiner alludes to the requirement to maintain standards, an issue we address in the final section about living with your professional decisions beyond your role immediately following the negative judgement.

The immediate aftermath

In the immediate aftermath of receiving news that substantial corrections or additions are necessary (see Chapter 12 for extended discussion of the various potential outcomes), it is likely that a candidate will be feeling despondent. After all, for major revisions, following several years of hard work there is still more to do, which could include some substantial writing and/or data collecting tasks. In a worse scenario, the researcher and/or the candidates standing as an autonomous researcher may be not doctoral standard, but worthy only of a lower postgraduate degree or even no degree at all. These obviously generate an increasing level of despair for all involved, including the examiners. These examiners have usually accepted that assessment role in the hope of learning about cutting edge research in their area and in the expectation that they will soon have the pleasure of welcoming a new colleague into the fold. Few accept the role for the pay which, in view of the large and skilled effort required, is paltry and even fewer, if any, do so to gain a chance of demeaning a colleague. Most hope that they can, through tailored critical feedback, support the candidate to future success.

In the past, different and changing circumstances made for different requirements of doctoral candidates, while the opportunities for comparing experiences were restricted. Now we have greatly improved communication systems which brook no excuse for any form of covert practices, implicit expectations and exclusive, secret society rituals, should there ever have been any. Those who have laboured long and hard to achieve doctorateness deserve respect, part of which is ensuring transparency, fairness and justice in the assessment system.

Of course, supervisors and examiners can also sometimes find the process somewhat disheartening, but these occasions are uncommon. Voice of Experience 8.3 illustrates that point.

Voice of Experience 8.3

Getting difficult cases into proportion

While thinking that working with doctoral researchers is the most stimulating part of my job, I do agree that there are occasionally times when you can find the tasks both challenging and distressing. But let's get this into proportion. I have supervised nearly 70 researchers to successful completion and examined probably twice as many. I have only had three sad withdrawals: one due to serious illness, another to a life-changing accident and one who suddenly and unexpectedly died. Another two I found it necessary to gently guide towards withdrawing as the kindest way of coping with their inability, one way or another, to achieve doctoral standard. This is only 7%, which is not a bad success rate.

As an examiner, I have had 14 that required re-submission for major corrections. One of the very early ones in my career never did complete and I regret that we examiners really let her down. Instead of being honest and saying that the work was too far from doctoral standard to be worth working further on, we cowardly examiners hoped that the extent of corrections required would encourage her to give up and she did. It was unfair of us to hold out inappropriate hope that might have been clung to. I have learnt from that mistake but fortunately have not had to confront a similar problem since.

Another two re-submission decisions required a lot of diplomacy and a degree of toughness because one candidate was supervised by a prestigious person, who had clearly been a 'hands-off' supervisor, and one was registered in a famous university but had had little support. On both occasions we were, as an examining team, given to understand by the internal authorities that re-submission was not expected to occur in their exalted world, so we had to firmly stand by our decisions. In all the other cases, the candidates did seem to recognise how the requested corrections would improve their theses. Therefore, in my experience it really has been only a small percentage of final doctoral degree assessments that were very difficult.

In recent years most examinations result in a requirement for some minor corrections, some small points that could be explained better or have been missed but mainly the problem stems from too hurried submissions to meet funding deadlines so that the last chapters, the important ones, are rather cursory and don't do justice to the rest of the work. It seems that increasingly it is being left to the examiners to provide the candidates with opportunities to polish up prematurely submitted theses.

A Scottish Psychology Professor

Lessening the trauma

One advantage to those who do have to work a little more and a little longer beyond the first 'final assessment' on corrections/amendments to gain the award of a doctorate is that they can know they are in good company since minor corrections are now the most common outcome of the first 'final' examination. Later, when the corrections have been accepted and the degree awarded, no one (beyond those immediately involved in the assessment) will ever know that their doctorate is any different to any other. Although some countries award doctorates with extra notes of 'specialness' (for example, cum laude), none produce titles such as 'Doctor-after-major-amendments' – something you might point out to candidates. However, any process of correction-making can be very disheartening, especially when there has been such a high level of investment of effort and time, so assessors should try to present their more negative findings in as supportive and motivating way as possible. For instance, the candidates can be lifted out of low feelings to look to the future by emphasising the advantages to be gained beyond simply gaining a pass by addressing the issues, such as making the work more publication worthy or doing justice to the good aspects of the research.

Thus, the tone of these encounters is critical. For a face-to-face viva situation, while it is important to establish an ambience in which the candidate is not frightened into inarticulateness, instead is encouraged to think calmly and clearly, it is also important not to mislead. We have heard candidates complain that they do not understand why they have so many corrections or did not pass a review because during a viva discussion the examiners seemed to appreciate their answers and did not convey any disagreement with them. Those examiners were, in our view, trying too hard to keep the candidate calm enough to proceed. This is a difficult tightrope to walk, especially with very nervous candidates or with work which is severely compromised.

One possible way forward is to be honest at the beginning by saying that there are some/several/quite a few issues that need to be clarified or resolved so that this occasion is an opportunity to raise the standard of the work by defending or, if necessary, revising ideas. It will still be helpful to start by commenting on the parts that are good or acceptable to encourage further engagement in the process. Keep in mind what you would like the candidate to say about the incident years later when recounting their experience; no one wants to be remembered for humiliating, harassing or bullying a candidate. Rather, whilst you cannot avoid the task at hand, you should be responsive to the candidate's position and be clear about what specifically is unsatisfactory in the thesis or does not meet the standard required, all within the context of what is acceptable or has been done well.

If the feedback on written submissions is in writing, the same kind of questions as in Information Box 8.1 can be included with a request that the document is revised taking account of those questions. In the worst-case scenario a point could be made that there are too many or too important issues to be resolved within the time limits to merit a pass. At least the candidate can see in detail what the problems were, before moving on to other things in their lives. In such cases it is doubly important to ensure that comment is provided on what has been achieved, what important ideas have been well presented, what they can be proud of.

Living with the consequences of hard decisions

For written or verbal feedback and comment on a failing piece of work, some consideration and articulation of how the experience of the research and the learning involved might contribute to the candidate's future life can be helpful, at least when they have recovered from the initial torment of the situation. For instance, there may be some aspect of the research that could be publishable, if not in a formal sense like a journal article then as a blog to alert other researchers about the difficulties involved in researching such a topic. Perhaps attention could be drawn to some transferable skills that the candidate has learnt and can bring to bear in their future professional life.

Spending time preparing such thoughtful responses can be helpful for assessors/ examiners too. When one is aware of the huge effort expended by candidates and the hopes with which they started out on the programme, it can be hard to disappoint, especially if you think that in another age with less strict completion deadlines or an otherwise more supportive environment, they might have eventually succeeded. Nevertheless, for assessors/examiners the greatest responsibility is to be just and clear in their decision-making.

You can console yourself with the thought that you are fulfilling a professional role and have professional obligations and duties to discharge. This respects and honours all those – past, present and future – who do meet the standards required in the designated time period. Letting work pass that clearly does not meet those standards is disadvantageous for the discipline, the institution and your own reputation. To be honest, being critical in a fair and balanced way, applying criteria appropriately and combining adherence to principles with humanity is a tough demand, and one that requires experience to develop, but it does enhance your own, the institution's and the discipline's reputation.

No one wants to be the bearer of bad news and witness distress in others. However, so long as you know that you have followed the regulations, have discussed and explored the situation thoroughly with colleagues and the candidate, and you have acted with integrity and have been just, then you should be assured that you have done a good job. In such very rare situations as when there may be unpleasant consequences, for instance if the candidate complains or appeals your decision, then you need to feel sure that you can provide your institution with evidence that you have followed the correct procedures so that they, in turn, can defend and support you in that professional role.

There are few, if any, professions that do not involve difficult situations such as delivering a negative decision. They go with the territory so to speak and accepting the responsibility for decisions and living with the consequences must be accepted as part of the role. However, that does not mean that you as an examiner are without support in your tasks; you are not alone. As we mentioned previously in dealing with the rigours inherent in assessing throughout the doctoral process, there are sources of support available. In Appendix A we have provided some suggestions about where you might find sources of support in new or challenging situations.

Finally, we emphasise that you avoid putting off the breaking of difficult news – the wait can be more destructive for both you and the candidate than dealing promptly with the actual situation. You should get to the point quickly – prevaricating does not lessen the impact. You could begin by saying something along the lines of 'I'm sorry to bear this disappointing news' or 'I know you will find this difficult, but we cannot grant a pass under the circumstances.'

We hope that you infrequently encounter such occasions but are brave when you do so.

Further reading

Denicolo, P. M., Duke, D. C. and Reeves, J. D. (2020) *Success in Research: Supervising to Inspire Researchers*. London: Sage
There is a dearth of books and articles about giving distressing information in assessment contexts. You could, however, make use of texts on communicating effectively, for instance:
Giblin, L. (2010) (revised edition) *Skill with People*. Mumbai: Embassy Books
Grenny, J., Patterson, K., McMillan, R. and Switzler, A. (2011) *Crucial Conversations*. New York: McGraw-Hill Education
Houston, G. (2019) *A study of the PhD examination: process, attributes and outcomes*. Oxford University. 190–224. (Unpublished thesis.). Available at: https://ora.ox.ac.uk/objects/uuid:07291f0e-e80b-4b06-a6af-b3ac8b90a00e

PART III

Assessment on completion – striving for empowering outcomes

9

What forms of doctoral assessment procedures might an examiner encounter?

In this chapter, you will be introduced to:

- Present pervasive requirements
- Common requirements internationally and those that differ
- The processes involved in examining appropriately to context
- Debates on the maintenance of standards despite differences

Introduction

As identified in Chapters 3 and 4, there is a deal of diversity in assessment of the doctorate during its process across discipline, programme and country. As we look specifically at final assessment of the doctorate, after thesis submission, differences are again present. In this chapter the diversity of final assessment across circumstances is addressed, including formalities to be aware of (i.e. institutional regulations) and contextual differences (i.e. disciplines and countries). As the goal is to ensure that a doctoral candidate from any discipline, in any institution, in any country, is as worthy of the title 'Dr' as any other, it is important to look at these variations, and come to an understanding of how, although different, they assess the same underlying but implicit learning objectives.

General requirements

In Chapter 1 we noted that, from the turn of the century, European universities have endeavoured to bring some equivalence to the doctoral process, particularly in relation to the very general criteria that each doctorate should be judged against. This initially had a practical purpose: to aid the mobility within Europe and across careers of researchers with recognised knowledge and skills. Under financial pressure from the impact of the global banking crisis 2007–08, as many national economies deteriorated and global competition increased, the purpose to some extent evolved into demonstrating the quality of research in those and associated countries through the rigorous training and assessment procedures undergone by their researchers. This, in turn, challenged and encouraged other countries' governments worldwide, such as those in the Pacific rim countries and South America, to turn some increased attention to doctoral education and how a doctorate is achieved. Thus, at conferences and in learned societies globally doctoral procedures were discussed more openly so that greater transparency has been achieved in a realm that once seemed more like aggregations of secret societies with arcane rituals.

We now know, with increased communication channels and greater collaboration, that there are some commonalities within countries, though we recognise that some individual interpretation occurs between disciplines and institutions, since each evolved its own rules and procedures over time. The customs, rites and ceremonials developed over decades, even centuries in some cases, are slow to change as was noted in Chapter 3, but most are recognisable as variations on a national theme. A similar state exists between countries, with some generally accepted practices, such as whether there is a one- or two-stage viva, further nuanced by national conventions. Often it is within disciplines that commonality exists, despite country conventions, for instance the general move towards publication-based theses in engineering and some biological sciences.

Through research and discussions with international colleagues we note that all doctoral candidates undergo a serious and stringent examination process that involves the production of a written argument (thesis or dissertation) scrutinised by more than one assessor. That scrutiny can result in the requirement for further work until a satisfactory piece of work that demonstrates an original contribution to knowledge, achieved through well-defended procedures, can be made accessible to the public.

Roles and responsibilities

There are several roles associated with the final examination, all of which you could be asked to undertake during your career. Typically, examiners might be internal to the institution where the doctoral researcher is registered (sometimes known as an internal examiner) or external to the doctoral researcher's institution (sometimes known as an external examiner). If there is a viva voce examination or public defence, there will often be a member of academic staff present who chairs the event and orchestrates the ceremony (who may be referred to as an independent chair or convenor).

All examiners are appointed based on their academic expertise, combined experience of examinations and impartiality. The use of supervisors as examiners varies from country to country. Where supervisors are permitted to serve as examiners there is almost always an examiner with no previous involvement with the project on the examination panel to provide a check and balance and to uphold the integrity of the examination process.

In the UK, to protect the impartiality of the examination process, supervisors are not permitted to examine their own doctoral researchers and no member of the examination panel can have an existing relationship with the doctoral researcher, whether this is personal or professional. Wherever you are asked to examine you will probably be required to self-declare that you have no conflict of interest in examining a specific candidate/project. It is not a problem if you know the doctoral researcher from your professional networks, for example if you have seen them present at a conference or are aware of their work. Eligibility to examine can, however, be compromised if you have worked with the doctoral researcher or their supervisors to the point where your independence is called into question. There are, of course, many borderline cases, especially in very niche research areas. If you are contacted to act as an examiner and have concerns about your eligibility, the best thing to do is raise your concerns with the appointing institution so that they can decide the issue, rather than risk impugning your integrity or putting the outcome into question.

The role of the independent chair and the examiners differ. The examiners are there to do most of the hard work during the examination process. If you are appointed as an examiner, your job is to:

- assess the thesis and any accompanying materials;
- assess the candidate during the viva, if there is one;
- come to a verdict as to whether the candidate should be awarded the doctorate.

The independent chair, on the other hand, is there to ensure that:

- any viva is conducted in line with the regulations;
- the questioning of the candidate is fair but rigorous;
- all administrative matters are taken care of;
- the examiners deal with any issues that arise.

Normally, the independent chair will be an experienced examiner, well-versed in the examination process. This is a role that can start to develop your skills and reputation as an examiner. By ensuring that you are thoroughly familiar with your institution's examination regulations you can volunteer to chair an examination in your department or school. Such experiences, without the burden of final decision-making, incidentally, stand you in good stead with your colleagues if you conduct the examination fairly. However, their main benefit is as learning opportunities for the further development of examination and supervision skills: what criteria are being used to judge answers in the viva and hence the quality of the presented work.

The material to be examined

The material that comprises the thesis varies by discipline, type of doctorate and sometimes institution. Whereas in the past the PhD tended to be presented and examined as a monograph, new ways of doing a doctorate have emerged, as suggested in the General Requirements section. Whilst there may have been some commonality to the thesis format some years ago, the diverse landscape of doctoral qualifications across, for example, the UK, USA, Australia and New Zealand means that theses vary too. We provide below examples of the most common types of thesis from our experience of UK examinations, but this list is not intended to be exhaustive.

Performance- or practice-based doctorates often have a creative piece that accompanies the more traditional, but shorter, dissertation that explores the creative process and its contribution to knowledge. The creative piece might involve musical compositions; creative writing in the form of short stories, novels or poetry; a live theatre performance; film, artwork and so on – the list is as long as people's capacity for creativity.

Practitioner doctorates, such as the Doctor of Education (EdD) and Doctor of Clinical Psychology (DClinPsy) might be presented as a portfolio including examples of assignments undertaken during the programme, a major research project, a reflective piece covering how the doctoral researcher has developed as a professional during their programme and how their research will contribute to professional practice as well as to knowledge.

PhDs by publication are also growing in popularity in some disciplines such as education and profession-based doctorates, as debates about the currency and relevance of the monograph in contemporary academe become more prevalent. In some countries, such as the Netherlands, the PhD by publication is well-established standard protocol. Submissions for PhD by publication will include a collection of the candidate's publications and some introductory and explanatory material. This material will normally set the publications within the context of the broader field, state the aggregate and individual contributions of publications and provide some reflections on the research process.

As you gain more experience as an assessor, you will get a feel for what is acceptable for a thesis in your subject area. We provide detailed guidance in Chapter 10 about the examination of the content of a thesis, but we suspect that you will be surprised by the variety of formats you could encounter within disciplines as well as between them. If we take the discipline of Education as an example, some of us in that field have assessed traditional monographs, portfolios for practitioner doctorates and collections of published works. Each different type of thesis invites us to adapt how we assess to suit the submission while maintaining in mind the standard of 'doctorateness'. Fortunately, most universities' regulations are good at describing acceptable submission formats for different disciplines and programmes. If you ever find yourself surprised by what you receive as an examiner, then it is worth checking the institutions' regulations to see if it is valid. Do contact the institution if you have any concerns.

As an assessor, you will most likely be asked to record your thoughts about the thesis before you meet the doctoral researcher in the viva, if there is one. Most institutions will provide you with pro-forma and a set of questions to help you to organise your thoughts, although these can sometimes be a little restrictive. We would suggest that you complete the paperwork as required by the institution but not to limit your comments on the work to what is formally requested. Remember, as an examiner you are acting as a gatekeeper for the highest academic qualification, so it is important that you are confident in the candidate and their work and that you have had the opportunity to ask the questions that you feel are important. We provide in Chapter 11 and in Appendix C further discussion about the process and some example questions that you might adapt for this.

The university will normally ask you to consider very general aspects of the candidate's work. This might include things like their understanding of their field; legitimacy of research questions and/or objectives; the appropriateness of the approach taken to investigate those questions/objectives; the validity of findings; and whether the candidate has made a knowledge contribution worthy of the award. Some institutions might ask you to consider whether the doctoral researcher's development has been well-evidenced through the thesis though this tends to be restricted to professional doctorates. If passing the examination will result in the candidate having a licence to practise a profession, then there may be other factors that need to be considered too. The university should offer you extra training and guidance if this is the case.

There are other regulations or processes that are widespread but, of course like everything in higher education, the devil is in the detail.

Common requirements and international variation

Every country has its own peculiarities regarding the final doctoral examination. A feature of the UK viva examination process, for example, is that it is closed. Almost always, the only people permitted to attend the viva are the candidate, examiners, in some cases the supervisors, and the independent chair, if used. There are generally at least two examiners, one internal to the institution and one external to it, with additional external examiners recruited if, for instance, the candidate is a member of staff or if the research covered several disciplines. Although the use of an independent chair is considered good practice, their actual use is yet uncommon and certainly seldom regulatory. Unlike in some other countries such as the USA and Canada, the supervisors are not examiners and are not permitted to question the candidate during the viva voce examination, while the value and appropriateness of their presence is hotly debated. In a few UK universities, supervisors are not permitted to attend the viva at all. Similarly, independent chairs are present solely to aid the proceedings by ensuring fairness to all participants and may not question the candidate. Similar rules apply in South Africa.

Whilst it would not be possible to enumerate every possible difference in examination protocol across the world, we have selected a few examples here to illustrate just how much variation exists.

In Australia, for example, there is generally no viva voce examination conducted by all the examiners, although a private oral examination conducted by internal examiners may ensue if there are specific issues to be addressed. (See also the Kiley et al. 2018 debate about the key issues involved in instituting a viva in Australian doctoral processes.) Instead, the thesis is sent to at least two examiners external to the researcher's university, often at least one being outside the country, and the researcher is not permitted to converse with the examiners whilst the thesis is being assessed.

The protocol in Spain differs too. Here, the researcher is examined in a public defence of the work by three examiners (one internal and two external to the institution). Members of the audience who possess a doctoral degree are then invited to ask questions of the candidate as a part of the examination protocol. Supervisors have no role as final assessors.

In the USA, the researcher is examined by a 'Dissertation Reading Committee' comprised of the main advisor/supervisor and the advisory committee internal to their institution. Candidates will normally deliver a public presentation before being questioned in a closed examination and whether the questioning session is public or private depends on the institutional regulations.

In Canada, each province or territory governs its own rules but generally there is a defence committee composed of several examiners, one of whom is external (though they may be virtual in consideration of the distances between institutions) and includes the supervisor. There is usually a public presentation followed by a closed formal examination.

In Germany, the examiners include the supervisor, two or three professors and often a postdoc and/or a doctoral candidate. There is a public defence, though often only close family, friends and colleagues attend.

Some countries regularly have a large number of examiners; for instance, in the Netherlands there can be up to eight in the panel while in Turkey and Macau there are at least five, with three from the advisory committee, an independent internal examiner and an external one. In all those countries the candidate usually prepares a presentation in advance.

We provide next some elaborations on the procedures that the examiners engage with.

The examination process

If you are asked to serve as an examiner, you may well have questions about what to expect from the process. As with progress monitoring, university regulations tend to provide ample information about the processes associated with the final examination but are less forthcoming about what questions are asked and how judgements are made. We explore those hidden, implicit aspects of the examination in the chapters that follow. For now, we attempt to explain the choreography of the final examination so that it feels more familiar to you.

While we refer here to the examination process it is important to remember that this is the culmination of continuous assessment throughout the doctorate. The UK examination process itself is a staged process, a continuum of judgement, as Houston (2018) described in her research on the UK viva. We reproduce, with her permission, her summary diagram as Figure 9.1.

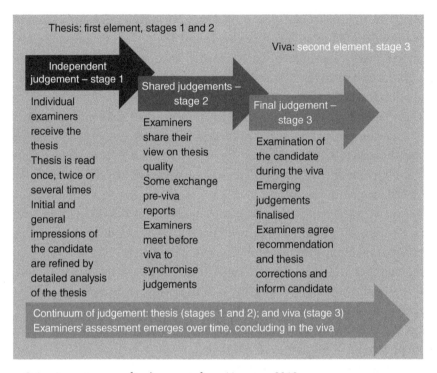

Figure 9.1 A continuum of judgement, from Houston 2018

There are various protocols associated with each stage that vary between institutions. Currently, most institutions send a hard copy of the thesis to examiners, typically allowing up to three months to examine it before the viva stage. Some may ask if you will accept an e-copy so consider in advance your tolerance for reading a very long script online. Although theses in maths and some sciences can be much shorter, involving equations rather than detailed discourse in some sections, social science or humanities theses can be around 90 to 100 thousand words (depending on institutional regulations or custom and practice), excluding appendices or addenda.

Each institution has its own rules about pre-viva reports. Some may expect them to be handed in on the day of the viva but increasingly they request copies to be exchanged between examiners before that, while many require that they are lodged with the university first, sometimes before the examiners confer.

At the final judgement stage, for minor corrections it is usual for the internal examiner to undertake this task, but major revisions require all examiners to sign them off. The examiners are entitled by most universities also to require another viva if necessary.

It is important to note that examiners do not actually make the award, though they may congratulate a successful candidate at the end of the examination process. In fact, the whole process is not complete at that stage because examiners must recommend an award to the governing body of the institution to ratify and make an award. (It would be highly unusual if the recommendation were not accepted – we are not aware of any such occurrence – but these professional niceties should be observed.)

Thus, regardless of whether there is a viva voce examination, the first job of an examiner is to examine the thesis independently and complete a report. We provide considerable detail about examining the thesis in Chapter 10. When there is no viva or if the oral presentation part of the rite of passage occurs after the decision is made (as in many institutions in Belgium, Sweden and the Netherlands and in some disciplines in Spain), then the examiners compare their assessments and debate until they come to a consensus. Institutional regulations deal with any situation in which no consensus emerges, usually involving an additional independent examiner.

If a viva voce examination or public defence is part of the process, you will have the opportunity to meet the other members of the examination panel prior to the examination. During this time, you and the other examiner(s) will compare your pre-viva reports and share your views of the doctoral researcher's work. You will discuss the questions that you want to ask the doctoral researcher as well as discuss your overall view of the work. In some cases, you might find that yours and the other panel members' views of the work differ. This is not a problem. The important thing is that you discuss why you have come to different conclusions and agree some questions that would give the doctoral researcher an opportunity to address any concerns emerging from this. It is often the case that a point of clarification added to the thesis averts problems for other readers.

If there is not an independent chair at the viva voce examination, then one of the examiners, normally the internal, will take on the responsibility for chairing as well. Typically, the viva will start with all those in the viva introducing themselves and some general questions to help the doctoral researcher feel at ease. The examiners will then ask the more challenging questions before calling the viva to a close. We provide in Chapter 11 a discussion about the value of vivas, including how the process can be both rigorous and compassionate so that candidates are supported to demonstrate effectively their qualities as a researcher. In some cases, doctoral researchers are encouraged to or must deliver a presentation of their work at the start of the viva. In our experiences, this approach tends to be welcomed by the examiners as it gives the doctoral researcher some control over the start of the viva – they know what to expect – and it helps to give the examiners an overview of the work. If you choose to do this, you may find that it may even answer some of your questions.

The revelation of the outcome of deliberations differs according to whether the viva or oral presentation comes before or after the opportunity, or requirement, to make changes to the thesis. In Australia, candidates are provided with the outcome of the thesis review but not the final result which follows any private oral presentation. In Germany, a mark is given from a review of the thesis before a viva which then contributes a further mark. The marks combine to give a final grade – corrections are seldom required after a stringent continuous review process. Similarly, a requirement for changes is seldom required in Spain but the thesis must be approved before a presentation is made to the viva board and the public, after which a final mark is given determining the level of the degree (see Chapter 12). In Denmark, and many other universities in Scandinavia, thesis corrections are required to be completed before the viva, a public occasion with rigorous questioning by the opponents/examiners, though by this time there is more or less an assumption that the candidate has passed since a party usually ensues thereafter involving family and friends as well as colleagues.

In other countries, such as the UK, Canada, South Africa and Turkey, and some institutions in the USA, the viva must precede any declaration of results. Once you have asked all your questions and given the doctoral researcher an opportunity to ask questions or make any additional comments, then the doctoral researcher (and in some countries the supervisor/s too, if not part of the assessment process at this stage) is normally instructed to leave the room. This gives the panel an opportunity to confer about the outcome. Each institution will have a set of acceptable outcomes that range from straight pass, through minor corrections, or major revisions, to a lower award (such as MPhil), or fail. These are discussed in detail in Chapter 12. Nowadays, most outcomes tend to fall into the minor corrections or major revisions categories.

Once the panel has agreed the outcome, the doctoral researcher is called back into the room to be informed of the outcome. The panel then, within a short period of time determined by the institution, must complete a report on the viva and produce a list of any corrections that need to be made to the thesis.

Our overview, while highlighting the most common features, does not exhaust all the possible variants of a doctoral examination so there remains some research for you to do when you receive a request to examine a doctorate in an institution other than your own. However, we have distilled the process in Information Box 9.1, recognising there may be other variations that could overlay this.

Information Box 9.1

Synopsis of main stages of doctoral assessment for final examiners

- Invitations to examiners distributed and agreed with, generally, a fixed time to complete the examination.
- Examiners receive the thesis and access to the institution's regulations.
- If appropriate a date for any viva voce or presentation is agreed.
- Examiners review the written work and write a report to be delivered to the institution according to regulations.
- Examiners confer and decide on outcome (provisional if corrections are required or if a viva ensues).
- Following any viva, or aggregation of marks following a presentation, or completion and acceptance of corrections/amendments, a recommendation is made to the institution's governing body.
- The award is made by the institution.

Preparing to examine in a new context

An invitation to assess a doctoral thesis in another institution, particularly if it is in another country, is flattering. It serves as a testament to your international standing and the high regard in which your work is held. However, it can be a daunting prospect to examine a thesis under a system with which you are not familiar. The first step in your decision process is to ensure that the topic is within the range of your expertise. The next step is to check that you have an appropriate space in your diary to accommodate the whole process, always allowing for the possibility that the thesis may not be available until some months after the date originally planned.

If the context is your own country, then it is relatively simple to check regulations on websites or to obtain them from the institution involved. If the context is another country, factor in that the language used, though one you speak, may be more challenging to understand than you would imagine. Regardless of venue, you should then explore with the person who contacted you any puzzling aspects of those regulations and, importantly, what specific expectations they have of you in the role. To help you find your way through an international examination, we provide some guidance next on how to approach them in Activity 9.1.

Activity 9.1

Seeking advice from colleagues with international examiner experience

Having checked the published institutional regulations and sought elaboration from your contact, the next step is to ask somebody who has done lots of international examinations to share their experiences and approach. (We provide an example below in Voice of Experience 9.1.) You might well find a colleague who has examined in the country in focus and further, given how multicultural our universities are, you could also find a person from that country.

The former should be able to tell you about the etiquette that pervades the doctoral examining process that might not be obvious in the written regulations and might not occur to your contact to mention. The latter, even if they have had no involvement in doctoral education, can tell you about the general expectations of professional etiquette within their country, such things as modes of address (formal or informal), greetings and farewells, who sits in which seats, which hand is used to give or receive a gift, and whether gift giving is part of the custom and practice or frowned upon, and so on. This can save everyone embarrassment. And it is interesting, and comforting, to have found these things out in advance.

We asked a colleague to provide an example of her experience of examining abroad. You will see in her Voice of Experience (9.1) below that it is helpful not only to find out about official rules and procedures but also about the social aspects of this important occasion.

Voice of Experience 9.1

Examining internationally

I have now examined quite a few doctoral theses for institutions outside the UK and was initially surprised at how different many of the processes are from what I had experienced domestically. My main suggestion for those examining abroad for the first time would be to be aware of this variety in practice and to read carefully all the documentation you are sent, which will usually explain the process in considerable detail.

When I examined in Finland, for example, I had to submit my feedback on the original version of the thesis several months before the viva. The candidate then had an opportunity to revise her work considering my comments. In the viva, I was made to work quite hard for my fee! I had to give a speech about the thesis to start with and then, after the candidate had also given a speech, I had to question her for about an hour or so. This was quite a daunting prospect as the viva was public, the room was filled with her friends and family, and I had to come up with all the questions myself – there was no internal examiner with whom to share the questioning.

(I also had to wear a black dress and gown and carry a special hat.) It was harder than usual to come up with probing questions to ask, as the candidate had already responded to my initial set of comments when she revised her thesis prior to the viva.

A further tip would be to be aware that there may be requirements to participate in social events, too, which may not be documented in the paperwork you are sent! At the Finnish viva, I was invited to a very nice lunch afterwards (at which I met the candidate's family and friends) and then a formal meal in the evening. At the evening meal, I was required to give another speech, although this time – thankfully – it could be considerably shorter!

I now very much enjoy examining outside the UK and see it as an opportunity to find out more about the histories and traditions of different higher education systems.

Professor Rachel Brooks, University of Surrey

Maintaining standards despite variations

Despite differences in procedures and ceremonials, the purpose of doctoral examination remains the same: to confer the award of a doctorate onto a new researcher who has reached the standard of being capable of conducting independent research, having demonstrated that ability through the production of artefacts/documents which evidence the quality of their research and a contribution to knowledge that is publishable in some form. It is the examiner's role to maintain that standard. There is an expectation within academe and by employers worldwide that there is equivalence between doctorates regardless of discipline, awarding institution and country.

The word equivalence is critical because there is no expectation of uniformity. Neither could there be when each thesis is unique in and of itself. This makes the examining process a demanding task but one that it is a professional obligation and honour to perform assiduously. To help you do that, we have provided in the following three chapters as much detail as we can garner about how to do it well.

Further reading

Houston, G. (2018) *A Study of the PhD Examination: process, attributes and outcomes. Doctoral Thesis.* Oxford University

Kiley, M., Holbrook, A., Lovat, T., Fairbairn, H., Starfield, S. and Paltridge, B. (2018) An oral component in the PhD examination in Australia: issues and considerations. *Australian Universities' Review, 60*(1): 25–34

10

What should we be looking for in a thesis?

In this chapter, you will find, in relation to the thesis (or other written bodies of work submitted for a doctorate):

- Its purpose and how it is demonstrated
- The parameters of institutional regulations
- General quality issues
- More detailed criteria by section
- Developing your own criteria
- Coming to a balanced conclusion

Introduction

In the previous chapter we discussed the different assessment formats to be found in both national and disciplinary contexts but noted that all of them required some form of written document. As we noted in the Prologue, depending on the context, this is named either a thesis or a dissertation which puts forward a proposition and its arguments. Put simply, its purpose within a doctoral degree is to demonstrate in a public form that a candidate has achieved 'doctorateness', that is, in summary: the ability to conduct autonomously and within restricted boundaries of resources, including time, research that is ground-breaking, in the sense that it results in a novel/unique, non-trivial contribution to knowledge, and that is publishable in some form.

Those resource boundaries, as we have mentioned previously, are to a large extent discipline-related and to some extent geographically-determined, for instance whether extensive 'kit' or access is required for research, as in many pure and applied sciences, or whether there is a large structured component with its own assessment included in the doctoral programme (e.g. as in the USA or more widely in professional doctorates). Further, restrictions on time to submission of the thesis or completion of the doctoral programme are becoming increasingly prevalent in universities worldwide in contrast to the more relaxed approach in previous times (before the 1980s in some cases).

In many ways a thesis (or monograph or collection of papers with an overarching document that critically appraises them, or similar document that deals with a performance or artefacts) is intended to demonstrate mastery of the 'craft' of research in much the same way that apprentices' 'masterpieces' did in the past for other crafts. In the case of the doctorate, the craft involves not only the various skills involved in undertaking research in a discipline but other professional research skills such as those required to produce a detailed written report to make a convincing argument. The structure of a thesis again has disciplinary conventions, which examiners should uphold while meeting the requirements of overarching institutional regulations.

Parameters in institutional regulations

We discussed in Chapter 3 the way in which institutions regulate both the process of the doctorate and its final assessment procedures. The latter determine the various roles within that crucial stage, including requirements for internal and external examiners to satisfy themselves that the thesis meets the doctoral standard. We noted developments in academia that impinge on the doctoral process, such as a general widening of participation leading to increasing numbers of candidates in a wider range of subject and professional areas as well as policy initiatives, so that consequently thesis styles have diversified in recent years. Thus, institutional/disciplinary parameters include, along with generalised quality considerations, presentational and structural attributes of theses mainly related to:

- traditions about format, length and section headings;
- practical issues such as line spacing and margins and whether e-versions or only hard copies are required;
- criteria governing the Abstract and Lists of contents, authorship and copyright declarations.

In contrast, we have recognised that the critical attributes that differentiate the doctoral award from those of other degrees that usually lead up to it are necessarily generalised so that disciplinary/geographical/professional variations can be accommodated. As summarised above these quality attributes include a requirement that the research project produces a (variously formulated: unique/original/novel/creative) contribution to knowledge and a further demand that the work is in some form publishable in peer-reviewed formats. However, for assessors, especially those who take on the final examiner role for the first time, more detailed guidance would be welcomed on how those contributions and publishability, and other indicators of mastery of the craft, might be recognised within an individually distinctive oeuvre or opus.

This we attempt to provide in this chapter by building on the general requirements to elaborate on what to seek as evidence in a thesis.

Quality issues

Most national and international guidelines for characteristics expected of a doctoral thesis include expectations that candidates will demonstrate in that work:

- a systematic acquisition and understanding of a substantial body of knowledge which is at the forefront of their field of learning;
- through advanced scholarship and research, the creation of new knowledge to satisfy peer review;
- evidence of the ability to exercise independent, critical power in analyzing and synthesising information;
- the development of a significant range of skills, techniques and practices related to research in that field of learning including the ability to develop further research through recognition of new problem areas and designing responsive procedures relevant to the task;
- the development of personal professional attributes relevant to research such as integrity and knowledge of ethical and safe procedures;
- the ability to communicate the procedures and results of research to peers.

Like the Dublin Descriptors that we presented in Chapter 1 (Information Box 1.2), these criteria are formulated at a high level of generality to accommodate disciplinary differences. They lack detailed indication of the kind of evidence that would substantiate the presence of those characteristics in the work. Indeed, some would contend that we require both the documented research and a viva voce to be sure that the candidate has demonstrated all these characteristics (see Chapters 9 and 11, and Houston, 2018).

Nevertheless, here we are concentrated on what can be discerned that indicates the required quality in the body of written work that is a major part of any submission for the award of the degree.

More detailed criteria

Before we consider what evidence could be found in each section of a thesis there are certain attributes of a reasonable thesis as a whole that can be discerned via a quick skim through before a detailed reading. The first concerns its readability – not its physical legibility (we are assuming that nowadays the technology available ensures that) but the style and structure of the writing that makes its meaning at least accessible to any intelligent reader even if it is not elegant prose. It should tell the story of the research in a logical way, including all the aspects that are necessary to understand the story, with user-friendly sign-posting and forward–backward referencing to make the large compilation of words navigable in an economic way. (An example might be the way we have indicated in this book where ideas have been introduced or elaborated in other chapters.) It should be clear in any thesis worthy of a doctorate that the writer has aimed for a coherent presentation, integrating information with consideration for the reader. In a good thesis a 'golden (or red in some countries) thread' will be evident with rational links between parts (chapters and sections of chapters) that produce an intellectual wholeness to the piece, telling a rich and coherent story. Again ideally, the chapter titles and subheadings should tell the story in summary but at least should indicate where important information, such as the contribution to knowledge, can be found. You might consider here the viewpoint of an experienced supervisor-examiner in Voice of Experience 10.1.

Voice of Experience 10.1

Working from an ideal notion of a thesis to a practical overview

When my doctoral researchers ask me what I would hope for in their thesis, I gently smile and say: it should describe your careful, cogent and well-justified research in a concise, precise, relevant and elegant way. Then I grin and say: well, elegance is difficult to achieve but repeated iterations of drafts with feedback should make it possible to achieve the other criteria.

I use those criteria when examining others' theses, recognising that, though beautiful prose is something we all must continue working towards, research at a doctoral standard should be expressed in a convincing way. For me 'convincing' means a combination of those other descriptors. I can tolerate a certain degree of long-windedness, but I will challenge vagueness, lack of justification, carelessness and lack of relevance, hoping that it can be readily amended enough to bring the thesis up to a pass standard.

Sometimes all I need as a response in the viva is a recognition by the candidate that they can or could express things better; other times some or much correction is required to ensure that other readers' understanding is not inhibited, or the research misunderstood or undervalued.

One of your Authors

Following up the point about justification within the thesis (of topic, approach, method and conclusions), at this broad review stage it is worth checking randomly some of the references in the text to ensure they are included in the bibliography. Next a scan of the bibliography can serve as a check that it covers the most prominent recent and relevant texts that inform the subject with which you have the expertise required of an examiner. This will provide an indication of the degree to which you might have to ensure accurate referencing as you read in more detail.

Indeed, this preliminary overview can tell you whether there is any point in continuing to that 'detailed read' stage. If you find that important sections are missing or that the prose is exceedingly difficult to follow, then you might have an opportunity to return the thesis for further work before you examine it as a final product. We use the word 'might' because rules vary between institutions and country contexts. In some places, such as in institutions in Denmark and Spain, the thesis is allowed to be (sometimes expected to be) corrected on the advice of examiners before formal submission and a public viva. In other places, notably many institutions in the UK, the examiners must bring any criticisms and evaluations to the viva, even if they are so concerned about the thesis content that they deem a viva to be a waste of time. Thankfully those situations are few and far between, but the recommended swift overview is useful when the thesis arrives with you if only to remind you to check those rules and then to allocate enough time to thoroughly review the work and make notes about its significant features, good and less so, section by section.

At the end of this chapter we will provide a checklist of over-arching features and sectional attributes, but it is worth saying before we discuss them in detail that a thesis that presents a perfect or even excellent standard in all of them is yet to be written. Because of the complexity and richness of any research at this level, combined with the variation in writing and language ability of candidates, examiners must weigh up the quality of the various components to decide if, on balance, the work is GOOD ENOUGH to merit a pass, with or without suggested corrections/amendments. Some aspects are less worrisome than others in determining whether the researcher has reached a standard in research prowess to be allowed to research independently, recognising that they will continue to learn and improve their practice, as we all must do. We will return to the issue of gaining a balanced evaluation at the end of the chapter.

Sectional attributes

In what follows we are using broad headings for sections which represent important aspects that should appear in any thesis. We are not suggesting that these will be chapter titles because information is collated differently in each discipline/context and, indeed, candidates do have some say in how they think subtopics link together in a logical way – a sort of poetic licence. Similarly, the degree of detail and length of each section or subsection will vary for the same reasons. Thus, under each heading we present indications of what criteria you might use, what attributes should be contained for preference in that section. Of course, any candidate may include specific items under different headings because of writing 'flow', for instance, so be alert that apparently missing information might appear elsewhere. In Activity 10.1 we encourage you to prepare your own way of dealing with this complex assessment task but first we share some ideas from our own experience that you might find useful to tailor to your own style.

It is useful to note down as you read any missing information (you can score it off later if it appears) and areas that could benefit from elaboration as well as any errors or points you would like to challenge. Some institutions allow you to mark up the thesis whereas others strictly require you not to do so. Sticky notes can help whether or not that is the case because they can be readily reviewed as a whole when your reading has been completed. Small sticky notes are useful to indicate pages which require attention to punctuation, spelling, syntax or other grammatical issues. Sticky notes of a different colour could indicate issues of substance such as incomplete or faulty argument. One of us has found it useful to organise feedback, the design of viva questions and the making of final judgements by using such a colour-coded set of sticky notes, each with brief annotations, for assessing the work. For instance, blue notes might be used for issues of theoretical argument, yellow for small queries, red for important challenges, and so on. These can then be combined into clumps to underpin and organise views for discussion with other examiners or the candidate or for writing a report.

The number of notes of each kind of issue can also provide some preliminary guidance on whether the thesis generally is sound, that is with few very important challenge notes apparent, or whether there are many 'careless' errors but no big issues, or several big issues that require further work for resolution, and so on. Indeed, a simple two colour 'big/small' issue set of sticky notes, perhaps numbered to refer to in a list of issues written as you read, could also suffice or perhaps you can think of a more technology-based way of accomplishing that. Consider options as you take on the challenges in Activity 10.1 that follows.

Activity 10.1

Preparing for action: a practical thesis-assessment guide

It would be unfair to suggest that assessing a thesis is anything other than an awesome, time-consuming activity. Further, since any thesis is a lengthy and complex document, it is hard to keep the story in mind that it purports to tell while dealing with the detail. Thus, it is useful to have some sort of strategy in mind that will help you do that – a kind of template for action.

Many people find it helpful to get the gist of the piece together first, sometimes by reading the Abstract, and then the first and last chapters. Others prefer to skim quickly through the chapter headings (if they are more than simplistic headings such as 'Literature Review') or even the whole thesis.

Think about your preference in this respect. You might try several versions over the course of the next few years to decide on what works best for you.

Then think about the general kind of attributes you are looking for and how you will document their presence and absence in some way. It is also worth thinking about what weighting you might give to different kinds of attributes. Certainly, the criteria used to determine the overall outcome seem to weigh issues of substance within the thesis (justifications of appropriate aims, methodology, etc.) more heavily than issues of presentation, though one can be sorely tested by copious typographical errors throughout the tome.

However, you will probably find it helpful, when considering the whole piece, to decide on a method of indicating some finer grading of good and less good, even seriously poor, aspects. These indicators can be quite simple guides for yourself alone if you decide to summarise your deliberations more formally later for the others involved. What you will find helpful is to decide in advance how you will annotate them and then be consistent in doing so.

It can be tempting simply to read the work through and hope that you remember all your thoughts at the end. That is not only inefficient but also unfair, because we all have a propensity to remember the first and last parts of a lengthy read rather than what comes between. Further, you are very likely to be required to justify any decisions you make to the other examiner/s and to the institution and to provide detailed feedback for thesis improvement to the candidate so adopting a systematic approach is advisable.

Let us now turn to sections that appear in some format in most theses, considering how you might analyze them as contributions to demonstrating 'doctorateness'.

Some details that should appear in a thesis

Here we combine the criteria used by several examiners who collectively have over 60 years of experience examining doctorates in a broad range of countries.

It is, thus, approaching a summary of a perfect thesis. This is something to bear in mind while reading and is addressed in a caveat as a final section.

Abstract

This should clearly describe main aspects of the thesis (purpose, theoretical and methodological base and general outputs and outcomes) within the institutional word limits (frequently between 200–300 words).

Contents lists

These should provide an accurate guide about where to find different topics and aspects such as figures, tables, diagrams and appendices.

Introduction

Although the length and degree of detail varies by discipline/context, it is usual to expect some indication of what stimulated the exploration of this project focus, why it was deemed important: in other words, a brief rationale for the research. Frequently, a summary of the whole thesis is provided chapter by chapter which provides readers/examiners with an indication of where they might find specific information about the project. Thus, it should be a map of the whole terrain to orientate travel through it.

In humanities, arts and social sciences there is often a useful indication of the background of the researcher that makes them particularly apt for undertaking it whereas this may not appear in the science and technology theses which use paradigms that favour neutrality/objectivity.

Literature review

Science Note: often the introduction and literature review chapters are integrated as one.

English Literature Note (This can also apply to theoretical/conceptual explorations, and political/philosophical/sociological treatises): often the entire thesis is, in essence, a critique of literature and so detailed and sophisticated argumentation relating to the literature will be evident in the majority of chapters.

Grounded Theory Note: a preliminary literature review that orientates the research would not be included (see the next subsection) but discussion of the literature in relation to the research results should have the same quality characteristics as described below.

Besides demonstrating a thorough knowledge of the field, including what are the most prominent schools of thought and who are the main protagonists, a good literature review will be succinct, penetrating, challenging, critical, using an analytical rather than a descriptive approach. It should be organised to show a developing argument for the hypotheses/research questions that follow. These may be included with this review or have a separate section, but the links should be obvious while the questions/hypotheses should be readily found in the thesis.

Primary rather than secondary sources should be used while recent references should predominate except where older, seminal work is acknowledged. Further, while quotations can be useful for illustrating or exemplifying points, they should be used sparingly (with page numbers) so that the main argument consists of the candidate's own words.

Statement of research problem or development plan for a creative piece

This should comprise a well-articulated rationale for the 'worthwhileness' of the research which culminates in either clear and succinct hypotheses or questions or a basic plan derived from/revealed by the preceding literature review. A notable exception would be in Grounded Theory research in which a literature review is not conducted because theory is intended to be deduced from observation, experience and so on through the research rather than a priori.

Development plans should have a novel theoretical or methodological or creative slant and/or bring together previously unrelated fields and/or a new area of application.

Theoretical justification of approaches and methods

The quality of this theoretical argument, the **methodology** rather than 'methods', is extremely important. It should include a closely argued rationale for the general approach chosen, giving reasoned case for rejecting other possible approaches. While in some disciplines the approach may be the traditional or only approach taken, the candidate should know and demonstrate why this is so.

A justification for the chosen research design should be presented, taking account of potential advantages and limitations as well as why other possible design factors have been rejected. Then the research techniques require a theoretical and practical argument about their relevance/appropriateness to the research problem.

If standard tests or procedures have been amended or innovative data collection techniques designed, then a rationale is required to demonstrate why that was needed and the revised or new versions justified. It may well be that standardisation to a new context/population will also be required to demonstrate reliability/validity/credibility.

Similarly, there needs to be a cogent rationale provided for the selection of the analysis procedures, choice of statistical tests, software, interview transcript deconstruction techniques, text mining approaches, and so on.

All this defence of decisions and procedures forms a foundation to indicate that the research process and results are trustworthy and have authority.

Description of research process

Arts Note: If a piece has been created (performance, a book, an artwork) or, for instance, an extended argument based on the literature has been presented then data collection, analysis and presentation may not apply. They would be replaced by the artwork or argument with a detailed and clear description of how they emerged.

Following on from the theoretical justification for the research process it is important, too, that the procedures for data or other information collection or creation are clearly set out and easy to follow, possibly including a flow-chart, Gantt chart or similar device if appropriate. Pertinent details should be included, for instance, in social sciences, how access was achieved, the number of subjects/respondents and their salient attributes or profiles, and the timing of interventions. In the sciences, what materials and equipment were used, and the nature and timings of procedures would be important inclusions.

If not included in the methodology, then this section should include as appropriate a discussion of potential ethical issues, how those issues have been acknowledged and dealt with, including the details of ethical approval, such as how permissions were obtained and what guarantees were given.

If not in this section, then certainly in the Discussion section later, there should be a presentation of the difficulties encountered during the research and how they were dealt with to avoid compromising the results and their credibility.

Analysis (if appropriate to the discipline)

Any mode of analysis performed should be congruent with research questions/ hypotheses and approach adopted, with theoretical justification (if this was not included in the methodology section) and with any assumptions or modifications defended. The details of the procedure should be presented, perhaps using examples here or in an appendix.

Presentation of data (where appropriate)

Graphs, tables and figures are extremely important in a science thesis or in any discipline research producing quantitative data. These should be clear, well-labelled and self-explanatory using only the legend.

Whether the data are quantitative or qualitative their presentation should be clearly structured with a transparent trail from raw data/information to research outcomes. For instance, details of why, from whom, what and where data were collected should be evident, preferably summarised in tables, figures or diagrams that are clearly labelled, numbered and referred to in the texts.

Discussion of outcomes or conclusion of argument

In this section the main points should be summarised and evaluated in relation to the previous literature. When the results are in the form of data/information then they should be interpreted in the light of recent, relevant research indicating what theories have been supported, substantiated, added to, challenged, amended or rejected.

The whole project should be evaluated with its limitations addressed with their consequences for the results explained.

It is often at this point that the *contribution to knowledge* of the doctorate is lucidly and unambiguously articulated though that may form a separate section with any suggestions for repeated or further research and implications of the results for theory and for practice.

Reference section and/or bibliography

In the References section all references in the text must be included in a consistent and appropriate style for the discipline, while no references should be included that do not appear in the text.

In some disciplines/institutions it is considered acceptable to include also a separate, short bibliography of texts that influenced the research in a special way but were not finally included as referenced texts.

Appendices

These should be numbered and appear in the order of first reference in the main body of the text.

The thesis as a whole

On completion of reading the whole thesis, an examiner should make a judgement about its overall presentation, whether the reader's need for understanding has been enhanced or inhibited by the care given to presentation (whether it is logical, coherent, accurate, accessible, guided, grammatical, for instance). A glossary of key terms or acronyms, for example, might demonstrate a recognition of the need for clarity.

Importantly, any reader should be left knowing without doubt what contribution/s to knowledge were expected, how they were achieved and to what extent.

Important caveat

No thesis is likely to meet all the requirements listed here; there will always be some parts that are nearer to achieving excellence than others. Some disciplines emphasise some aspects/features more than others. Some parts are more important than others because they indicate the strength of the thesis' argument and the credibility of the results/conclusions. All theses are imperfect in some way. Examiners dream of receiving a thesis that is precise, concise, relevant and elegant but frequently elegance is lost to time pressures or lack of language skills. Similarly, succinctness may give way to a perceived need to include every detail at least once. Often, for instance, a thesis demonstrates a well-thought-through research plan, skill in its implementation but, for whatever reason, say time or motivation pressures, can result in scant final sections.

The examiner's challenge is to decide what is good enough to deserve a doctorate – as it is or with a bit of extra effort?

Coming to a balanced conclusion

An important restraint to the expectation of perfection is provided in some form within institutional regulations. A phrase frequently used is that the thesis should demonstrate a quality and quantity of output 'that can reasonably be expected from an individual after the equivalent of 3–4 years' full-time study'. Thus, we must not expect a description of research that could be accomplished by a large team of researchers, and/or with a huge amount of funding, and/or over an extensive period.

It is perhaps crucial to add here that neither should we expect all research hypotheses to be proven or all questions to have irrefutable answers. While these may be the fodder of publication mills there are likely to be well-founded, carefully conducted and documented doctoral research projects that find that expected connections do not exist or that answers are more complicated than is commonly thought. That does not mean that there was no contribution to knowledge, quite the reverse.

Accepting that there will inevitably be some sections or aspects of a thesis that could be improved, it is then the examiner's job to decide if those improvements are trivial enough to allow for a straight pass or very minor corrections or whether some further, clearly and explicitly defined work, small or larger, could bring the thesis up to an acceptable standard for a pass.

It might be salutary at this point to engage in Reflection Point 10.1 and then Activity 10.2.

Reflection Point 10.1

What was good enough for me

For a few moments, think back to your own thesis or that of a greatly respected colleague, should you not have completed a thesis yourself. Consider first what you are most proud of or admire most about that thesis. Then be honest and reflect on how it could have been improved if you (s/he) had had more resources, including personal skill or knowledge at the time.

Then contemplate how the positive aspects more than balanced out the less positive ones.

Activity 10.2

What was good enough for others

In this chapter we have presented the attributes that demonstrate a very good thesis. Use them to review two or three recent theses that have been produced in your department or school and have passed. Consider how their different very positive and quite good aspects outbalance the less good, even poor aspects. You might check with colleagues what the candidates were required by examiners to do in order to bring their original theses up to scratch, bearing in mind that that phrase means 'adequate, tolerable, or sufficient' rather than 'perfect, impeccable, fault-free'.

Now it is time for you to take charge of developing your own doctoral assessment criteria.

Developing your own criteria to suit your circumstances

We recognise here that doctoral assessment criteria will vary to reflect differences in disciplines, such as between theoretical physics and the performing arts, between different doctoral degree forms, such as lab-based or practice-based doctorates or doctorates by published work, and over time, for instance as technology develops.

We also acknowledge that becoming a confident doctoral examiner takes experience and time. However, it is always important to the integrity of your assessment work that you can justify your decisions with evidence. That evidence comes through developing and adhering to a set of criteria that fit the circumstance.

From the information provided in this chapter, your own experience and any discussions you have had with colleagues in your discipline, begin to construct a template that you could use whenever you are required to examine a doctoral thesis. You could test it out by volunteering to give a candidate in your department a mock viva: use your nascent criteria to formulate questions. Later you could check how the actual viva went and how useful your questions were, either in stimulating revisions that helped it pass, or predicting questions from the examiners or in reflecting revisions required, or all the above.

For ease, you might like to copy out and draw on the summary of criteria derived from our preceding discussion that is provided as Appendix B.

Further reading

Houston, G. (2018) *A Study of the PhD Examination: process, attributes and outcomes. Doctoral Thesis.* Oxford University

Pearce, L. (2005) *How to Examine a Thesis.* Maidenhead: Open University Press/ The Society for Research into Higher Education

Tinkler, P. and Jackson, C. (2004/2009) *The Doctoral Examination Process.* Maidenhead: Open University Press/The Society for Research into Higher Education

11

What are the purposes of a viva voce and how can it be conducted rigorously and compassionately?

In this chapter, in relation to the viva voce, you will find:

- The value and prevalence of forms of assessment involving a defence or viva
- Rationales for various forms of defence
- Potential expectations to use as objectives
- Examples from good practice
- How assessment and feedback can be positive forces in developing the independence of researchers and for successful completion

Introduction

In most countries and disciplines, doctoral graduates will experience a summative, oral examination in some form to complete their assessment. The nature of the oral (which we will now refer to as a viva for ease) varies considerably, from a public celebration to which friends and family are invited, to a private event attended only by the candidate, their examiners and perhaps one or two others with formal roles (see Chapter 9). The purposes of the viva are many, ranging from the purely practical, for example, checking the thesis is the candidate's work, to an opportunity for deep discussion of the topic among peers, a 'rite of passage' that confirms the candidate is capable of independent research and, in recent times, a demonstration of professional performance as a researcher.

You should ensure that you are indeed available and capable of being an examiner of a specific doctoral thesis, with all the expertise, integrity and independence it entails, before you formally, or even informally, agree to take on the role. It does indeed require setting aside enough time to ensure you are able to do a good job, both in the thesis reading and reporting and viva stages. Besides hours dedicated to properly reading and critiquing the thesis, between at least three and several working days of uninterrupted work depending on discipline and quality of the thesis, other preparation is necessary to help ensure the optimal experience for the doctoral candidate whom you hopefully will be inducting into the new world of being doctoral. This time, however, is not wasted; the experience of examining will help you develop your own skills as a doctoral examiner, as a supervisor and as researcher. To spark your interest, consider the questions in Reflection Point 11.1 if you yourself experienced a viva.

Reflection Point 11.1

The final assessment – the influence of vivas

Think back to your own viva, if you had one. How did this experience impact on your next steps? Do you feel that it has had a lasting effect on your view of yourself as a researcher? Was it positive, neutral or negative in its impact? What made it so?

The purpose of a viva

The assessment combination of examining the written thesis followed by an oral viva voce is very different to most assessment situations. By reading and critiquing the thesis in the first instance, you as an assessor will have already come to a preliminary judgement about the eventual outcome of the assessment process. In some cases, you may be explicitly asked to declare this initial judgement. In most cases this early judgement will indeed be a good indicator of the eventual outcome, as research shows that the viva outcome usually confirms the examiner's view obtained through reading the thesis (Trafford and Leshem, 2008; Houston, 2018). If this is true, why do we go through the extra effort of having a viva at all? What is the benefit if, in general, the exercise usually leads to confirmation of the existing opinion?

Viva as confirmation of authenticity

The most basic answer to this question is that the viva ensures that the candidate was indeed the person who did the research and wrote the thesis. Although this may seem cynical and perhaps pedestrian, with such a high-stakes assessment of years of study conducted while working closely with supervisors and often other members of a research team, it becomes critical to not only verify that the work presented is that of the candidate, but also to clarify the nature of the candidate's contribution to the development of the research, interpretation and ideas described within the thesis.

The examiners are the gatekeepers of the discipline, ensuring that any who carry the title doctor are indeed able to conduct independent research within their field and represent their discipline as a significant figure in it. This is an important responsibility. The viva provides the opportunity for examiners to confirm that the doctoral candidate has done the work necessary to be awarded the title 'doctor'.

Viva as an assessment measure

Beyond confirmation of authenticity, the viva is an assessment measure beyond that of the written thesis. There are several skills and attributes of an independent researcher that can be best tested, or perhaps can only be tested, in a viva situation. These skills require the researcher to respond to questions they may be unprepared for and pushed to think more deeply about different viewpoints. Further, they can be required to reflect on the strengths and weaknesses of their work.

A viva allows the examination not just of the candidate's in-depth understanding of their field, but also allows the examiner to explore how well the candidate can place their work within the context of the larger discipline and even the context beyond the discipline. There should be some evidence of this skill within the thesis, but the viva allows for a more extensive exploration of these skills, pushing for detail that may not have appeared in the thesis. (Note that institutions are beginning to require a formal 'impact of research' statement to be included within their theses.) Questioning the lines of logic laid out in writing allows exploration of the candidate's ability to re-interpret or see things from a different viewpoint. Challenging the candidate and requiring them to expand on their written argument allows for a demonstration of a more sophisticated level of understanding than written work alone.

Vivas also allow examiners to explore parts of the written thesis that are slightly weaker than other parts. When writing such a piece of work, it is highly likely that some areas will be less developed than others. This may be due to a lack of understanding on the candidate's part, but equally it may well be that this knowledge has become so second nature, so obvious to the candidate that they have failed to explain this in writing to the level of detail required by someone external to the project. Within the viva, the examiners can determine which of these two circumstances holds. The result is quite different in terms of corrections required. If the candidate fully understands the issue, but has not adequately written the explanation, this is a relatively small correction. However, if the weakness in the thesis stems from a fundamental lack of understanding, or indeed a misunderstanding, then it may require much more work, involving new knowledge and skills, to raise the thesis to the appropriate level.

Other 'researcher' skills that cannot fully be tested solely through written work include those of defence and debate and the researcher's ability to communicate with a variety of different audiences. Learning how to defend and debate the rationales for all the elements of research is vital to succeeding as an independent researcher. It is important for all researchers to be able to communicate why they have made the choices they have and to weigh up the positives and negatives of those choices versus those of the alternatives. Equally, they need to be able to communicate their research journey and justify the importance of their findings to a wide variety of people (see the Dublin Descriptors in Chapter 1). The viva enables examiners to assess these different skills, challenging researchers to answer these all important 'why' and 'so what' questions.

Having said all that, only in unusual or borderline cases does the viva really tend to be the decisive assessment component since, as we previously noted, it is generally confirmatory, although it may have a much larger impact on the specific corrections required. In borderline cases, the examiners can more deeply explore the problems they identified in the thesis and come to a more informed decision about the appropriate outcome. Therefore, the viva serves to help examiners guide the development of the thesis, hopefully to enable the eventual successful completion of the doctorate.

Viva as a means to support the final developmental stage to independent researcher

Although it is often seen as the last step in the doctoral journey, the viva is in practice more of a transition point. It is the end of the bulk of the research and a showcase of the wide range of skills a doctoral researcher has acquired over their years of study. It is the start of the very final stage of the doctorate, which usually entails some form of final corrections/modifications to ensure the thesis is in a state that is suitable for sharing with the world through various open access platforms, or 'public' library. It is the beginning of a new journey for these **early career researchers** as they look beyond the doctorate and decide where their newly minted degree will take them next. The viva examiners play an important role in supporting this transition period and helping newer researchers excel as the doctorate comes to an end and the world opens up in front of them.

Often, the guidance needed and value of high-quality examiner feedback for the final corrections of a thesis are underestimated in terms of their importance and the skill it takes to provide. If there are serious problems with a thesis, the viva serves as a way for the examiners to question and probe, working to understand how best to guide a doctorate researcher to make it to the necessary level, or instead gently but firmly break the news to them that their work is not going to reach doctorate level (see Chapter 8). When a thesis is of overall high quality, the viva can help examiners identify how to advise the doctoral researcher to polish it, bringing any weaker areas up to a standard the candidate can be proud of while highlighting the fullness of the work. For instance, they might be asked to strengthen the final arguments in the last chapter or to suggest how professionals as well as other researchers could benefit from reading their work and applying their findings. In such cases, clear and constructive feedback provided by the examiners is essential to the final development of the doctorate, enabling the candidate to achieve their best outcome and highest quality thesis possible.

Looking to the future, good viva examiners often question doctoral candidates about logical next steps for the research and the potential impact of their findings beyond their discipline and, indeed, beyond academia. These types of questions can help doctoral candidates reflect on their work and speculate about future steps that they may or may not wish to follow. Although the viva is largely retrospective, in order to determine if a doctoral candidate is truly able to act as an independent researcher, part of the viva must assess the candidate's ability to formulate future research and to utilise this research in different ways. This can lead to ideas for future publication, collaboration or potential work with or within other sectors.

Viva as a rite of passage

Lastly, the viva is to some degree a rite of passage. It is the final trial that a doctoral researcher enters and then exits, all going well, recognised as a full member of the disciplinary community, an independent researcher. This may seem to be a trivial purpose for the viva; however, the authors know of people who felt their vivas were not rigorous enough and as a result feel as though they have not truly earned their title. Therefore, it is critical that examiners understand this purpose and do their part to ensure that the exam is conducted with the gravitas and sincerity it deserves so that the candidates are empowered and encouraged to demonstrate their skills to their full ability. Then they feel worthy of the degree they have rightfully earned.

Preparing for the viva

Understanding expectations of roles and responsibilities

The way in which vivas are conducted across countries, institutions and even disciplines vary considerably. In fact, it is quite interesting to discuss with international colleagues the many variations of this final examination of the doctorate, thinking about what true best practice is in terms of assessing whether a doctoral candidate does indeed possess the skills of an independent researcher. We suggest a simple but effective way to learn more about other practices in Activity 11.1.

Activity 11.1

Exploring the differences between institutional and national doctoral examination systems

Have a coffee with a colleague who has experience of another institution or, better yet, another country's way of examining doctorates. What are the key similarities and differences to those conducted in your institution? Are the different practices or rituals intended to achieve similar outcomes?

In Chapter 9 we discussed the details of roles and responsibilities in the final examination process. Whether you are an internal or external examiner, you will be responsible for reading through and assessing the thesis (see Chapter 10), devising questions, working with your examining team to plan and prepare a high-quality process, conducting the viva in a fair and rigorous way, and working with the examining team to ensure the outcome reflects the quality of the candidate and their work. Quite a lot of work then, really, is an understatement. Never fear, the sections below will take you through all of this; however, just a small spoiler, the key to all of this is good preparation and communication with your examining team!

Identifying key areas for discussion and designing questions

As discussed in Chapter 10, you will find a wide range of different aspects of the thesis that warrant more discussion, perhaps because greater clarity is required, or the argument presented was incomplete or weak or it may be simply an area you are extremely interested in that you would like to explore in greater depth (remembering this is the opportunity for an intellectual exchange with a new researcher too). All in all, you are likely to find in the end that it is not generating questions that is difficult, rather it is narrowing down the questions such that important areas are all covered within a sensible timeframe. This is especially true when you consider that your co-examiner(s) will have their own questions they would like addressed, and while these may well overlap with yours, it is highly likely they will also have unique but critical areas to add to your list of questions and topics.

This all means that prioritisation is going to be important. It is easy to get caught up in the research, focusing on the detail, but what you are assessing is whether the candidate possesses and has demonstrated the skills and qualities of an independent researcher. Therefore, it is worth going right back to those Dublin Descriptors introduced in Chapter 1, thinking about what is critical to explore to be confident that the researcher in front of you has demonstrated the outcomes defined there. Prioritise questions in these areas. The goal of your questions should not be to catch the candidate out, or to trick them. The doctorate is complicated enough. Straightforward questions that require thought, consideration and sound argument will be enough.

Trafford and Leshem's (2008) research on viva questions shows that as examiners become more experienced, they ask fewer 'how' and 'what' type questions and more 'why' and 'so what' questions. Questions dealing with rationales help you to assess the doctoral candidate's decision-making, as well as their ability to reflect on past actions and to make future judgements as an independent researcher.

Impact questions (colloquially known as 'so what' questions) help you better understand the novel contribution made and its influence on the wider field and the world at large, as well as exploring the ability of the candidate to conceptualise their results in a meaningful way. It is worth taking the time to think carefully about the questions you want to ask while thinking about what skills, knowledge and attributes you want to see the candidate demonstrate in answering these questions. It is likely there will be changes on the day but having a good pre-planned outline will help ensure you will be able to form a fair and logical judgement. We provide in Appendix C some commonly used viva questions provided by experienced examiners.

Pre-viva meeting with co-examiners

It is essential to ensure you have time to meet with others in your examining team and plan the viva process. This is often done for ease on the day, since everyone is together in one place or in touch by video- or tele-conferencing. However, there may be some advantages to meeting (perhaps virtually) in advance of the actual viva date. Having a bit more time provides an opportunity to think how to best accommodate the different topics all of the examiners want to explore, to decide jointly how to approach any identified problems and to ensure that any points of disagreement between members of the examining team are thoroughly negotiated well in advance of the start of the viva, before the candidate is present. It may be that an hour before the viva is enough to do all of this; however, it may be that having this extra time will greatly increase the quality of the viva for everyone. This is worth discussing with your examining team in view of any specific regulations the institution may have. It is also extremely important in cases, becoming now more frequent, such as distance learning doctorates that are examined remotely. Frequently the regulations for conducting remote vivas are more constraining to all participants because of the perceived potential for deception or malpractice as well as the need to prepare for malfunction of equipment.

Within the pre-viva meeting it is important to ensure that all members are well-informed and clear about the process and regulations, as well as having an agreed outline and strategy for the conduct of the viva itself. This role is often taken by a viva chair or the internal examiner. If the viva is a private affair such as in the UK, attention should be paid to ensuring that you and other examiners provide an environment and atmosphere conducive to the candidate performing their best: see Chapter 6 for information about building rapport within the viva and Chapter 5 about inclusive practice during a viva. The physical environment may be outwith your control if the institution requires a public viva but the general atmosphere or ambiance can be set by prior discussion between examiners or opponents, as they may be called. The goal should be to empower and enable the candidate to demonstrate their ability to be an independent researcher. You should think about how to structure the interview process, including the room set up, alongside determining the final questions set. You also should decide on a general but flexible timeframe, outlining how much time you will, ideally, spend on each topic. It is helpful to avoid straying too much from such a schedule in order to ensure that you get through everything you need to on the day while keeping the questioning section within psychologically comfortable boundaries. Although viva lengths tend to vary by discipline traditions, few people (candidates and examiners included) can concentrate much beyond two hours without a break. We summarise some important guidelines for pre-viva meetings in Top Tips Box 11.1.

Top Tips 11.1

Conducting a pre-viva meeting

- Determine by email or a phone call the general response of each examiner to what is contained in the thesis.
- Suggest that, in advance of the pre-meeting, the examiners share satisfactory/good points and main concerns to enable comparisons to be made.
- Ensure that examiners have enough time, depending on the degrees of satisfaction or concern expressed and the degree of agreement indicated, to talk through and agree in advance of the viva date both the main aspects of the thesis to be explored and the practicalities of conducting the viva.
- If there are several or many points of criticism emerging, encourage discussion about which are critical for the award, which require more explanation or clarification to be acceptable or which could simply be noted as requiring some specific post-viva work, such as the addition of information that was clearly available but simply not included.
- Debate what would be deemed as acceptable answers to such critical questions and what potential outcomes would be depending on the quality of the response.
- Plan the viva ensuring 'settling-in time', a logical order of questioning, who would lead each topic area and roughly how much time would be required for each group of questions. Ensure that it is clear to all what are the most important issues to address and when.
- Check that all examiners have had their voices heard and understood.
- Make sure that examiners are familiar with the procedures required by the institution and its regulations.
- Verify that examiners are content with the ethos planned for the encounter.
- Confirm the practical requirements that examiners expect will be attended to, for example availability of water, other refreshments, privacy notices, and so on.

Conducting the viva

Managing the candidate

It is important to realise how stressful a viva is for the doctoral candidate. This is the day they have been preparing for throughout the course of their doctoral journey and all that anticipation and anxiety can hit them quite hard, particularly right at the beginning of the viva. Therefore, it is important to establish an atmosphere that enables the candidate to perform their best. A review of the last sections of Chapter 6 would be useful at this point before considering some of the detail below.

It is often helpful to start a viva with one of the examiners formally introducing everyone, using the name that each person wishes to be addressed by during the viva, whether that be 'Prof Smith' or 'Jane', avoiding any embarrassment or confusion. It is also good practice to go over the procedures and some of the basic viva protocols, including how the session will proceed. It can be helpful to let candidates know whether they are able to consult the thesis during questioning (it is usual to allow this), or ask for more time to think, or clarification of a question, and that comfort breaks are allowed. The candidate may know all these rules already; however, it is a good way to give time for the candidate to relax within the viva environment and ensures that they can be relaxed enough to ask for a break if needed.

It is helpful to start with some positive and reassuring, but truthful, words, such as 'We enjoyed reading your thesis' or 'We found your research very interesting'. It is not good practice, however, to state or even to hint at the actual outcome of the viva, prior to the conclusion of the assessment process. This is because, even if the thesis was fantastic, until you talk to the candidate, you are not able to fully confirm such an assessment. You do not want to put yourself in the position of having to take back a statement that they have passed should the viva uncover something untoward. The authors do know of rare occasions when the thesis was fine, or even good, but the candidate was unable to demonstrate the necessary contextual/textual understanding and/or adequately interpret their data. Thus, the candidate was required to do further work that was not initially anticipated by the examining team. Therefore, it is best to be resolute in withholding a decision until you are sure rather than anticipating an unknown outcome.

Once all these niceties are out of the way, you will want to start with the presentation by the candidate, if such is required or allowed as good practice, and then move on to questions. Thinking of one or two opening questions that help the candidate to start talking, and therefore relieving some of the stress response, can be useful to a strong start. Questions about what they enjoyed most about their research, or alternatively why they wanted to pursue a certain topic or methodological approach get the candidate talking and hopefully that will start to diminish their nerves since there is no right or wrong answer to each of these questions. Instead, they tap into the researcher's passion for the subject and in that way can give insight into them as researchers, as well as helping them overcome the challenging first few minutes of the viva.

Usually the start is the most difficult time for a candidate, however, it can be that you notice them getting flustered at some point in the middle of a viva. Perhaps they have become worried they are not performing well or struggled with an answer that then threw them off track. It may be that they have a different interpretation of terms used by examiners (a common issue in a global examining environment) and become confused by how they are being used in this process. It is usually acceptable to have a break within a viva and if the candidate is visibly upset, a break would be in order. During the break you or a fellow examiner or even the supervisor, if they are available, could talk with the candidate to try to reassure them so that the viva can resume with them feeling more able to answer questions. (See the scenario in Activity 6.4.) We can confidently say that in vivas it is common to have some areas where the candidate answers well, and some where they answer less well, and some questions that are not answered well at all. This rarely affects the overall outcome because they simply lead to just a few corrections here or there. See Chapter 6 for details about making the viva more inclusive for candidates with specific anxiety and/or neurodiversity issues.

If you do have a break, when restarting you may want to start with a theme or topic that the candidate is more confident with instead of diving straight back into the area that caused the distress. Of course, you still must cover these tough topics, but hopefully the break and gentle restart will help get the candidate back into the right frame of mind. As an examiner you want to make sure you are assessing the true potential of the candidate rather than their reaction to a uniquely stressful situation. Consider the points made in Information Box 11.1, as examples of how potentially difficult situations can be averted by thoughtful intervention and questioning.

Information Box 11.1

Dealing with misapprehensions

The first scenario we address is all too common in the viva situation in which the candidate is naturally anxious: s/he mishears the question and responds by discussing something that the examiners had not asked about. Rather than leaping in to convey that the candidate is in some way at fault, a simple thank you for that answer and a re-wording of the original question, perhaps making it clearer, averts escalation of anxiety.

In contrast, the second scenario – no less common – involves an examiner misunderstanding something written in the thesis or, indeed, asking why something is not included that actually is there. A thesis is a big, complex read, and examiners are human. It is appropriate to apologise for the mistake. It is possible that a suggestion could be made about

(Continued)

clarifying what is written, but only if on reflection it really is unclear in the text or emphasising a useful point that might be missed in the complexity of the text.

For both scenarios and all others, it is helpful to treat the candidate as you would a valued colleague, as soon they may well be.

Managing the questioning

Different examiners from different institutions and different cultural backgrounds put more or less emphasis on testing a candidate's ability to defend. However, one should think about the impact of aggressive viva techniques on newer researchers, and conversely the impact of a less rigorous examination. Research shows that people's experience of the viva does not necessarily correlate with the outcome of the viva and that expectations and the examiner's approach can greatly influence how the researchers feel about their viva experience (Murray, 2015). The viva does act as a rite of passage for researchers and, therefore, it is quite important to strike the appropriate balance that provides due rigour without undue aggression to ensure that all candidates who pass this assessment are privileged to the full value of the process.

This will mean negotiating with your examining team an appropriate approach to the questioning, ideally in advance of the viva, as suggested in the Top Tips above, and ensuring that all members of the examining team stick to this agreement, including yourself. Many University regulations have within them a statement about the candidate being given adequate time to consider and answer questions. As academic judgment cannot normally be appealed against, it is this regulation that often is utilised during appeals with candidates claiming that they were not provided with adequate thinking time. This means it is incredibly important that examiners ensure the candidate has the space and time they need to perform their best. Besides protecting against an appeal, it also means you get a better chance of understanding the full potential of the candidate.

Further, because the academic judgment is so critical, it is important that all the examiners involved recognise the expertise of each other and are familiar with any alternative paradigms or schools of thought accepted in their field. Bearing in mind that the candidate is the star of this show, it is important that examiners can put aside any intellectual/theoretical differences such as this so that they do not inadvertently skew the discussion. Equally, examiners must be respectful or assertive, whichever is appropriate, of the others' status in the proceedings whatever their status in the world of academe. Each has an equal right to ask questions and to their opinion on the quality of the thesis and the answers to viva questions. As discussed elsewhere, while the external examiner's role is to ensure inter-institutional equivalence of doctorateness, it is the internal's role to ensure due adherence to the institution's regulations and procedures, but both should evaluate the thesis and the candidate as a potential independent researcher. Undue deference or assertiveness is out of place in this situation.

However, convention has it in many disciplines that the external examiner is allowed to ask the final question while frequently either the independent chair, if there is one, or the external examiner thanks the candidate for their contributions and describes the next stages in the procedure: the outcome and requirements. Maintaining the essence of compassion at this stage in the encounter, it is helpful to indicate how long the examiners' deliberations might take so that the candidate is not kept outside the door anxiously waiting and can take a comfort break and or refreshments in the interlude (as can the examiners!). We summarise some important advice in Top Tips 11.2.

Top Tips 11.2

Practicalities and sensitivities for examiners

When you receive the thesis

- As soon as possible, quickly review the thesis to ensure that the topic is one in which you have expertise and the presentation is tolerable. If you must return it unassessed because of a problem with either of these things, it is best done soon.

The review of the written thesis

- Allow plenty of time for the process – a rapid overview and then a detailed review compiling comments and questions will take at least three working days.
- Write your preliminary report before any discussions with the co-examiner.

Working with co-examiner

- Ensure that the procedures for conducting the viva are agreed in advance, that is, who deals with what, when, to ensure that the viva flows smoothly.
- Agree prior to the viva, how the joint report will be written. Agree who will draft the report and the procedure for agreeing the final report. The main points to be covered, including any amendments, can then be quickly decided during the short period after the main dialogue when the candidate temporarily leaves the room. Trying to draft the report together while the candidate awaits the result can unnecessarily worry them that you are having difficulty coming to a joint decision.

(Continued)

The first few minutes of the viva

- Make sure that the candidate knows how you expect them to address the examiners, including yourself, in the viva. If you are the Internal Examiner, they may be used to using your first name to address you but be unsure in this special context.
- At the start of the viva explain the format of the viva. Tell the candidate that you would like them to answer each question in two or three sentences, that you will ask them to elaborate if necessary and that you will gradually cover all their work.

The main dialogue

- Phrase the questions to encourage short answers from the candidate that focus on a specific issue, then ask for elaborations if necessary. Start with a few 'what' and 'how' questions to get the candidate talking. (What got you interested…? How did you start…?)
- After the initial pleasantries are over a helpful format can be to ask what the thesis is about: What is the main argument? Which literature was the most influential in guiding or informing the research topic? How did the candidate get evidence to make the crucial points? What is the connection between the results and the conclusions?
- Once these major points have been covered, turn to specific presentational issues – graphs etc, referencing, sectioning, that might need addressing. Concentrate on 'why' and 'so what' questions as the viva gathers pace.
- Towards the end, it is useful to turn to the future and what developments might come from the conclusions.

How it feels to be an examiner

- You must deal with the candidate's nervousness and recognise the candidate's needs for comfortable seating, water and, in cases of long examinations, a chance to break.
- For a new examiner the feelings of responsibility can be overwhelming, to the candidate, the institution and the discipline/profession.
- Discourse can have many pitfalls. It can be especially stressful when there are differences in hierarchy and gender that are acting contrary to convention, for example when a candidate is older than the examiner, or the external examiner less senior than the internal examiner. It is important to be clear about the seniority/equality of roles within the viva. Remember you are there in your professional and expert capacity; be confident in that.
- If the supervisor is present it can be difficult to cope with their body language even if they are not permitted to speak. Position the seating so that neither the examiners nor the candidate is facing the supervisor. You could suggest the supervisor takes notes on the questions and the complimentary comments of the examiners for the candidate to refer to afterwards, thus, giving the supervisor a positive role!
- Be prepared for strong reactions from the candidate to any comments that might imply criticism of their thesis. They may believe that ANY criticism implies failure and react accordingly.
- If you are an internal examiner you often know the candidate quite well. Be aware that you are in a role that may be completely unfamiliar and unexpected to the candidate and may change their perception of you.

Coming to a decision

As we described in Chapter 10 about weighing up the critical and less important aspects of a thesis, the examiners will be required to reflect on the answers provided during the viva debate to consider whether their concerns have been allayed, whether those answers or the equivalent need to be incorporated into the thesis alongside any other requirements they may have, such as correction of typographical errors, to achieve a thesis satisfactory to grace the institution's shelves. Here the institutional requirement that it demonstrate a unique contribution to knowledge which merits publication in some form should be revisited. More importantly, their decision should concentrate on whether the candidate has convinced them that they have indeed demonstrated the ability and qualities of an autonomous researcher. As we have noted throughout this book, one of the important attributes that feedback throughout the doctoral programme should seek to achieve is that the researcher should be able to critically evaluate their own work. If the candidate can do that in a viva without detracting from the work they have done, then at least one significant quality will have been demonstrated. By the end of the viva, the examiners' skilled questioning and their ability to draw out the best in the candidate should make transparent the final decision and any additional requirements before the award is granted.

The impact of a viva on candidates and examiners

Being asked to be an examiner for a doctoral thesis is a great honour. It is recognition of your expertise within your field and of respect within your academic community. It is also an opportunity to read and discuss cutting-edge research, with an enthusiastic new researcher. This is an extremely important assessment role and in taking on this role you will be for ever linked to this doctoral candidate in some small way, if only in their memory and their life stories.

In terms of assessment roles, there are few that match being an examiner for a final doctoral viva in terms of responsibility and impact on an individual's future. This impact is not simply derived from the academic judgement required to reach a formal result, but is a consequence of the whole viva experience, which often influences a candidate's future development and even their perception of themselves as an independent researcher (see Murray's descriptions of Viva experiences in the Further Reading and the Voice of Experience 11.1). Therefore, this is not a task to be taken lightly.

Voice of Experience 11.1

Too little or too much: aiming for a balance in vivas

I was always a Type A student – determined to do very well despite expecting a real grilling in my viva since my research was extremely novel. The examiners were charming, starting off by chatting about the creativity shown in my research methods. Then they chatted about the field as a whole and how it needed a new approach. I sat in trepidation waiting for the intellectual inquisition. They then chatted about the potential impacts of my research, asking my views on what they might be. This is it, I thought, the nice cop/bad cop approach – the tricky questions will come next. Then they got up and shook my hand, congratulating me on achieving my doctorate. Stunned, I left the room. Since then I have felt short-changed – something of the imposter syndrome left as a residue. Now I feel my research deserved more than that perfunctory engagement with it.

Thenceforth I determined not to underestimate the impact on the candidate of the examiner's role the in viva. When examining I try to do justice to the effort made to reach the submission stage, no matter what the outcome of the examination turns out to be.

Voice A – a university pro-vice chancellor

Ahmed's thesis was a delight to examine. He had been punctilious in his writing up, ensuring he did justice to the challenging desert context and the demanding lives of his participants while remaining objective and precise in his research practice and interpretation of results. I felt that there were a few small issues that deserved a little more attention, but these were mainly presentational. This was confirmed in the pre-viva discussion with the external examiner and so I began the viva looking forward to the ensuing discussion.

After I had introduced everyone and tried to put Ahmed at ease without giving away yet the happy outcome we had predicted, the external asked a run of questions – practically one for each page up to the end of the introduction. This took some time. She then allowed me a questioning opportunity, so I quickly led us through the main aspects of the literature review, expecting that she would then move into the methodology – but no, again we went page by page through the literature section asking interested and interesting questions although by now we were 2 hours into the viva. This pattern continued. Eventually Ahmed requested a break for prayers when I was able to suggest to my colleague, over refreshments, that perhaps we should move on more rapidly. That had a marginal impact but in the end the viva took 5 hours.

I was both exhausted and worried that Ahmed might complain about the length of the viva. But no, it turned out that he was absolutely delighted that someone had shown such interest in his work. I doubt whether many candidates would feel the same, especially if they did not, as he did, get a straight pass with an allowed short period to correct some typographical errors. He remained in contact with his examiners when he returned home. Ever since, I have though ensured in pre-discussion with fellow examiners that we agree a maximum time for the viva process.

Voice B – the internal examiner of an international student

In neither of the cases in the vivas described above had the examiners set out to be anything but rigorous and compassionate; they simply defined and enacted those virtues differently to the others involved. It is a cliché, but nevertheless especially worth thinking about when conducting a viva, that we should consider walking in the other person's shoes.

In the next chapter we elaborate further on conventions and etiquette in relation to the potential outcomes and how they are delivered and dealt with thereafter.

Further reading

Houston, G. (2018) *A study of the PhD examination: process, attributes and outcomes*. Oxford: Oxford University

Murray, R. (2015) *How to Survive your Viva*. Maidenhead: Open University Press

Tinkler, P. and Jackson, C. (2004) *The Doctoral Examination Process*. Maidenhead: SRHE and Open University Press

Trafford, V. and Leshem, S. (2008) *Stepping Stones to Achieving Your Doctorate: Focusing on Your Viva from the Start*. Maidenhead: Open University Press

12

What are the potential outcomes and what will be your continuing role?

In this chapter, you will find information and discussion about:

- Criterion-referenced professional decision-making
- Range of outcomes
- Time as an arbiter
- End-game roles and responsibilities
- Submission and completion issues
- Publishability judgements
- Dilemmas and challenges
- Presenting results productively
- Life beyond the final decision
- Reflecting on the past – tension of escalating demands
- Looking to the future

Introduction

In this final chapter we address the topics raised in Stage 3 of Figure 9.1, Houston's continuum of judgement, concerning the recommendations that examiners make about a doctoral thesis and the process of explaining these to the candidate. Further, we address the aftermath, exploring both fulfilling and potentially difficult situations, leading up to formal completion and any further contact beyond that. First, though, it is important to consider the complexity of the decision process involved in reaching a consensus view about the way forward with other examiners.

Negotiating a decision

Let us first consider the nature of the evidence on which we will base our decision about whether doctorateness has been achieved. Each examiner has before them the extensive notes about the written work (and possibly artefacts and so on depending on the degree type – see Chapter 3) and the candidate's performance in any presentation or viva. These are likely to be based on a selection of the kinds of criteria we provide in Appendix B, some of which will have been met in full, others less so and perhaps some not at all. This might suggest that the final decision is criterion-referenced. That is, that the candidate's performance is measured against a fixed set of predetermined criteria or standards rather than being norm-referenced, which is a comparison of the performance scores with the average of those of other candidates, those scoring average or above passing.

Certainly, as far as we are aware, there is no mean, median or mode score yet determined for doctorateness but neither yet has a standardised test been invented that includes all the criteria written in concise form and weighted for contribution to a final score (thank goodness that we are not yet so systematised and automated). Nevertheless, it does mean that as examiners we are reliant on a complex system of criteria that we evaluate a candidate against according to our professional experience and expertise (our norms) that may or may not be in complete harmony with that of our colleague examiners (with their own norms). Sometimes it seems amazing that we have managed to survive this system for so long.

However, to lighten the concern a little, we can make some loose comparisons to the driving test, another criterion-referenced test administered by a professional person who judges whether a learner driver's machine-handling and road skills, traffic awareness and attention, their dexterity in performing a three-point turn, for instance, and ability to make an emergency stop are adequate enough to earn them their driver's licence. Most days, whether as a pedestrian or driver, we can spot others whose driving skills we can and do criticise, wondering how they got their licence, while knowing full well that our own skills can sometimes, if only occasionally, be lacking in refinement.

Contemplating that scenario reminds us that we are not seeking perfection in every aspect of a doctoral submission. We need to decide whether it is good enough to let the candidate out into the world as an autonomous researcher. To make that decision we need, then, to decide which of our criteria are critical (those they must be able to demonstrate that they can do well) and which can be refined with experience. You might begin the identification of your most important criteria by undertaking Activity 12.1.

Activity 12.1

Identifying your most important criteria

Using your library resources and the advice of your colleagues, select a couple of theses from your own department, preferably one that comes highly recommended and one that is deemed OK. It will be helpful, as you will find later, if the theses were submitted in the last five years. Skim through the introduction, the methodology and then concentrate on the discussion and conclusion chapters, noting:

- how far from perfect you think these are;
- facets that you think are great – examples of good research practice;
- facets that you think could be improved;
- aspects you found troubling or at least irritating.

Considering then that these have already been regarded as passed at doctoral level, this gives you an idea of a standard by which to measure any you may examine yourself.

- To improve your skills further you could use the criteria presented in Appendix B to evaluate one of those theses in more detail.
- If you find that there are quite a few of the criteria that are not met very well, consider what mitigating circumstances, perhaps some exceptionally well-designed or creative parts, may have allowed that thesis to pass.

Before we go further, we should emphasise that you are unlikely to examine a thesis, even as an internal examiner, that bears a lot of resemblance to the one you have chosen to practise your skills on. Although doctoral researchers in your department might well refer to previous successful theses for guidance on style and other presentation issues, their topics will differ as will the process and progress of their research. Further, the theses you will examine are likely to require some modifications to bring them up to the standard of those currently on the departmental completed list. Indeed, most of them will have undergone some modification since they were originally submitted. This leads us to the issue of potential preliminary outcomes of the initial examination process. The words preliminary and initial are there to indicate that there can be several stages, as we introduce next, between the thesis in its submission state and in its completed form.

The range of possible outcomes

Although the terminology may differ slightly between institutions, the potential outcomes after the first examination are limited and very similar in general degree of seriousness, in terms of quality and time allowed for remedy. Table 12.1 summarises this situation in the UK, drawing on institutional regulations (regs), experience and discussion in supervisor and examiner forums.

Table 12.1 Summary of general outcomes and consequences of UK first examination

Outcome	Time allowed for review (up to)	Re-examined by	Frequency of occurrence	Next step
Pass	n/a	n/a	Very infrequent	Proceed to award
Pass with typo rectification allowed	Between 1 week to 1 month, depending on institution regulations (regs)	Internal examiner or delegated to lead supervisor	Infrequent	Proceed to award
Minor corrections	3 months or to 6 months, regs dependent	Internal examiner	Extremely common	If and when accepted, proceed to award
Referred for major amendments	1 to 2 years, regs dependent	All examiners	Quite common	Can result in re-viva, and/or minor corrections before proceeding to award
Offer of Lower degree (MPhil or MSc (res) or MRes)	n/a or minor corrections	One or more examiners	Seldom	After any corrections successfully undertaken, proceed to award
Fail	n/a	n/a	Rare	De-registered

Similar outcomes occur in other countries though, as we noted in Chapter 9, in some countries there is a strong expectation that in-course assessment procedures will result in few referrals or failures. They expect that major problems will have been 'weeded out' beforehand, while minor issues are dealt with in a preliminary review before the formal final examination process. Further, in some countries, for example many institutions in the Netherlands, Austria, Spain and Germany, the final pass is graded, usually as 'good' or 'especially good' in the appropriate formal language.

As a rule of thumb, minor corrections tend to be such things as the addition of a paragraph or two here and there in the thesis, or the re-writing of a section or two to clarify and emphasise important points, alongside some phraseology revision and perhaps attention to the reference list in some way. In contrast, major amendments could comprise those sorts of things as well as some additional work such as the collection or correction of major data, the re-writing of large portions of the thesis or the insertion of considerable additional material. Those are the requirements in many universities' rubrics. However, other considerations might complicate matters as we explore in the section that follows on negotiation.

First, there are several aspects related to time that we think important to note. The first is that the frequency of occurrence of these outcomes has changed over the last 30 years, with the proportion of the two pass categories reducing and that of the minor corrections category significantly increasing and major corrections becoming more frequent. One speculated potential cause is the advent of readily available word-processing packages which allow for corrections to be made more readily than previously when hard-bound, typed copies were the norm. In more recent years the rush for 'timely submission' to comply with the three to four years Full Time Equivalent registration period recommended as the seventh of the Salzburg Principles (2005), and then later imposed as the funding period by national research funding agencies, has often been blamed for 'premature submission' of theses. Many examiners are beginning to feel they are having to provide more guidance than previously on how to bring the thesis up to standard. This, of course, has implications for supervision, as we note in our sister volume on Supervision in this series (*Supervising to Inspire Doctoral Researchers*).

Another temporal issue is the variability in time allowed for amendments. We will discuss this next in relation to how the final decision is negotiated.

The negotiation of decisions

As we noted in Chapter 9, examiners are generally expected to have come to a view independently about the quality of the entire thesis and its various sections. This view may be modified by the candidate's performance in any viva or oral presentation/examination. They are then required to come to a consensus view about the outcome to be communicated to the candidate. It is not unusual for examiners to have perspectives that span two categories, perhaps one happy to allow typographical errors to be amended prior to confirmation of a pass, while another considers that some minor amendments are required – which prevails depends on the evidence and the strength of each argument presented.

Similar cases are when two other boundaries are straddled: perhaps Major amendments and the offer of a lower degree; or Lower Degree and Fail. Again, the evidence must be carefully reviewed, and each case considered, often with two conflicting considerations in play, upholding the standards of the discipline and being compassionate to someone who has worked on the research for several years and has much at risk. This is a demanding professional decision, the balance going either way depending on circumstances. It is often in these situations that the supervisor or research director is called in to ascertain whether there are any mitigating circumstances that can be considered. While the thesis must be brought up to the higher standard, only exceptional factors such as the failure of equipment or the lengthy absence of supervisory support can be considered at this point while the normal traumas of adult life are believed to impact on all candidates fairly equally and should have been covered through 'time out' or temporary suspension procedures.

A less challenging decision-making process often prevails when deciding between the two requirements for corrections/amendments, because practicalities usually prevail. The decision pivots on what must be done to make the thesis 'good enough', how long that might take the individual in his/her personal circumstances and how long the regulations allow for the task. For instance, if the candidate is full time with few demands on their time and funding enough to survive while the regulations allow six months for minor corrections then that is the likely decision. In contrast, if the candidate is part time with a demanding job and family commitments while the regulations only allow for three months' grace, then it might be considered more compassionate to recognise that explicitly and opt for the category of major amendments.

A similar decision might be made if the candidate's visa is about to run out so that work must continue at a distance, perhaps with fewer resources. Remember that if the candidate does not complete the changes within the regulated time then the doctoral submission could well be deemed to have failed in its entirety. Some examiners might consider it best to include the candidate at this point in the deliberations if there are no obvious official objections. Treating candidates as fellow, if junior, professionals will leave them less bruised by the process, as we continue to advocate in the next section.

In most cases, the panel will have agreed on the outcome. However, on rare occasions, examiners fundamentally disagree about the standard of a candidate's work. In such cases, the chair will normally explain this to the doctoral researcher and the institution will review all the paperwork via an examination committee and may appoint a third examiner to adjudicate. If you find yourself in this situation, the most important thing to do is make sure that you clearly justify your point of view in the post-viva report to aid any subsequent review. Understandably, the doctoral researcher will find this outcome very unsettling, so it is important that the next steps and associated timeframes are clearly explained, and that the institution is alerted to this outcome so that the doctoral researcher gets the support they need. See Voice of Experience 12.1 for an example of such a situation.

Voice of Experience 12.1

Disagreement between examiners

My first, and I hope only, experience of examiners disagreeing came early in my new role as Chair of the Exam Board of an education doctorate. I had met with the examiners prior to the viva and each had provided a list of questions they felt it useful to ask. I helped them to assemble them into a sensible order and, just before the candidate arrived, I asked if they had talked about the potential outcome they envisaged. The internal examiner revealed that he was, by and large, expecting good answers to his questions which would result in a verdict of minor corrections. The external agreed that he hoped for good answers but demurred to give a possible result.

I was delighted as the viva progressed and the candidate gave confident and what seemed to be cogent answers – it all seemed to be going well. The shock came when the candidate had left the room and the examiners began to confer. At first there seemed to be agreement on the good quality of the answers which could readily be converted to short insertions or clarifications in the thesis. Having noted these down, I was just about to suggest that we bring the candidate in to announce she had passed with minor corrections when the external dropped his bombshell. He required those corrections and a substantial portion of the thesis re-written because, he declared, it was prolix!

The internal seemed as flabbergasted as I. Once he gathered his wits, he asked what the other meant by prolix in this case. 'Too many long words, too complex sentences, each section much longer than it need be. It could never be published.' The internal drew a breath and suggested that though he thought that some sections should be clarified, as they had already agreed, the rest could remain as it was, including the unusual but evocative vocabulary. The air became heated so, when it became clear that neither would back down, I had to intervene to suggest that a third opinion might be needed to settle the situation.

In the event, the third opinion was that the disagreement was based on aesthetics – different views on what constituted good English rather than on the quality of the research per se so the verdict of Minor Corrections was reached – but only after the candidate had been terribly distressed not just at her own predicament but because she felt she had caused trouble to the department. She completed her corrections to the internal's satisfaction but asked for her certificate to be posted to her rather than receiving it in the formal ceremony. A sad ending to her studies and a learning experience for me. At the outset of a viva I now always clarify the criteria for each award level and ensure that possible outcomes are discussed in detail and agreed in principle so that the final stage is not destructive. I also make sure that my own supervisees keep any inclination towards grandiloquence or rambling to a minimum.

A pro-Vice Chancellor

In that Voice of Experience, a point was made about publishability, which is indeed one of the most common overarching criteria in university regulations, usually expressed as 'containing work worthy of publication'. In many science disciplines publication is expected during the research project and supervisors tend to ensure that doctoral researchers produce journal articles, in the worst case if only because their own name will be included in the list of authors. In other disciplines researchers tend not to benefit from that advantage because publication traditionally ensued after completion, although this situation is changing as publication becomes a sought-after employment credential in some situations/ disciplines. In most cases it would be unusual for the thesis to be published in its entirety. In Arts and Humanities subjects a monograph might well be derived from the thesis but normally several papers can be gleaned from a thesis as different topics within it are suitable for different journals. (You might be interested to follow this up in our sister book in the series: *Publishing for Impact.*)

Although researchers might be encouraged to present at conferences and to develop sections of their work into journal article form, publication lead times can be very long, up to two years after acceptance, and lengthening as pressure is brought to bear globally on academics to publish. Thus, expecting extant or imminent publications at the point of submission in most disciplines is more a dream than a reality. However, that can be something that a thoughtful examiner might help with once a successful outcome has been achieved (and certainly something to enquire about during the viva). We will elaborate on that in a later section on life after the final decision but first it is important to consider whether and how recent changes in the doctoral process have impacted on the final examination process.

Changes that have impacted on the final examination

In Part I we noted transformations in the requirements of successful doctoral researchers in response to changes in business, industry and the funding structures of higher education. In summary, the doctoral researcher is no longer an apprentice learning the intricacies of research activities and techniques in order to become an academic but is rather intended to become a professional with a range of research and professional skills able to bring to bear a vast range of attributes, as exemplified by Vitae's Researcher Development Framework (for details see our sister volume: *Developing Transferable Skills*, Denicolo and Reeves, 2014), in a multiplicity of contexts. Although institutions are charged with supporting the development of those professional, transferable skills, assessment of them has been mainly left to those conducting progress reviews with the final examination only including recognition of presentation and verbal argument skills in those institutions that have an oral viva component. In our view, and of concern in the sector, this provides a limited perspective on 'doctorateness' and the effort the candidate has expended during their programme.

All researchers, including those submitting their theses, are expected to demonstrate the value of their work through an indication of its impact (references woven through Chapters 1, 2 and 3 and the focus of our sister volume: *Achieving Impact in Research*, Denicolo, 2014) in their discipline and for the wider society.

Furthermore, these additional obligations are expected to be achieved within restricted timeframes. Formerly, research took as long as it took, but, as we recorded previously, most funders now require submission (the lodging of the final work) within three to four years, or part-time equivalent, while universities must demonstrate that even those whose research is self-funded in some way conform to that rubric. This edict has stimulated a rush to submit which frequently means that the written review of the research is less punctiliously prepared. However, this is an issue for supervisors whose role should be to ensure a viable thesis topic for the time allowed and is raised in our sister book (op cit) on supervision. In Appendix D we provide a list of common faults found in theses. In recent years it has been those related to the final sections, discussions and conclusions, that have been affected most, with the discussion being cursory and often lacking critical edge. While inadequate attention to proof-reading can be irritating to examiners so that corrections are required, these are very minor compared to the need to radically review the whole of the final chapter. While researchers might know in their heart of heart that this will not only improve the thesis but will be a clear indication of their achievement of doctorateness, the prospect of such a major undertaking when they had thought they were finished can be distressing.

Conveying the examination outcomes in a sensitive manner

We noted in Chapter 8 that, after all the investment that researchers make into their doctoral study, any decision less than a pass (perhaps after typos corrected) is likely to cause disappointment if not anguish. In that chapter we advised on ways of conveying unpleasant news that would apply also in these later stage cases. Further, since examiners arrive at any oral/viva examination stage having already reviewed the thesis, it is possible to couch questions and feedback on subsequent responses to candidate's answers in ways that indicate that the thesis could be improved and made more pride-worthy with some extra work. Without labouring the point, questions and responses such as the following put a positive spin on required corrections (assuming the replies are at least adequate) and prepare the candidate for engaging with necessary improvements:

[Question] 'How might you express that idea so that any lay person could grasp its import?'

[Response] 'I really like that – it could be very helpful to future readers.'

And

[Question] 'It seemed an enormous leap to me from what you presented in this paragraph and what comes next. Can you help me by justifying the links between them?'

[Response] 'That helps and with further consideration you could make the connections very clear.'

And

[Question] 'If you had had a bit more time, how would you have made the impact argument stronger?'

[Response] 'That does sound convincing – it would be a pity not to include it.'

Whichever examiner role you are taking, ensure that you do not give candidates false hope that all is well while at the same time you should continue to endeavour to encourage them to give of their best so that they might redeem shortcomings in the written version by their verbal elaborations. This is a demanding path to tread, as many professional activities are, but there can be compensations.

If the outcome is any form of pass, including minor corrections, be sure to offer congratulations and join in immediate celebrations. The usual protocol is that the external examiner, when present, gives the news of the result and thus, if you take on that role, you should check carefully with other examiners exactly what the official title for the outcome is and what its consequences are. You should explain to the candidate that the examination board makes recommendations to the university but that they are unlikely to be rejected. If, for instance, corrections are required say clearly but briefly what they encompass and what the completion deadline is. You should reassure the candidate that they will receive a written, detailed version about this and, for your part, ensure that this happens because your role may not yet be complete. We have found it useful to require candidates to provide with their re-submitted theses a copy of the list of corrections annotated to indicate where in the vast tome those changes have been made, thus easing the re-examination role somewhat.

Re-examination roles and responsibilities

If all that is required is that typographical (and spelling) errors are corrected, the task of checking those changes frequently falls to the lead supervisor though some institutions require sign-off from the internal examiner who is also solely responsible for ensuring that minor corrections have been appropriately dealt with. To lessen the tension and avoid official recursion, some internal examiners allow for off-the-record checks of draft corrections so that they can be signed off when they are officially submitted.

The review of major amendments is a greater challenge that is shared by all the examiners who must agree that these are satisfactory before completion and award of the degree can take place. In some circumstances the changes are so significant that they may also require a further viva. The regulations of most universities suggest, therefore, that candidates should not be told that no further viva will be necessary until those changes have been ratified and accepted.

While supervisors have no further official assessment role at this stage (unless the regulations include them in the examination panel), it is expected that they will continue to support the candidate until completion has been agreed.

A further point is germane here: while examiners have it in their power to return corrections and amendments until they are satisfied that their original criticisms have been resolved, they cannot at this stage introduce new requirements.

However, once the institution has accepted their final recommendation and, hopefully, have been able to grant the award, examiners can maintain contact with the new doctors, as you will see in the next section after considering our summary in Top Tips 12.1.

Top Tips 12.1

Approaching the final stage of the doctorate as an examiner

There follows a summary of advice for the final examination of a doctorate that we hope also captures the essence of the approach to assessment that we have conveyed throughout the book.

- Prepare for examinations as seriously as you would any important, life-changing occasion.
- Make sure that you have all the relevant information about institutional regulations and disciplinary and national conventions.
- Carve out enough time, plus a little more than you expect, to do justice to each step of the process.
- Ask of the work only what you could reasonably expect of a relatively basically resourced, individual endeavour lasting the full-time equivalent of three to four years.
- Remember that assessment involves evaluation and recognition of positive aspects as well as deficits.
- In personal encounters, treat the candidate, as well as fellow examiners, with respect and consideration as a fellow professional.

- Consider what questions, feedback (written and verbal) and ambiance would empower the candidate to respond to the best of their ability.
- Expect, value and negotiate professionally any differences in perspective or opinion expressed by the candidate and other examiners.
- If a submission cannot make the standard even with the strongest retrieval opportunity, then you must stand by this judgement in respect to all those whose work does achieve the standard.
- Check before formalising the decision that candidates who are required to make amendments are not put at further risk because of lack of facilities or time.
- Recognise the valuable facets of the research even if/especially when the outcome is not at pass level, congratulating the candidate on what they have achieved and providing constructive feedback on less satisfactory aspects.
- Imbue any formal occasions with the dignity they deserve. Recognise that though this may be a regular event for you, for the candidate it is likely to be a special, unique experience that will be retained in memory for a lifetime, whatever its outcome.

Finally, when the verdict is agreed, given and accepted, and the paperwork complete, you should celebrate and congratulate yourself and your colleagues on a professional job done well. It is important to take a moment to enjoy the magnitude of the task you have carried out on behalf of your discipline and the institutions in which you examine. You are a pivotal person in the final phase of the doctoral life cycle, and that vital role deserves to be recognised.

Life beyond the final decision

While one of the benefits of examining doctorates is the learning accrued which helps you become a more effective supervisor and fellow researcher, one of the joys that can result is that of continuing to work with a new researcher whose research interests, skills and attributes you have had the privilege to become familiar with through the examination process. You can advise them on appropriate publishing avenues and career opportunities if they decide to stay in academia; they may become your co-author or co-editor; they may become a trusted colleague or, indeed, friend as they recognise and know your sterling research attributes and assessment integrity. You may also be asked to provide an academic reference for researchers whose work you have examined. It is, therefore, a good idea before you dispose of all the paperwork with a sigh of relief for a job well done to create and store a summary to remind you of main points later. The researcher's name, thesis title, abstract and bullet points about the qualities demonstrated in the thesis and during the viva should suffice. Such things are important for recently qualified doctorates; they will remember examiners as well as supervisors and how they were treated by them for many years to come.

Looking to the future

As we draw this book to a close, we would be remiss if we did not alert you to further changes in the world of doctoral assessment brewing in the background. We have alluded in the text to an upsurge in interest in the use of technology to allow remote vivas/orals which could well improve the use of more international collaboration in examining, thereby perhaps reinforcing the global equivalence and currency of the doctorate. As yet, only a few institutions, usually in remote geographical areas, have regulations that encompass such procedures; both the procedures and regulations are experimental and likely to develop further.

There are discussions at conferences and other congregations of academics about the continuing appropriateness of the thesis as a vehicle to examine doctorateness. You might consider joining that debate.

There have also been discussions about the professionalisation of those involved with the support and assessment of doctoral researchers, elsewhere but notably within the European Universities Association, Council for Doctoral Education. You might be interested in the reflections of the Tarragona Think Tank on such professionalisation: http://llibres.urv.cat/index.php/purv/catalog/book/294.

As we have been compiling this book, we have become increasingly alert to the dearth of research on doctoral assessment so have included throughout references to those that you might join us in finding interesting. We have also noted a growing recognition that such an important and complex academic role deserves greater attention to its development than it currently has within institutions. The many recent developments in doctoral education, and those yet to come, mean that the continuing professional development of assessors and examiners is crucial. We invite you to not only engage with it but to correspond with us to improve it further.

Further reading

Denicolo, P. M. (2014) *Success in Research: Achieving Impact in Research*. London: Sage

Denicolo, P. M., Duke, D. C. and Reeves, J. D. (2020) *Success in Research: Delivering Inspiring Doctoral Supervision*. London: Sage

Denicolo, P. M. and Reeves, J. D. (2014) *Success in Research: Developing Transferable Skills*. London: Sage

Duke, D. C., Henslee, E. and Denicolo, P. M. (2020) *Success in Research: Publishing for Impact*. London: Sage

APPENDIX A

Some sources of support for assessors and examiners

Internal resources

Experienced colleagues are best placed to advise about internal regulations and processes, especially those who sit on committees and boards dealing with Doctoral Programmes. These could be either or both of Research or Teaching/Learning committees or boards.

One of those could be approached to be a **mentor** for your initial forays into assessing or examining at the doctoral level.

You may be able to contact them through your departmental/School or Faculty Research Office.

There may be a **community of practice** of colleagues within your locality who are interested in developing their knowledge and skills of assessing and examining at doctoral level. If there is not one already, consider joining with a few colleagues to establish one. While occasional discussions over, say, a lunch break can be useful for airing concerns or ideas about best practice, an e-link of some kind on which you can share queries and ideas can be effective, especially if someone needs to consult on a problem fairly rapidly.

There may be workshops available in your institution to promote good practice in this area. These might be run by a Doctoral College/Graduate School or through Staff Development or Human Resources.

Your librarians will be good sources of advice about local resources and information leaflets and books. They may also be able to direct you to information about digital technologies for developing online assessment practices which have the potential for creating advance community-orientated approaches to assessment.

External resources

In your region you should explore whether there are any accredited programmes for recognising skill in assessment and examining, especially at doctoral level. These may be part of workshops and programmes for doctoral supervisors/advisors. For instance, in the UK, Advance HE provides such a resource:

UK Professional Standards Framework (UKPFS) Dimensions of the Framework for Doctoral Supervisors (2016). See: www.heacademy.ac.uk/download/uk-professional-standards-framework-ukpfs-dimensions-framework-doctoral-supervisors

In Eire, several universities provide accredited programmes as Licenses to Practice, for instance for viva chairs or Doctoral Examining.

Professional bodies similarly provide best-practice workshops, though unaccredited, run by experienced colleagues for their peers. For instance, in the UK the Society for Research into Higher Education (**SRHE**) and the UK Council for Graduate Education (**UKCGE**) regularly provide such opportunities to meet colleagues to discuss issues arising in the organisation and practice of assessing and examining at doctoral level. For more, visit:

UK the Society for Research into Higher Education (SRHE): www.srhe.ac.uk/events/

UK Council for Graduate Education (UKCGE): www.ukcge.ac.uk/Events/Default.aspx

In Europe, the European Association of Universities Council for Doctoral Education (EUA-CDE) can be contacted for information about conferences, meetings, seminars and webinars that have relevance to this topic: https://eua.eu/events.html

You can find out about potential support too from the African Doctoral Academy (ADA) at: www.sun.ac.za/english/SUInternational/ADA/the-ada/about-us

In Australasia, HERDSA (the Higher Education Research and Development Association of Australasia) will also point you to meetings and resources in that region. See: www.herdsa.org.au/about-herdsa

Further, https://wonkhe.com/about-us/ – a website by and for workers in higher education dealing with HE policy issues.

APPENDIX B

Summary from Chapter 10 of criteria used by many examiners for assessing the written thesis

Overall, a thesis should have:

- a careful, clear presentation that recognises the reader's reading and understanding needs;
- the contribution to knowledge expected and achieved be made explicit.

Sectional attributes

Abstract

clearly describes, within the word limit, main aspects of the thesis (purpose, theoretical and methodological base and general outputs and outcomes).

Introduction

rationale for undertaking study clearly explicated;

a brief overview of thesis provided, demonstrating the 'story line' chapter by chapter.

Review of relevant literature

succinct, penetrating, challenging, critical, analytical approach demonstrating thorough knowledge of field;

organised to show a developing argument for the hypotheses/research questions.

Statement of research problems or plan for development of a creative piece

clear and succinct hypotheses or questions or basic plan derived from/revealed by the literature review;

well-articulated rationale for 'worthwhileness' and novelty of research.

Approach and methods of enquiry adopted

rationale for general approach closely argued giving reasoned case for rejecting other possible approaches;

justification of research design presented, taking account of potential advantages and limitations of research techniques;

ethical issues and procedures.

Data collection (where appropriate)

clearly set out and easy-to-follow description of actual process with relevant details included;

difficulties encountered and how they were dealt with so that the research was not compromised.

Analysis of data (where appropriate)

mode of analysis theoretically justified;

any assumptions declared and justified;

congruent with research questions/hypotheses and approach adopted;

details of procedure lucidly presented.

Presentation of data (where appropriate)

clearly structured with evident data trail;

tables, figures, diagrams to summarise data clearly numbered and titled and referred to in the text.

Discussion of outcomes or conclusions of argument

main points summarised and evaluated;

interpretations made of raw data;

links made to literature previously presented;

reflections on the research process;

suggestions for repeat or further research based on this research;

implications of results for theory and for practice;

clear articulation of contribution to knowledge.

Impact statement/chapter (where appropriate)

details potential impact, benefits and beneficiaries of research;

links research to the wider context and outlines future possibilities for research.

References

all and only references in the text included in an appropriate and consistent style.

Appendices

all appendices clearly numbered in the order of appearance in the main text.

APPENDIX C

Some thematic questions from viva voce examinations

Set out below are some of the general framework questions typically asked in a viva. Some answers will generate further questions and the examiners will also have specific questions arising from their own special areas of interest or from issues they have been alerted to by reading the text.

Introductory questions

Scene setting, allowing candidate to begin talking with enthusiasm, to explore motivation, etc.

Some examples are:

- What led to your interest in this topic? What stimulated your decision to explore this specific area? Why do you think this topic is important?
- What is your personal/professional position in relation to these issues? What prior conceptions/experiences did you bring to the study? What did you do to ensure your personal/professional links did not bias your research?
- What is the essence of/main points about/significant aspects of your thesis?
- Could you summarise your research in one sentence?
- Talk us through your main research questions and their origins.

Literature review questions

Exploring the theoretical framework or basis of the work, how conversant the candidate is with the field and its literature. Some examples are:

- Are there any specific theorists in your literature review who stand out as particularly important? Why? How have they influenced your work?
- What is the main orientating theory for the study? Which theory or theories does your study illuminate/add to/challenge?
- What are the main issues in the area? Are there particular controversies? How does your research stand in relation to these?
- What shaped/guided your literature review? Why did it cover the areas it did? (and neglect others?)
- Who is the most influential writer, in your opinion, in this field and why? You don't mention Dr X – why is that?
- What are the three most important publications in relation to your thesis?
- Which publication is closest to your work? How does your work differ?
- How did your research questions/hypotheses emerge?
- What crucial research decisions did you make and why?

Questions about methodology and data collection

To elicit a justification for approach taken and to explore the skill with which data collection was undertaken, any opportunities and constraints encountered, how these were dealt with. Some examples are:

- What led you to decide to choose that paradigm or philosophical approach and reject alternatives?
- Talk us through the process of designing the project and what are the design's strengths and weaknesses?
- How did you select your sample, and why, and why that sample size?
- Provide a summary of techniques/methods chosen and rejected and why.
- What difficulties were encountered in the data collection; how were they overcome; how did these influence the interpretation of results?
- Were there any pleasant surprises deriving from the fieldwork?
- What skills were learnt prior to or during the course of the fieldwork?
- Were there any important ethical issues or health and safety problems to handle that you knew of in advance? What were they and how were they addressed?
- What is the justification for the choice of analysis techniques, and what is of special salience in the results? Were there other alternative analysis techniques possible and why were they rejected/not included?
- How did you categorise/filter the data? Did the themes emerge from the data (a posteriori) or had you decided them in advance (a priori) (and why to both)?
- What ethical/safety issues arose during the project and how did you deal with them?

Questions about your findings/conclusions

- Please summarise your key findings.
- Was there anything surprising in the data, any anomalies? Any omissions and how might they influence the outcome?

- How do your conclusions relate to other relevant models/theories? Your findings are inconsistent with those of Dr X and Prof Y; how do you explain that? Your findings appear to be inconsistent with X theory or model; does that mean this theory or model is wrong?

Questions on the significance of the work/contribution to knowledge

- What is your most important contribution to your field? What is your contribution to knowledge; why do you think you've made a novel contribution and what is it that makes it novel?
- Can you describe the most important finding of your research in one sentence? When you found X, did it surprise you? How do you explain that?
- What are the important implications/key findings of the work? What would somebody from this field find interesting about these results? What does it suggest in terms of improvements for practice? What is newsworthy about it?
- How generalisable are your results and why?
- What lessons can be learnt by other researchers about the research product/ process?
- If you had another chance, what would you have changed about your project, and why? What would you advise someone who wanted to test out your findings in a different setting or context?
- Your data show some inconsistencies. How does this affect the accuracy of your model or the confidence that you have in it?
- Please summarise for us the possible criticisms of your research.
- What further work is inspired by what you have done? Are there any findings which demand urgent research attention to address them further? Any issues you had to set aside for future exploration?

Concluding questions

What have been some of the main things you have learned as a result of carrying out this piece of research?

- Have you published/disseminated anything from the work yet? Which parts do you feel could make worthy publications? In which journals? What plans do you have for dissemination?
- What are the potential benefits/who are the potential beneficiaries of your research and/or what impact would you like your research to achieve?
- What would you say is the greatest strength of this work? With hindsight, what are its limitations? What excites you most about this work?

- Is there anything that you would like to highlight from your work that we have not covered so far?
- Why did you want to do a doctorate, what benefit has your study brought you as an individual and a professional, and would you do it again?
- Is there anything you wished we asked about your thesis/research project?

APPENDIX D

Common thesis problems

The following are some of the issues frequently raised by examiners of doctoral theses, collated by the authors, from over a spread of disciplines, and over 300 examinations. Within each section they are presented in an order that approximately indicates degree of seriousness of faults in theses, from serious to less serious.

Presentation

- Account not taken, or unjustified assumptions made about, readers' knowledge: jargon, acronyms and topic details not clearly explained.
- 'Golden/Red thread' of argument from introduction to conclusion/discussion difficult to follow or not apparent.
- Lack of guidance to the reader using signposts, links, references forward and back.
- Careless proof-reading.

Literature review/s

- Descriptive rather than critical literature review.
- Review does not follow/produce a line of argument leading to (refined) research questions.
- Search system and procedure not described in enough detail or at all.
- Selection criteria for references unclear (or loosely applied).

Research questions/hypotheses

- Not clearly or sufficiently focused.
- Lack of transparent, well-articulated link between previous literature/research and research questions/hypotheses.
- Little indication of ownership of research.
- Assumptions made not clearly articulated.

Design, methods, procedures

- Rationales for approach, design and methods inadequate or muddled.
- Lack of evidence to support selection of approach, design, methods, participant/subject or instruments, particularly data analysis techniques.
- Long-winded descriptions when tables or diagrams would be clearer.
- Application of instruments from other work without calibration or standardisation to context.

Results

- Not clearly presented – lack of, or poorly presented, summaries or tables, graphs, diagrams, etc.
- Results and discussion/conclusions not clearly differentiated.

Final chapters

- No clear and detailed indication of the contribution made to knowledge (and/or practice if appropriate).
- Lack of depth to discussion and conclusions – superficial.
- Cursory back reference to the literature to indicate what has been supported, exemplified, refuted, etc.
- Implications for theory/practice not discussed in enough depth.
- Alternative explanations of results not considered in the discussion.
- Critical review of the research undertaken not included or cursory or unrealistic.
- Suggestions for future research not included or cursory.

Glossary

Advisor: In North America and other countries, this is the academic who supports and advises a doctoral researcher. See also: *Supervisor*.

Apprenticeship model: The teaching and learning model of novice learning by following and working with an individual, experienced practitioner.

Assessment: Formative: evaluation of a learner's comprehension, academic progress and learning needs in order to provide feedback and guidance to aid improvement. Normally this occurs in-process though it can be used by examiners at the end of a doctorate to guide future learning. **Summative:** evaluation of a learner's progress at the end of a stage or a course in order to recommend onward progression to the next stage or an award to mark completion.

Completion: A term that can be confusing because it is defined differently by different authorities. Often completion is used synonymously with submission, i.e. the point at which the thesis is submitted and prior to the final assessment. Alternatively, it may be the point when all the requirements of a doctorate have been successfully achieved and the award confirmed.

Critical feedback: Responses that note quality aspects of a piece of work, including what was good and what could be improved.

Cultural sensitivity: Knowing, being aware and accepting that cultural differences and similarities between people exist without assigning them a value, positive or negative, better or worse, right or wrong.

Culture: An active process of meaning-making; the sum of attitudes, customs, and beliefs that distinguishes one group of people from another.

Dissertation: A written report about a project carried out at master's level in the UK, for instance, and at doctoral level in the USA, for instance. See also: *Thesis*.

Doctoral College: Part of a university devoted to doctoral researchers as a focal point for a range of support and other services.

Doctoral programme: All the learning and research experiences which make up doctoral study.

Doctoral researcher: Someone engaged in pursuing a doctoral qualification. Previously/sometimes known as a doctoral student or candidate.

Doctorate: The highest-level award to signify successful completion of a programme of study involving research.

Doctorateness: A word coined to denote all the characteristics/attributes associated with the highest-level award for a course of study that includes research.

Dublin Descriptors: Adopted as the Qualifications Framework of the European Higher Education Area, they offer generic statements of typical expectations of achievement and abilities associated with awards that represent the end of each academic level or cycle.

Early career researcher: Generally, a postdoctoral researcher in the first stages of their career but, in some literature, doctoral researchers are also subsumed into this grouping.

Epistemology: The branch of philosophy concerned with the study of knowledge: its nature, justification and rationality of belief. An individual's epistemology is what s/he believes are the limits of truth and proof and what is recognised as only opinion.

Ethics: The moral principles that guide and govern a researcher's behaviour in the conduct of their research projects.

Evaluation activity: A process undertaken to judge the quality of a process and its products.

External examiner: An academic from a different university to the candidate who assesses the doctorate products, ensuring that they meet the criteria recognised as universal for such an award.

Feedback: The range of comments and recommendations provided by assessors or evaluators in response to a piece of work they have been asked to judge.

Generic skill: A skill that can be deployed in many settings.

Graduate School: Part of a university devoted to either all postgraduates or only doctoral researchers as a focal point for a range of support and other services.

Graduate student (Grad student): See *Doctoral researcher*.

HASS: Short version of Humanities, Arts and Social Sciences.

Impact in research: The demonstrable contribution that research makes to society, its culture, health, wealth and environment.

Independence: A condition in which a person demonstrates self-efficacy and an ability to work autonomously, that is, without supervision or direction.

Independent chair: An academic who manages the process of the viva voce but who has no role in the assessment of the doctoral research under scrutiny.

Internal examiner: An academic who works in the same university as the doctoral candidate but who has made no direct contribution to the research process other than assessment of its outputs. The examining role includes ensuring that the doctoral products fits the regulations of the university for that award.

Interdisciplinary research: Research that relates to more than one branch of knowledge. It crosses the nominal, artificial boundaries of disciplines or subjects so that knowledge and procedures from more than one discipline can be brought to bear on a problem.

Internationalization: The action or process of making something relevant to and/or practised in more than one country.

Inter-sectoral research: Research that crosses the nominal, artificial boundaries within society such as academia, industry, commerce, government, the health and social services sectors, and so on.

Knowledge economy: An economy in which growth is dependent on the quality, quantity and accessibility of information rather than on the means of production.

Literature review: A critique of key themes and an evaluation of important studies within a specific body of literature and their relevance to a piece of research.

Massification: The process of increasing access to a wider, and therefore more numerous, section of the population.

Mock viva: An exercise in which candidates are asked questions about their research as a practice for the formal final viva voce.

Multi-disciplinary research: Relevant to and involving more than two branches of knowledge. See *Interdisciplinary research* which may involve only two branches of knowledge.

Ontology: The branch of metaphysics dealing with the nature of being.

Outcomes: The consequences of research; the way things turn out or end product/s.

Outputs: The immediate products of research, usually data or information.

Paradigm: A philosophical and theoretical framework of a scientific school or a discipline within which theories, laws, and generalisations, and the research methods performed to produce them, are formulated.

Pedagogy: The method and practice of teaching, especially as a theoretical concept.

Peer review: Evaluation of scientific, academic, or professional work by others working in the same field and therefore conversant with its paradigm/s.

Plagiarism: The practice of using other people's work as if it were your own. It is a form of stealing and includes copying other's work without references to credit the source.

Postdoctoral researcher (postdoc): Someone who has successfully achieved their doctorate and is working as a researcher, usually in a university or research organisation in a paid position.

Postgraduate Research Director: An academic who oversees the postgraduate work within a specific area such as a department, faculty or university.

Postgraduate Researcher (PGR): See *Doctoral researcher*.

Primary supervisor: See *Principal supervisor*.

Principal supervisor: The academic who is ultimately responsible for the guidance, support and development of a doctoral researcher, though others, for instance co-supervisors and/or collaborative supervisors, may also contribute.

Project: The bounded research starting with a research question or hypothesis and culminating in a completed report, known in some countries as a thesis and others as a dissertation.

Proposer: Used in some countries, for example Belgium, as the person who supports and guides a doctoral researcher. See also: *Advisor* and *Supervisor*.

QAA: UK Quality Assurance Agency – an organisation supported by government and charged to assure the quality of education in publicly funded schools, colleges and universities.

Research Excellence Framework (REF) UK: A 5- to 6-yearly UK national ranking of all higher education institutions to determine core funding.

Ranking involves peer review of submissions not simply metrics such as research income, publications, citations, student numbers, the environment and impact. The process was recently reviewed by an independent authority, led by Lord Nicholas Stern: www.gov.uk/government/uploads/system/uploads/attachment_data/file/541338/ind-16-9-ref-stern-review.pdf

Research methodology: An argument presented about the selection of approach and methods for a research project that demonstrates the study's validity by explaining the reasons for that selection and for rejecting alternatives.

Researcher Development Framework: A tool which indicates the main attributes/skills of a researcher over a working life developed under the auspices of Vitae amongst other things to aid researchers identify areas for further development.

Rubric: A set of instructions or rules; a statement of purpose or function.

Salzburg Principles: The recommendations for good practice in doctoral education established by the Bologna process for educational reform in the European Higher Education Area.

Satisfactory progress: Progress evaluated as meeting at least a minimum standard required at a specific educational level.

Self-efficacy: The extent to which you believe you can determine an outcome and can complete tasks and fulfil goals.

Seminal research: A piece of work/research that is ground-breaking, pivotal, and/or inspirational and that exerts influence over the discipline.

SRHE: Society for Research into Higher Education – UK based.

STEMM: Short version of Science, Technology, Engineering, Maths and Medicine.

Submission: The point when a thesis/dissertation is presented for formal final assessment.

Supervisor: A person charged with guiding and supporting a doctoral researcher from induction to completion, sometimes known as an 'advisor'. Any researcher may have several supervisors, though one should be recognised as the principal or main supervisor.

Thesis: A written report about a project carried out at master's level in the USA, for instance, and at doctoral level in the UK, for instance. Also, a proposition or argument.

Transferable skill: A skill learned in one realm, job or profession that can be applied in another.

UKCGE: UK Council for Graduate Education.

Vitae: A UK-based organisation for developing the careers of researchers with links worldwide.

Viva voce: An oral examination for an academic qualification. It typically involves the candidate responding to questions about his/her study area and sometimes involves a presentation by the candidate. A closed viva refers to one conducted in private involving only the candidate, examiners and perhaps a chairperson, and less frequently one observer, say a supervisor, or note-taker. An open viva can involve any number of observers.

Writing-up: The period towards the end of the research process where the complete version of the thesis is compiled. Even 'completed' chapters will need to be edited together to make an elegant, flowing and readable whole.

Index